Balanced Scorecard Strategy For Dummies®

W9-CKE-388

Building the Balanced Scorecard

Building your balanced scorecards requires that you take these fundamental steps so that they will be strong and deliver the benefits you want and need for your business to thrive and grow:

1. Develop your vision, mission, and guiding principles.
2. Develop your strategy map.
3. Develop your scorecards for the four legs.
4. Develop your balanced scorecard measures and dashboards.
5. Establish your leadership and management team's alignment, authority, and responsibilities.

Top Five Reasons for Using the Balanced Scorecard

Sometimes you have to convince people to use the balanced scorecard approach. Often you have to keep encouraging people as to why such an approach can benefit your company and its goals. If you find yourself in either of these situations, here are some great responses:

✔ To grow your business, increase your market share, improve your business processes, and to have fanatically loyal customers

✔ To have a clear picture of what your business is really doing and why

✔ To effectively manage your business and beat the pants off the competition

✔ To establish a system for measuring your business performance so that you make the right decisions, on time, every time

✔ To enable your people to do the right things right, the first time

Top Five Tips for Balanced Scorecard Success

Don't lose sight of these tips as you follow through with the balanced scorecard approach:

✔ Don't view the balanced scorecard strategy as a flavor of the month approach to quick and easy answers to your problems.

✔ Be persistent and be thorough in establishing your strategies, tactics, and key performance indicators.

✔ Communicate your scorecards and dashboards throughout your business and advertise how you're doing, what you're doing, and why.

✔ Use teamwork and involve your people in your balanced scorecards.

✔ Never give up the ship!

For Dummies: Bestselling Book Series for Beginners

Balanced Scorecard Strategy For Dummies®

Cheat Sheet

Top Five Scorecard Analysis Tips

Analysis is a vital part of the balanced scorecard and is something you'll be doing often. Here's how to keep your analysis running in the right direction:

- Always look for any key performance indicators that are not measuring up and performing as required.
- Perform root cause analysis on those key performance indicators that are not performing as required.
- Look for positive and negative trends in your key performance indicators.
- Use statistical analysis or the Six Sigma tool set to gain a better understanding of your data and information.
- Take the time to really understand what the information is telling you.

Key Tips for Building Dashboards

Another key component of the balanced scorecard is building dashboards. Here are some tips to make your building of dashboards a success:

- Keep your dashboards to one page and one page only!
- Focus on the data and information and resist the temptation to put in a lot of useless color, glitz, and fancy presentation graphics.
- Make sure your dashboard information jumps out at you and doesn't require a lot of scrutiny and analysis to understand what it's telling you.
- Be careful in selecting any dashboard software solutions, making sure that the software and its provider fit your needs, not only for today, but for many years to come.

For Dummies: Bestselling Book Series for Beginners

Balanced Scorecard Strategy

FOR DUMMIES®

by Chuck Hannabarger, Rick Buchman, and Peter Economy

BICENTENNIAL
1807
WILEY
2007
BICENTENNIAL

Wiley Publishing, Inc.

Scorecard Strategy For Dummies®

by

Wiley Publishing, Inc.
111 River St.
Hoboken, NJ 07030-5774
www.wiley.com

Copyright © 2007 by Wiley Publishing, Inc., Indianapolis, Indiana

Published simultaneously in Canada

No part of this publication may be reproduced, stored in a retrieval system, or transmitted in any form
or by any means, electronic, mechanical, photocopying, recording, scanning, or otherwise, except as per-
mitted under Sections 107 or 108 of the 1976 United States Copyright Act, without either the prior written
permission of the Publisher, or authorization through payment of the appropriate per-copy fee to the
Copyright Clearance Center, 222 Rosewood Drive, Danvers, MA 01923, 978-750-8400, fax 978-646-8600.
Requests to the Publisher for permission should be addressed to the Permissions Department, John Wiley
& Sons, Inc., 111 River Street, Hoboken, NJ 07030, (201)748-6011, fax (201)748-6008, or online at http://
www.wiley.com/go/permissions.

Trademarks: Wiley, the Wiley Publishing logo, For Dummies, the Dummies Man logo, A Reference for the
Rest of Us!, The Dummies Way, Dummies Daily, The Fun and Easy Way, Dummies.com and related trade
dress are trademarks or registered trademarks of John Wiley & Sons, Inc. and/or its affiliates in the United
States and other countries, and may not be used without written permission. All other trademarks are the
property of their respective owners. Wiley Publishing, Inc., is not associated with any product or vendor
mentioned in this book.

For general information on our other products and services, please contact our Customer Care
Department within the U.S. at 877-762-2974, outside the U.S. at 317-572-3993, or fax 317-572-4002.

For technical support, please visit www.wiley.com/techsupport.

Wiley also publishes its books in a variety of electronic formats. Some content that appears in print may
not be available in electronic books.

Library of Congress Control Number: 2007932466

ISBN: 978-0-470-13397-2

Manufactured in the United States of America

10 9 8 7 6 5 4 3 2

WILEY

About the Author

Chuck Hannabarger: Chuck (Tyler, Texas) is founder and president of PSI Associates, a business consulting and training firm founded in 1992 with headquarters in Tyler, Texas. As a business consultant, Chuck has consulted with many of the Fortune 100 companies and is recognized throughout the world for his work in the areas of Balanced Scorecards, Six Sigma, Lean Manufacturing, Business Process Reengineering and Project Management. Chuck's course on Project Management has been offered at UC Berkeley, Pepperdine University, San Diego State University, and Michigan State University, to name a few. He received his BSBA and his MBA in technology management from the University of Phoenix. To schedule Chuck or one of his associates to discuss your business improvement needs, contact him at www.PSIAssociates.com or e-mail him at Charles.Hannabarger@psiassociates.com.

Rick Buchman: Rick, who lives in Woodland Hills, CA, has worked with many of the Fortune 100 companies for over 20 years, as both an organizational member of executive management, and as an external consultant, in designing, developing, and implementing operational excellence and continuous improvement programs worldwide. He received his bachelor's degree in mathematics from Western Illinois University, his MBA in business from California Coast University in Santa Ana, CA, and has completed all but the dissertation for his PhD in management as well. Currently, Rick is working as a consultant with several major global clients toward designing and implementing their continuous improvement programs, focusing on lean leadership and improving the flow of value to deliver products and services to their customers worldwide. You can reach Rick at creative_edge00@yahoo.com.

Peter Economy: Peter is Associate Editor for the award-winning magazine Leader to Leader, Senior Consultant for The Jana Matthews Group, a member of the National Advisory Council of the Creativity Connection of the Arts and Business Council of Americans for the Arts, and bestselling coauthor of *The SAIC Solution: How We Built an $8 Billion Employee-Owned Technology Company,* as well as *Managing For Dummies, The Management Bible, Enterprising Nonprofits: A Toolkit for Social Entrepreneurs, Writing Children's Books For Dummies,* and many others. Peter invites you to visit him at his Web site: www.petereconomy.com.

Dedication

From Chuck: Dedicated to my father and mother, Don and Emma, who have always been in my corner, and to my wife Denise, our children and grandchildren, without whose support and understanding I wouldn't have been able to write this book.

Authors' Acknowledgments

We give our sincere thanks and appreciation to our publishing team at Wiley, including Joyce Pepple, Michael Lewis, Jennifer Connolly, and Darren Meiss, Josh Dials, and to our Technical Editor, Bill Lareau.

Chuck: Thanks to Rick and Peter for their friendship, steadfast support, and dedication to making this project happen.

Rick: Thanks to Mona, my mom, and my family, who helped me think through the many ideas, models and tools of the balanced scorecard, and who always cheered me on.

Peter: Thanks to Chuck and Rick for their diligent efforts throughout this project—no matter where in the world they happened to be at the time (and let me tell you, these guys get around!).

Publisher's Acknowledgments

We're proud of this book; please send us your comments through our Dummies online registration form located at www.dummies.com/register/.

Some of the people who helped bring this book to market include the following:

Acquisitions, Editorial, and Media Development

Project Editor: Jennifer Connolly

Acquisitions Editor: Mike Lewis

Copy Editor: Josh Dials

Technical Editor: Bill Lareau

Editorial Manager: Michelle Hacker

Editorial Supervisor: Carmen Krikorian

Editorial Assistants: Erin Calligan Mooney, Joe Niesen, Leeann Harney, and David Lutton

Cartoons: Rich Tennant (www.the5thwave.com)

Composition Services

Project Coordinator: Patrick Redmond

Layout and Graphics: Carl Byers, Brooke Graczyk, Joyce Haughey, Stephanie D. Jumper, Laura Pence

Anniversary Logo Design: Richard Pacifico

Proofreaders: Aptara, John Greenough, Jessica Kramer

Indexer: Aptara

Publishing and Editorial for Consumer Dummies

> **Diane Graves Steele,** Vice President and Publisher, Consumer Dummies

> **Joyce Pepple,** Acquisitions Director, Consumer Dummies

> **Kristin A. Cocks,** Product Development Director, Consumer Dummies

> **Michael Spring,** Vice President and Publisher, Travel

> **Kelly Regan,** Editorial Director, Travel

Publishing for Technology Dummies

> **Andy Cummings,** Vice President and Publisher, Dummies Technology/General User

Composition Services

> **Gerry Fahey,** Vice President of Production Services

> **Debbie Stailey,** Director of Composition Services

Contents at a Glance

Table of Contents

Introduction

• •

*T*here are many reasons for reading a book about implementing Balanced Scorecards in your business. Perhaps you've read or heard about Balanced Scorecards, and you want to know more about how they can improve your business processes and enhance the bottom line. Or maybe you have taken a new job and inherited a Balanced Scorecard system that isn't working right — and that is taking far more time to maintain than it's worth. Or you might have a highly tuned Balanced Scorecard system in place — complete with well-designed dashboards — but you would like to get some advice on how to fine-tune your Balanced Scorecards and continually improve them.

Balanced Scorecard Strategies For Dummies was written to respond to each of these needs — and many more. The book avoids the business fad-of-the-month approach common in many works of this type, instead focusing on tried-and-true solutions to the most common situations and problems that real business leaders face: solutions that will stand the test of time and be just as effective tomorrow — or a year or decade from now — as they are today.

Balanced scorecards have emerged as one of the most effective business tools available today. The bad news is that there is much confusion out there in the business world as to exactly what a Balanced Scorecard is, and how to design and implement ones that work. The good news is that this book solves these problems — and more.

We specifically designed this book to provide you with the very best and most up-to-date ideas, concepts, and tools for designing and implementing Balanced Scorecards — successfully, and with a minimum of muss or fuss. Apply them, and we are certain that you'll be able to benefit from their significant promise — achieving the high level of business success that Balanced Scorecards can unlock in any organization.

About This Book

Balanced Scorecard Strategies For Dummies is full of useful information, tips, checklists, and figures for everyone who aspires to implement Balanced Scorecards and dashboards in businesses of any kind in any industry. If you work for an automobile or computer manufacturer, this book is for you. If your business delivers healthcare or software development services, this book is for you. If your business is large or small, old or new, product or service oriented, this book is for you. For a fraction of the cost of an hour's time with a top-rank consultant, this book provides you with an easily understandable road map to today's most innovative and effective Balanced Scorecard and dashboard techniques and strategies.

This book is perfect for all levels of managers and business professionals. New managers can easily find the basics that they'll need to know to be successful, while more experienced managers will find higher-level material that can be used to make an existing Balanced Scorecard program even better. Despite the old saying about teaching old dogs new tricks, you can always make changes in your approach to doing business that will make it better and more effective.

Whether you're new to the job or a seasoned pro, it's our hope that you'll learn something new that will help you improve your business — making you and your team more valuable in the process. Don't worry about making an occasional mistake as you push for needed changes in your organization — we all make mistakes from time to time. The secret is to learn from mistakes and to avoid making them again. When you do make a mistake, simply pick yourself up, laugh it off, and learn from it. We wrote this book to make learning easier so you won't have to learn the hard way.

Conventions Used in This Book

We use the following conventions throughout the text to make everything consistent and easy to understand:

- All Web addresses appear in monofont.
- New terms appear in *italic* and are closely followed by an easy-to-understand definition.
- **Bold** text indicates keywords in bulleted lists or highlights the action parts of numbered steps.

When this book was printed, some Web addresses may have needed to break across two lines of text. If that happened, rest assured that we haven't put in any extra characters (such as hyphens) to indicate the break. So, when using one of these Web addresses, just type in exactly what you see in this book, pretending as though the line break doesn't exist.

What You're Not to Read

We've written this book so that you can find information easily — and readily understand what you find. We also simplify it so you can identify "skippable" material, that is, text that you can come back to later when you've got some extra time on your hands (as if you had a lot of *that!*). *Sidebars* are the shaded boxes that appear here and there. They share fun facts, but nothing that's essential to the success of your Balanced Scorecards. Enjoy them when you have the time!

Foolish Assumptions

We wrote this book with some thoughts about you in mind. For example, we assumed that you are a manager, executive, or other business leader who is motivated to discover some new approaches to improving your organization's processes and enhancing its bottom line. We also assumed that you're ready, willing, and able to committing yourself to making your organization more efficient and effective, and in helping others to do the same.

How This Book Is Organized

This book is divided into six parts — jump in wherever you want. The following sections explain what you'll find where.

Part 1: The ABC's of Balanced Scorecard

The use of Balanced Scorecards has become more popular than ever for measuring the whats and hows of business, and for good reason — they work. This part provides a basic understanding of the four legs of Balanced Scorecards — the customer leg, the financial leg, the internal business processes leg, and the knowledge and growth leg — and provides you with the best ways to understand your needs and to make plans for implementing your own Balanced Scorecards.

Part II: The Customer — The Critical Leg

Every business needs customers to exist — without customers, after all, who would pay for the products you manufacture or the services you deliver? This part describes the customer leg in detail, including understanding your role with customers and measuring what they want and need. We describe how to build your customer scorecards and dashboards, how to understand what they tell you, and the pitfalls to avoid.

Part III: Financial Measurement — The Foundation Leg

The financial leg of the Balanced Scorecard is the cornerstone of any business, and it determines its health, performance, and long-term viability. This part addresses financial measurement and the use of metrics — along with management's role in determining and implementing them. We describe how to develop and implement financial scorecards and dashboards, and point out a number of pitfalls that can derail even the best-laid of your Balanced Scorecard plans.

Part IV: Internal Business Processes — The Value Creation Leg

Believe it or not, your business's internal processes can and do create value for your customers — or not, depending on how well they are designed and implemented. In this part, we address the role that Balanced Scorecards can play with internal business processes, and how you can use them to create value. We also address the pitfalls to avoid in this leg of the Balanced Scorecard.

Part V: Knowledge, Education, and Growth — the Learning Leg

While most organizations have a natural tendency to focus on financial performance, it is critical that they not ignore knowledge, education, and growth. In this part, we consider the manager's roles and responsibilities in implementing this "learning leg" of the Balanced Scorecard, showing how scorecards and dashboards work together, as well as a variety of pitfalls to avoid.

Part VI: The Part of Tens

This part contains quick resources that provide information in an easy-to-digest fashion. Explore some tried-and-true tips for Balanced Scorecard success, mistakes to avoid, and ways to overcome barriers to your improvement efforts.

Icons Used in This Book

To make this book easier to read and simpler to use, we include some icons in the margins that can help you find and fathom key ideas and information.

These tidbits provide expert advice to help you save time, money, or frustration in the Balanced Scorecard process.

This icon highlights important information to store in your brain for quick recall at a later time.

Avoid mistakes by following the sage words of advice that appear by this icon.

Check out the true stories that accompany this icon so you can learn from the business experiences of others.

Where to Go from Here

The great thing about this book is that *you* decide where to start and what to read. It's a reference you can jump into and out of at will.

If you're new to the wonderful world of Balanced Scorecards, you may want to start at the beginning of the book and work your way through to the end. If you're experienced pro, then you can look up any topic you like and find your way directly to it. Just head to the table of contents or the index to find the specific information you want. Whichever approach you take, you'll find a wealth of information and practical advice. Simply turn the page and you're on your way!

Part I
The ABC's of Balanced Scorecard

The 5th Wave   By Rich Tennant

"The next part of your employment test is designed to determine your sense of humor."

In this chapter . . .

Balanced scorecards have become not only popular within companies both large and small, they have become essential to measuring and managing the what's and how's of business. Having a basic understanding of the four legs for balanced scorecards — the customer leg, the financial leg, the internal business processes leg, and the knowledge and growth leg — is the first step in establishing your balanced scorecard strategy for your organization. After we cover the basics, we consider the best approaches to understanding your needs and making plans for implementing your own balanced scorecards.

Chapter 1

Goals, Scores, and the Balanced Scorecard

An old saying goes something like this: If you're not keeping score, you're just practicing. If you ask us, truer words were never spoken — especially in today's topsy-turvy business world. To make (and keep) your business a success, you need to not only keep score, but also predict your score in advance by setting goals and then achieving them on a consistent basis. And we're not talking about easy-to-achieve goals and scores. No! We're talking about goals that stretch your imagination and push your creativity and ingenuity to the limits — as well as the creativity and ingenuity of your employees.

Can you imagine what the people working at NASA in the 1960s thought when they were asked to build a rocket and space capsule that would transport Americans to the moon — in less than ten years? We can imagine them wondering exactly how in the heck they would pull it off, but never doubting that they would. NASA put a massive stretch goal before them, and they achieved it. Balanced Scorecard Strategy is the tool that will allow your company to set and achieve stretch goals.

In this chapter, we give you an initial peek at Balanced Scorecard, preview its four legs, and offer a glimpse of how you can ensure that your company's scorecard stays balanced.

Getting Familiar with Balanced Scorecard

What's a Balanced Scorecard? Glad you asked, because in this section you'll get your first glimpse at what a Balanced Scorecard is and how it works. You'll see that scorecards aren't rocket science, but they do require some good business structure, analysis, and planning in order to get it right.

Just what is Balanced Scorecard, anyway?

To better understand what a Balanced Scorecard is, maybe you should first learn where it came from and why. The Balanced Scorecard was first developed in the early 1990s by two guys at the Harvard Business School: Robert Kaplan and David Norton. The key problem that Kaplan and Norton identified in today's business was that many companies had the tendency to manage their businesses based solely upon financial measures. While that may have worked well in the past, the pace of business in today's world requires better and more comprehensive measures. Though financial measures are necessary, they can only report what has happened in the past — where your business has been — and they are not able to report where it is headed: It's like trying to drive your car by looking in the rear view mirror.

In order to provide a management system that was better at dealing with today's pace of business and to provide business managers with the information they need so that they can make better decisions, Kaplan and Norton developed the Balanced Scorecard. Note that we said that the Balanced Scorecard is a *management system* — not a *measurement system*. Yes, measurement is a key aspect of the Balanced Scorecard, but it is much more than just measurement: it is a means to setting and achieving the strategic goals and objectives for your organization.

So, what is the Balanced Scorecard? In short, it's a management system that enables your organization to set, track and achieve its key business strategies and objectives. Once the business strategies are developed, they are deployed and tracked through what we call the Four Legs of the Balanced Scorecard. These four legs are made up of four distinct business perspectives: The Customer Leg, the Financial Leg, the Internal Business Process Leg, and the Knowledge, Education, and Growth Leg.

Leaning on the four legs of the scorecard

Your Balanced Scorecard Strategy relies upon four different yet integrated perspectives: The Customer Leg, the Financial Leg, the Internal Business

Process Leg, and the Knowledge, Education, and Growth Leg. These four legs of the Balanced Scorecard are necessary for today's business executives and managers to be able to plan, implement and achieve their business strategies. The four legs will make the difference between whether your business succeeds or fails. The following list takes a closer look at the four legs:

- ✔ **Customer scorecard:** Measures your customers' satisfaction and their performance requirements — for your organization and what it delivers, whether it be products or services.

- ✔ **Financial scorecard:** Tracks your financial requirements and performance.

- ✔ **Internal Business Process scorecard:** Measures your critical-to-customer process requirements and measures.

- ✔ **Knowledge, Education, and Growth scorecard:** Focuses on how you train and educate your employees, gain and capture your knowledge, and how you use it to maintain a competitive edge within your markets.

Achieving Organizational Balance

When reflecting on the many companies we've worked with (and we've worked with a lot!), we notice that many organizations tend to be unbalanced — that is, they focus only on two legs of the Balanced Scorecard: their financial measures (see Part III) and their internal business process performance (see Part IV). As a result, they miss the mark in measuring and tracking other critical parts of their businesses — things like their customers (see Part II) and their internal knowledge and growth (see Part V).

These four elements, or *legs,* have to be measured, analyzed, and improved together — continuously — in order for your business to thrive. If you ignore any one of these four legs, it will be like you're sitting on a four-legged stool with a broken leg. You'll eventually lose your balance and fall flat on your face. And, last time we checked, lying flat on your face is no way to run a business!

You not only have to measure these critical four legs, but also set strategies, goals, objectives, and tactics to make them happen. And while you're at it, you have to make sure that your strategies and tactics are congruent. They have to work together and create a single thread, tying them together in ways that make sense. This isn't an optional exercise; it's essential. The future of your business depends on it.

Following a total balanced-scorecard approach gives your business the balance needed to ensure that these critical areas get the attention they deserve. Organizational balance isn't all that difficult to understand, but achieving it . . . well, that's a different story. (And we don't have enough pages in this chapter to tell *that* particular story!) Balance takes effort and persistence and can be achieved in any business, in any country, at any time. The old saying "It won't work in this place — we're different from all those other guys out there" just doesn't wash. If you think that way, your competition will thank you — all the way to the bank!

Analyzing Your Customers: Critical Leg

Each of the four legs have equal importance in your Balanced Scorecard (after all, if they didn't have equal importance, they wouldn't be balanced), but your customers are your reason for being, your *raison d'etre*. Without them, you'd have to close your business's doors and go home to stare at the television all day long. Yet, as important as they are to you, customers often get lost in the swirl of the many everyday tasks you accomplish in your business. You may lose sight of who you do all this stuff for: your customers. Many companies don't have a clue about what the customer really wants — including those who make the product, fulfill the service, and have the greatest impact upon the customer.

Ask yourself this question: "Does every person in my company know what our customers want and how their work affects the customers?" Go ahead, go out into your workplace and ask your employees this question. What answers do you get? Something generic, like "Yeah, um . . . we need to deliver quality, I guess." Or something specific and measurable, like "I have to make sure that I get this part between 0.10 and 0.12 millimeters." Do you see the difference? If not, your customers certainly do, as do your competitors.

You have to know what your customers want from you — what they demand in terms of quality, cost, and delivery – and you have to know what they will be wanting from you in the future. To do this, you first need to find out who your customers are — in and out of your organization — and who they will become. For more on analyzing your customers for this leg of the scorecard, see Chapter 5.

Knowing who you sell to

Identifying customers seems like a pretty basic task that all companies should have mastered, right? Here's a news flash: Many don't do it. Tracking sales and identifying existing markets aren't very difficult duties, but many companies don't continually track these elements. Situations change. Customers change. Markets change. And woe be unto those companies that miss those changes, for they'll soon find themselves in a downward spiral to bankruptcy. They'll wake up one day and wonder what happened.

Cracking the whip on nearsighted business practices

Perhaps you've heard the lament about the poor old buggy whip manufacturers that operated around 100 years ago, when some character named Henry Ford was driving around Detroit, Michigan in his new fangled "automobile." Ford ended up putting most of the buggy whip manufacturers out of business. Instead of remaining stuck in the past — hanging onto old products and old markets — those buggy whip manufacturers should've looked toward the future and stayed focused on their real expertise: making things out of leather. Had they followed that path, they may have redirected their production into leather seats and padding for Ford's automobiles. Long story short, the whip manufacturers may have not only survived, but also thrived in the new era. Unfortunately, they insisted on making buggy whips — a going-out-of-business plan in a fast-changing market.

In today's globally competitive business environment, where the customer has a multitude of choices, it's imperative that you know who your customers truly are. It doesn't matter if you're a senior executive, a middle manager, or on the front lines making products or delivering services. If you don't know who your customers are, how can you ever satisfy them? (Hint: You can't!) For more on how to identify your customers and how they fit into the scorecard, check out Chapters 5 and 6.

Focusing on future customers

While taking a look at your existing customer base (see the previous section), you also need to be keeping your eyes on the future. Ask the following questions pertaining to your business and industry:

- ✔ Where are your markets heading?
- ✔ What new trends are emerging in your industry?
- ✔ What's the state of technology, and how will it impact your customers and your business?
- ✔ Can you identify ways to leverage what you currently do and move into other markets to get additional customers?

The bottom line: You need to look at what your company really does and don't limit yourself to a particular market, industry, or customer base. Look outside your sandbox, understand what's at the core of your business, and look for other markets and customers to sell to. To take a look into your company's crystal ball, head to Chapter 6.

Considering your internal customers

You have more customers out there than you may think, and you need to identify and account for them all. For instance, executives often don't realize that they have customers within their own companies. As an executive, mid-level manager, or front-line supervisor, each employee who reports to you is your customer. Now there's a shift in thinking, huh? Your job is to provide your employees with the tools they need to satisfy their internal and external customers. Specifically, they need knowledge, skills, authority, equipment, budget, and so on — tools that allow them to do their jobs right the first time.

Your employees have internal customers, too. Your business operations often are a combination of processes, requiring many different operations and people to get work done. If an employee does his job and hands off his work to another employee so that she can do her job, isn't she his internal customer? Shouldn't their company measure what the internal customer wants and needs and how well the internal supplier satisfies them? Shouldn't the first employee know what his internal customer wants from him so that they can do their jobs with the least amount of hassle? Shouldn't the work provided to fellow employees be fit for use, just like you want your products to be fit for the end users — the people who pay for what you do and pay your bills? The answer to all these questions is a resounding "Yes!"

A key part of the Balanced Scorecard Strategy is getting in touch with *all* your customers, including those within your company. Know what your customers need so that you can keep the end users satisfied and motivate them to buy your products and services time after time.

Following the Money: Foundation Leg

Businesspeople track their money like their lives depend on it . . . and they do. Managing the money is foundational to any successful business. Knowing where you get your money from — how much you bring in — and where you plan to invest it, is essential. The problem with many companies is that they focus too much on the financial leg and not enough, if at all, on the other three legs of the Balanced Scorecard.

When you start to look at your financial leg, it's always best to start at the strategic level. Here are some questions you can ask of your business at the strategic level. These questions will help you to focus on your long term financial goals and objectives for your organization and will allow you to set the operational and tactical measures for your Balanced Scorecard Strategy:

- ✔ What are your financial strategies?

- ✔ Do you plan to invest and grow your business? If so, in what products/services and in what markets?

- ✔ Are you in the more mature stages of your products/services lives? Are you milking them for all the cash they can deliver?

- ✔ Are your products/services in decline, causing you to sweat the future because you don't know what's next on the horizon and you're wondering if you'll still be in business this time next year?

These are basic financial questions in the business world, and you better know the answers to them. The financial leg of the scorecard will give you the help you need to track the right financial measures. For more on the financial leg of the scorecard, head to Part III.

For some reason, many businesspeople consider financial workers to be a necessary evil. They'd like to keep these number crunchers in a closet with a sign on the door that says "Enter only in case of extreme emergency." Don't hesitate to open lines of communication with your financial people. If you want a head start on this leg of the scorecard, learn their language and find out what gets them excited. For example, figure out how to translate your need to invest in new equipment into their language — like discussing improved cash flow and return on investment. You'll find that financial advisors are real easy to talk to.

Measuring your financial health

Market shares, costs of goods sold, financial ratios — such as the price-to-earnings (or PE) ratio — cash flows, return on investment and assets, internal rates of return — it's enough to boggle the mind (or at least give it a good workout)! These are just a few of the common measures that can show up in financial scorecards. An operational manager must understand them all and know how they affect business.

Your senior executives and financial people decide what financial measures your company chooses to focus on. The required measures differ from company to company. Heck, they can even differ between different organizations within a company. Regardless of the measures that you use, you need to understand how to measure your financial health and tie it to your Balanced Scorecard strategies, plans, and tactics.

When you cut through all the different measures, though, you're left with some pretty basic stuff:

- ✔ Earnings
- ✔ Profits
- ✔ Cash flow

All the possible financial measures can be tied back in some way to these three simple measures. How you account for them is up to your bean counters and accountants. Maximizing them is your job. Do you want to grow your company's revenues? Sure you do. But how can you do it? That usually relies upon increased sales and market share — selling to new customers and forging boldly into new markets. What you do in your business depends on where you want to be 5, 10, 20 years from now and the expected market conditions when you get there.

Working in isolation: Departmental benefit and company downfall

A material control manager for a company that builds airframes was losing around $60,000 every month in rivets (the things that hold the aircraft together) because employees would drop them and they'd fall to the floor. After they hit the floor, the rivets couldn't be used until they were swept up and gathered and sent to an inspection area, where people would inspect and bag them to be put back into the system for use. The manager wanted to get a handle on this system, but the approach he took wasn't optimal.

The company stocked and distributed the rivets by providing bins throughout the plant so that workers could get them without going very far. They could walk a few feet to the rivet bins, grab a bunch, and quickly go back to work. When you consider that there were over a million rivets per airframe, this system made a lot of sense. So, what did the material control manager do? He set up a system that got rid of all the rivet supply locations by creating two rivet locations that limited the number of rivets any one worker could obtain at one time.

With the new system, the workers had to walk miles every day to get their rivets. Along the way, they took coffee breaks and spoke with friends they ran into. They wasted time in huge amounts, but the company labeled the material control manager a hero because losses went down significantly. But what about the costs to the other operations? Assembly and manufacturing costs went through the roof because the proper amount of work wasn't getting done. The system put schedules in jeopardy, and the end result was millions of dollars in losses — all so the material control manager could control his department's costs. By any measure, the material control manager made a bad decision and hurt his company and its customers more than he helped.

Don't Lean too heavily on customers

A company in India was shipping kits to a major customer. In order to appear responsive, the company would ship kits immediately to the customer whenever they became available. The company wanted to score high on customer-satisfaction and process-shipping-performance indicators. Some of the kits had several dozen parts or assemblies, so the department transported partial kits whenever it could, sometimes several times a day. This system continued for some time, even though the company noticed rising costs, because the managers thought they were supporting the customer's needs. In fact, the system was causing major havoc — not only with the company's shipping process, but also with the customer's receiving process. The customer had to rent out additional space just to manage the partial kits and all the parts and sub-assemblies that it received but couldn't put into final assembly.

A Lean workshop identified the problem and determined that the company should just ship complete kits. The company used a Kanban (called a _pull system,_ based on customer demand) rather than a _push_ approach to the customer. The customer could now apply the kits to its final process immediately when needed.

Common mistakes made in finance

One of the most common mistakes in the business world is that leaders focus too much on short-term returns on investment and on quick fixes. The drive to maximize shareholder value and acquire quick, easy money makes for some interesting decisions for sure. And when we say interesting, we mean destructive. These decisions tend to foster short-term thinking and dissuade companies from making long-term investments that would improve the health of the companies. Improvements in equipment, people, and processes are ignored.

At the operational and tactical levels, the most common mistake is managers focusing on their own performance metrics without wondering whether achieving operational goals could hurt the overall performance of the organization. We call this mistake _sub-optimization._ One reason for this behavior is the desire to pit business units against each other to "motivate everyone to improve performance."

You need to be mindful of the impact that achieving individual goals has on the overall goals of your company. For instance, always ask how goals link directly to the goals of the business, measuring profitability, on-time delivery, and quality of the products and services you deliver to the customer.

On a related note, here's another common operational mistake: Depending on a department manager to make decisions instead of requiring the input of all the key department or functional managers. In some companies, the operations manager will decide to ship or not to ship based on operational goals, neglecting factors such as quality, expediting costs, or customer capability to handle the product.

Tracking Your Internal Business Processes: Value-Creation Leg

Many companies track some of their internal business processes, but they often ignore many of the things they should be measuring and tracking — especially all the non-core processes within their businesses (those things that you have to do in your business that don't add value to your product or service): paperwork, databases, purchasing, quality departments, warehousing, distribution, and even management. The support processes just seem to keep doing what they do, with no one really paying attention to how well they function. In many cases, business processes are ripe for improvement and can offer up some tremendous returns when companies start digging into them.

That's what the internal business process leg of the Balanced Scorecard is for. In the following sections, we take a look at how your internal business process create value and how you can install effective measures to monitor and improve your processes. We will also discuss the need for looking into the future and anticipating change and the top five problems that managers have in tracking their processes.

Assessing the current state of your business

In order to reap the benefits of process improvement, you first have to know where your company is right now. You have to assess your current performance so that you can determine where problems lie and what you must deal with now. You should measure the time it takes to get things done and how your quality levels compare to what your customers demand.

And for many businesses that look inward, what they find is poor quality. Poor quality costs money — often big piles of money. Studies show that poor quality often costs companies more than 25 to 30 percent of their revenues. However, you can recoup much of that revenue by paying attention to where the losses are generated and fixing the problems. Specifically, you can examine your internal costs, external costs, appraisal costs — the list goes on and on.

If you improve your quality, through methods such as Six Sigma or Lean Manufacturing, you'll reduce your costs and the time it takes to move products through your operations and to get them to the customers. After realizing that much of your processing doesn't do anything but cost you time and money, you can focus on the things that create value to the customer. You can develop and deliver systems and processes that provide maximum value to the customer, with high levels of quality, while maximizing your profit margins and increasing your customer base.

For much more on quality improvement, check out *Quality Control For Dummies*, by Larry Webber and Michael Wallace (Wiley).

Installing effective measures for tracking processes

When it comes to tracking your processes, you need to install some effective measures so that you'll know how you're doing in two key areas: time and quality. You need to measure time because time is money – the longer it takes you to deliver your goods and services to your customers, the greater the costs. You need to measure quality because if you don't, your business won't be along for very long. Every business has some measures of quality, but many of the measures commonly used are too late in the game to be of any help in getting to the meat of cost reduction and quality improvement: they tend to be reactive, rather than proactive. When you get down to the nitty-gritty of your business at the tactical levels scorecards, you want to get to the measures that allow you to be proactive..

Some common measures of time that most businesses use are as follows:

✔ **Lead times:** The amount of time between the placing of an order and the receipt of the goods ordered by the customer .

✔ **Cycle times:** The total time from the beginning to the end of your production/service process, as defined by you and your customers. Cycle time includes *process time,* during which you work on a unit to bring it closer to an output, and *delay time,* during which a unit of work must sit idle until you're ready to take the next action. In a nutshell, cycle time is the total elapsed time it takes you to move a unit of work from the beginning to the end of a physical process.

✔ TAKT time: "Takt" is a German word for an orchestra conductors baton. Takt Time refers to the rate — or beat — at which your processes must be able to operate at in order to meet customer demands for your products or services: It's the output requirement from your processes to meet your customer demand.

Some common measures for quality used by most businesses are as follows:

- Defects per unit produced (a preferred measure to use because, unlike tracking defective units which may have multiple defects for any defective unit, defects per unit tracks the individual defects by type, thus allowing for better analysis and improvement)
- How many defective parts per million
- Defects per million opportunities
- Scrap and rework costs
- Warranty and sales returns

You'll undoubtedly have several of your own measures as well, depending on your business, your industry, and the customers you serve.

Anticipating your business's future state

Knowing the current state of your business is only part of tracking your business processes; you also have to look at where your customers, markets, and industry are headed. What's happening on the technology front? Which of your suppliers' actions may have an impact on your business in the future? Understanding the impact of the future is the job of any business executive, manager, or supervisor, so you have to stay plugged into the available information sources. Here are some sources that provide glimpses of the future:

- Business journals and magazines
- Industry journals
- Seminars and workshops
- Conventions and trade shows

The key to anticipating your future is fully understanding where you are today and what's going on around you (see the previous sections). You have to continually move your focus from the horizon to the microscopic details of your business and back to the horizon again. While you're at it, keep your eyes and ears open for any new technological developments coming down the road. Sometimes, breakthrough technologies will travel far above the posted speed limit; if you're not careful, they may run you right off the road.

The top five process-tracking problems

After looking at the problems that can and will occur while you're tracking your process performance (remember, if something can go wrong, it will), we've identified five that tend to be the most predominant. No matter where we go in the world for business, we run into these measuring issues:

1. **Not involving the process workers in the measurement of their processes and work.** You shouldn't rely solely on automated data-gathering systems, staff, and quality departments to own and measure process data.

2. **Not analyzing the process data for statistical control.** You should use simple process performance-analysis tools, such as line/bar charts and control charts.

3. **Having micro-process tunnel vision.** Don't focus solely on the micro-scopic details of the processes; look also at the overall systems and how the processes work together within those systems. Very often, changes made in processes to improve their performance can actually hurt the performance of the business as a whole. You have to make the right process improvements for the sake of the business, not the sake of the individual processes.

4. **Getting the wrong data.** A big problem is measuring the wrong processes, such as those that don't relate to customer needs and wants. A good example of this is a company who spent a ot of time and money to measure and improve the finish on the product they sold to another company. Unknown to the supplier was the fact that the first thing the customer did with the product was that they roughed up the finish on the part so that they could use it in the assembly of their products.

5. **Not getting real-time data.** You need to measure often enough to get real-time information on your process performance.

If you eliminate these five key problem areas in tracking your process data, you'll put your company ahead of many others in the world that don't get it right. Congratulations! You've made a giant step forward.

Managing Company-wide Knowledge, Education, and Growth: Learning Leg

Managing your knowledge, education and growth is a vital, yet often ignored, aspect of any business. We've all hear the stories of organizations that were severely hurt by the retirement or attrition of a key individual that had tons of knowledge about the business and – oops - that knowledge went out the door with them. It has become such a critical issue that whole new systems designed solely for the purpose of knowledge management have been created.

Unfortunately, many companies just don't do a good job — or any job at all, for that matter — of managing the knowledge, education, and growth of their business. This is, without a doubt, the most neglected and ignored leg of the Balanced Scorecard. And companies wonder why they have an employee-turnover rate of 300 percent or more along with massive quality and cost issues! They are amazed when a competitor introduces a new feature or technology. In these organizations, it always seems that the employees are to blame in the eyes of management. In fact, nothing could be further from the truth.

The ones to blame for being blind-sided by the competition, the high turnover, poor quality, and cost issues are the managers who hire and lead their people. They're responsible for training the employees and making sure they have the necessary tools to do their jobs right. They are the ones responsible for keeping their eyes and ears open fo new developments in their industries and markets. The time has come to take a look into the mirror. If your organization is having troubles because your people don't seem to know what to do, when to do it, and how to do it, or you always seem to be behind the eight-ball when it comes to your competition, it's a pretty good indication that you haven't been paying close attention to this leg of the Balanced Scorecard. By paying attention to this leg of your Balanced Scorecard Strategy, you will prevent these issues from occurring in the first place – and that's why you use the Balanced Scorecard!.

In the following sections, we cover the importance of taking care of your employees' and their development, measurement for your knowledge, education and growth scorecards, and keeping this leg of your Balanced Scorecard on track.

Understanding the importance of taking care of your own

You need your employees not only for the work they do in your business, but also for their ideas and creativity. For your company to be successful, your workers need to be highly trained and skilled in the following areas:

- ✔ In the tasks they perform
- ✔ In measuring their processes
- ✔ In communicating
- ✔ In team-based problem solving
- ✔ In getting along with others

Plenty of competitors have this truth already figured out — that you must take care of your own to be successful — and they're ready to use this knowledge to their advantage.

For all the talk you hear about how companies value their employees, we still deal with many companies that ignore the development of their workers. It all starts in the very beginning, when they hire new employees. Many people get jobs because managers like them, not because they have the necessary skills for the jobs. On the other hand, a new hire may have the necessary skills, but he or she doesn't quite fit in with the culture of the organization. For many reasons, companies try to hammer round pegs into square holes. The result? A lot of headaches for everyone involved.

Allow us to be honest here: The days of workers leaving their brains at the door and just doing the work as management instructs are long over. And thank goodness for that! Can you afford to ignore this vital leg of the Balanced Scorecard? We don't think you can. But what do *you* think?

Measuring knowledge, education, and growth

Measuring the knowledge, education, and growth in your company is very different from the measures of the other three legs of the Balanced Scorecard. With the other legs, you focus on achieving excellence in performance. With this leg, though, you focus on excellence in capability, in terms of where you're going and how you'll get there.

To measure the knowledge, education, and growth aspect of your Balanced Scorecard, you need to follow these steps:

1. **Evaluate the core competencies your organization relies on to provide your products and services.**

2. **Examine your workforce to see what you have currently with respect to these core competencies.** What are your strengths, and where do you need to increase competency and capability?

3. **Determine where you have gaps between Steps 1 and 2.** When you understand what you need, you can compare the needs to your employees' current job skills and knowledge — skills and knowledge that you need not only to get work done, but also for your company's future capabilities.

4. **Choose an appropriate strategy to close the gaps.** You can count on one of the following:

   • Employee development (training, for example)

   • Talent and capability acquisition (buy a company with the specific competence you need)

   • Recruiting (hire subject-matter experts)

5. **Plan and execute your strategy.** Make sure you adjust accordingly along the way, because your work here ties into the other three legs of the Balanced Scorecard.

Appropriate, accurate, and timely measurement here makes the difference between whether your organization leads or follows in a market. For instance, we have seen recently where two hotels competed in a highly tourist-based market. The one hotel chain focused on fundamental services, and trained its workforce on precision, courtesy, and the rules of the hotel. The other, while still focusing on courtesy, trained its workforce on what is going on around the city, where to go for good food, entertainment, shopping or sightseeing. The second hotel chain had done a bit of market analysis, and determined most of the clients were from out of town, and wanted to get out and see the town. So, while the first hotel excelled in service and room amenities, the second hotel surpassed the first by a rate of two to one in their fill rates, because their employees were well versed in finding out what the client really wanted, and then helping the client get it.

It also determines how you measure progress and how fast you can detect and correct for any deviations from the expected scorecard performance objectives. Be sure you examine the following areas of your company:

✔ A good place to start is to look at what your company makes — the products and services it provides. To whom do you provide? In what markets? To what degree? Owning 85 percent of a market requires a different approach — perhaps expansion to other markets — than if you own only 5 percent (in which case you may look to expand your market share). Also, understanding the types of products you provide in your markets can suggest other applications, expansions, and opportunities.

✔ You need to know the geography of your market share. For example, you may own 15 percent of the global market, which may consist of 90 percent of the Central European market for your product. In this case, you need to think about how your group will need to approach the other 85 percent in ways that are different, given the different geographic and cultural aspects of these prospective clients.

Some companies design and use a simple matrix with employee names in the vertical column (Y-axis) and required job skills in the horizontal row (X-axis). They populate the matrix so that they can determine basic worker capabilities and the work their employees can perform, as well as gaps that need additional knowledge, skills, and capabilities — acquired through planning and executing employee development plans.

Staying on the right course in the fourth leg of the scorecard

Due to the pace of business (fast — *very* fast), you need a plan for measuring growth, education, and knowledge, and you need to monitor your progress against it. To stay on the right course takes effort and constant vigilance. As employees come and go due to internal transition, promotions, and attrition, the front-line managers must have the tools necessary to assess and develop employees. The real nuts and bolts of this leg of the scorecard are in the hands of the immediate supervision, whether they be process workers, supervisors, or managers.

All guys and gals who have employees reporting to them should have a knowledge, education, and growth dashboard that examines current needs and how they're met, as well as future needs and how the managers should be developing their people to meet those needs.

Using Dashboards to Apply Balanced Scorecards to Your Business

One of the most effective ways to ensure that your business is on course on all four legs of the Balanced Scorecard is through the use of dashboards. *Dashboards* provide you with critical, current information about the operation of your business, just as your car's dashboard gives you critical, current information about your car. Business dashboards allow you to keep track of how things are operating and let you know what needs attention — either through immediate action on your part (your engine light comes on, so you turn your engine off) or through action in the near future (your gas-tank icon lights up, so you need to put gas in before you run out). See Figure 1-1 to see how dashboards fit into the Balanced Scorecard.

People see and use all kinds of dashboards in their daily lives; here are a few examples:

- In aircraft cockpits, allowing pilots to make course or altitude corrections to stay on their planned flight parameters.
- In air-traffic-control centers, which use radar tracking systems both as a tool to manage the multitude of aircraft coming and going and as a

dashboard to provide continuous status reports of where each aircraft is and its respective heading and altitude.

✔ On your television, in the form of stock-market reports that flash across the screen to tell you what the value of a stock is at any given moment.

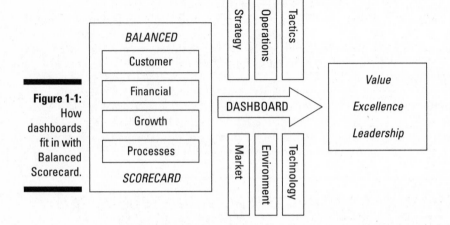

Figure 1-1:
How dashboards fit in with Balanced Scorecard.

In business, dashboards provide the same intelligence but in different ways, depending on the information and how you'll use it. Companies use dashboards as a way to manage their daily, weekly, and monthly activities according to the guidelines and key process inputs established in their Balanced Scorecards and business-performance expectations. Here are a few business dashboard examples:

✔ A water treatment company may set up a dashboard to monitor liters per minute of water treated and the quality and flow parameters, tying directly to the company's revenue stream for the amount of water treated per minute.

✔ A hotel may set up a dashboard to examine occupancy on a daily basis and issues that come up. For instance, the hotel could focus on turnover, theft, and other operational issues that tie into the bottom line.

✔ An automotive manufacturer can establish dashboards at different levels so that it can see activity by the minute on the assembly line while tracking and adjusting sales rates daily. The dashboards allow the company to still manage development of new products to condensed cycle times, with better integration and time to market.

When applying dashboards across a Balanced Scorecard's four legs, don't take the easy way out and try to get one, all inclusive dashboard that tries to capture everything on one page. Your business is far too complex for that. Developing dashboards that go across process and systems and that link among the strategic, operational and tactical levels take some thought, careful preparation, and lot of planning, measurement and diligence. You probably won't get them perfect the first time you try them. They will need to be adjusted and refined. As your business changes, so must your dashboards.

The really cool thing about dashboards is that after you create them, your job of monitoring your business, knowing where your problems are, and taking appropriate action in a timely manner will become much easier. And what you'll really come to appreciate is that dashboards will keep those "We're here to help you!" staff and management types from breathing down your neck. Now that's something worth shouting about!

The following sections dig a bit deeper into the topic of dashboards.

Market, environmental, and technology considerations for your dashboards

As you plan for, develop, and implement your Balanced Scorecard Strategy and related dashboards, you need to consider many factors that that will affect what you focus on and measure. Here they are:

- ✔ **Market:** You need to look at your particular market performance characteristics, including new-product-introduction cycle times and any quality and delivery issues (long lead times, for example). You should tailor your dashboard to support your business-specific market needs to give you a competitive advantage. Be sure to include aspects that would give you a clear advantage in the marketplace, and use these aspects to drive your decisions.

- ✔ **Environmental impact:** Look not only at your local region, but also across the broader environmental arena in which customers use your products and services. This includes the business environment and its implications regarding Sarbanes-Oxley and other legislative edicts issued in recent years (in the United States), as well as any regulatory constraints specific to your business. You can design your dashboard to monitor and manage your risks in these areas; early-detection and -correction systems can help you avoid potentially damaging and costly mistakes in your operation.

✔ **Technology:** The final consideration focuses on technology specific to your industry and your products and services, and actually integrates with the other two considerations. Your dashboard needs to reflect the technology associated with your business — not only to provide real-time updated intelligence, but also to enable you to stay competitive by providing technology intelligence as early as possible and where it may impact your business most.

For example, when new products in the cellphone business boasted of Bluetooth capability over traditional wired headsets, companies raced to incorporate this technology into their latest models. The fastest gained dramatic advantage in the market, albeit only temporarily. But these companies were able to set the standard by which everyone else had to strive to.

Your dashboard must be able to indicate technology shifts and enablers in all four legs of the scorecard — especially in the customer and process areas because providing a poorly supported new capability is worse than not having it at all.

Reviewing strategy, operational, and tactical scorecards and dashboards

Okay. Let's take a minute or two to review the scorecards and dashboards among the three levels: the strategic, operational and tactical levels. The strategic level scorecard is developed by senior executives and it's the driving force for all of the other scorecards, dashboards and their measures. It's the "big elephant" in the room. At the strategic level, you will develop your strategy map and then use that map to determine the measures and tactics that you will use for tracking your strategies and tactics at the strategic (executive) level, the operational (mid-management) level, and at the tactical (front line) level.

The key consideration when looking at your strategic, operational, and tactical scorecards/dashboards is linkage — or what we call "stringing the single thread." *Linkage* is achieved by ensuring that your measures at the strategic, operational and tactical levels are tied together and supportive of one another, as well as being linked across the four legs of the Balanced Scorecard. These scorecards/dashboards have to be well-integrated or they won't do the job you want them to do.

The things you do and measure at the tactical level, such as defects or errors per day, have to support and achieve the things you have on your operational dashboards, such as the quarterly departmental goal of reducing overall defects by 25 percent; the operational scorecards/dashboards must achieve the things you need at the strategic level, such as reduce the costs of a particular product or service line by 75 percent within three years. Also, you have to know how much the tactical and operational measures will contribute to achieving your strategic goals and objectives — by how much and when.

The following list presents a process called Catchball that will help you accomplish the linkage you need among the strategic, operational and tactical levels and across your organizational functions.:

✔ **Strategic Leadership Team**

Objectives:

- Define strategic goals, objectives, and metrics for the four legs of the scorecard (often defined by competitive and best practices benchmark studies).

- Deploy goals, objectives, and metrics throughout the strategic leadership team.

- Identify the actions and steps necessary to achieve the goals, objectives, and metrics.

- Pass down to the operational level.

✔ **Operational Level Team**

Objectives:

- Determine if the strategic-level passdown is achievable. If not, resolve the issues and pass back up to strategic level team to get concurrence and consensus. If so, set operational-level goals, objectives, and metrics.

- Deploy goals, objectives, and metrics to the operational team.

- Identify the actions and steps necessary to achieve goals, objectives, and metrics.

- Pass down to the tactical level.

✔ **Tactical Level Team**

Objectives:

- Determine if the operational-level passdown is achievable. If not, resolve the issues and pass back up to operational level to get concurrence and consensus. If so, set tactical-level goals, objectives, and metrics,

- Deploy goals, objectives, and metrics to the tactical team.

- Identify the actions and steps necessary to achieve goals, objectives, and metrics.

- Make it happen!

Chapter 2

Building and Balancing Scorecard Strategies

*T*he problem with many companies — at least those that choose not to use the balanced-scorecard strategy to manage their businesses — is that they're unbalanced. No, "unbalanced" doesn't mean that their buildings are leaning over like the Tower of Pisa. When companies are unbalanced, they don't pay attention to some very important aspects of their businesses. And like the town drunk trying to walk a straight line to get to the next bar, an unbalanced company will fall down and get hurt — sometimes seriously hurt.

For instance, they may pay attention to their financials and internal processes, but they may totally ignore their employees' needs for learning and growth or do a haphazard job of finding out what their customers really want. As a result, unbalanced companies employ poor strategies and make a lot of wrong decisions. They get blindsided by things that seemingly come out of nowhere, and they spend time and money trying to figure out what went wrong and assessing blame. And after they fire the "culprits," they keep on doing the same things that got them into trouble to begin with.

The bottom line: Balance is essential. But to achieve the balance your company needs, you first have to understand a few things: how to determine and link your strategies across the four legs of the Balanced Scorecard, what to do if you lose your balance, and how to deal with the shifts in your markets that affect your long-term strategies. In today's fast-paced business world, ever-changing landscapes will require you to make changes. You have to be pretty swift of foot to keep up.

This chapter takes you into the world of strategies and how they drive your Balanced Scorecards — in other words, it helps you understand the few things you need to make your company balanced. You also get some good tips on how to stay ahead of the ever-changing tides of your markets and the external forces that will come along and force change upon your organization.

Understanding How the Four Legs Interact and Link to Strategies

At the core of every Balanced Scorecard is the need for a company's senior executives to develop corporate strategies for all the legs of the scorecard. You can't just set up the four legs with measures and then go off and do your thing. That "thing" you do has to be tied to your key scorecard strategies, and your strategies have to be linked in such a way that you know how they affect the four legs of your Balanced Scorecard.

So, before you begin developing strategies for your business, you need to get an idea of how your strategies affect the four legs of the Balanced Scorecard and how your resources play a vital role in making those strategies work. Use the information in the following sections to establish a firm view of how your strategies and resources relate to the Balanced Scorecard.

Putting strategies in the driver's seat

Figure 2-1 shows how your company's leadership, scorecards, dashboards, and measures for the four legs provide the pillars that support your company's vision and strategies.

How heavily are each of the four legs influenced by your strategies? Get ready for our favorite MBA school answer: It depends. It depends upon the strategy, on your business, and on the things that influence them, both internally and externally. The key is that you give each leg its due consideration, figuring out how each of your strategies impacts each leg and then developing the plans, tactics, projects and measures that will achieve your long-term goals and objectives.

The following list gives you an idea of the things that need to be done when putting your strategies into the driver's seat:

 ✔ Develop your vision, mission, and guiding principles for your organization (usually done by the executive team with the help of mid-level management)

✔ Develop your long-term strategies and goals based upon strategic analysis and planning (usually done by the executive team with the help of mid-level management)

✔ Develop your strategy map, operational and tactical plans, goals, and objectives analysis and planning (done by mid-level management with help from their direct report employees and senior management)

✔ Develop Balanced Scorecards and dashboards (done by mid-level management with help from their direct report employees and senior management)

✔ Implement plans, measuring and monitoring progress and updating scorecards and dashboards as necessary

✔ Adjust strategies, plans, and tactics as necessary to achieve success

This is not a one-time event! It is an ongoing process that becomes an integral part of the way you manage your decision-making process and run your business.

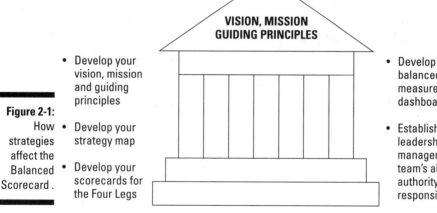

Figure 2-1: How strategies affect the Balanced Scorecard .

Focusing resources on your strategies

Identifying and focusing your strategies on all four legs of the scorecard is only part of the equation (see Figure 2-2 as well as the section "Developing Your Strategy Map" for more on identifying and developing strategies) — although it's no small accomplishment in itself. You also need to ensure that you align and focus your resources when implementing your strategies. This means focusing like a laser beam on achieving your strategic goals and objectives by applying the resources needed to succeed. Resources to be budgeted include things like:

- Money (you knew that one was coming, didn't you?)
- Time (yours, and your employees')
- Administrative support and supplies
- Training and education of your employees (scorecards and dashboards, team and process improvement skills, job skills, etc.)
- Space to meet and operate, and places and systems for display and communication of scorecards and dashboards
- Integrating scorecard and dashboard software with your information technology systems and databases to allow ongoing monitoring of your strategic and four legs goals, objectives, and performance

Now, we're not saying that you open up your wallet or purse and start writing blank checks. Like any other business function, a good amount of business financial planning and cost accounting goes a long way. The level to which you allow your teams autonomy to handle their funding and make decisions on their own depends upon their maturity and development in handling such decisions.

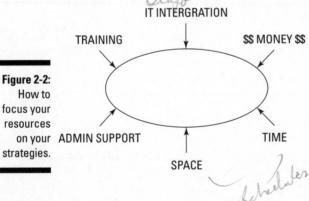

Figure 2-2:
How to focus your resources on your strategies.

Borrowing from Other Companies' Success

As you focus and align your resources to achieve your scorecard strategies, you'll zero in on some key areas. Robert Kaplan and David Norton, the fathers of the balanced-scorecard approach, identified five principles that are common to companies that have enjoyed success through the use of Balanced Score-cards. In the following sections, we list the five principles and explain how you can benefit by taking the same approaches to Balanced Scorecard strategies.

By using the approaches outline in these principles, your Balanced Scorecard becomes not only a method, but also a system for the long-term strategic view of your organization. It becomes a process wherein you translate your company's vision, communicate and link your strategies to your business-planning processes, and develop feedback based on what you learn along the way. During the entire process, you communicate, communicate, communicate — and then communicate some more.

Translating strategies into operational terms

The first principle is translating your scorecard strategies into operational terms — in other words, into tangible and measurable terms.

You translate factors like the following into terms that you can measure and manage for value creation:

- ✔ Reducing cycle times translates into reducing the number of minutes or seconds it takes to complete the detailed steps within a process

- ✔ Increasing market share translates into increasing the percentage of a market for your specific product or service and the need to forecast for the expected increase in volume, potential needs in human capital, training, plant and equipment, and so forth

- ✔ Increased innovation translates into the number of new ideas, methods or features that better satisfy the customer or that improve the business

- ✔ Improving employee and customer satisfaction translates into increasing the number of retained employees and customers (reducing turnover rate), or improving employee and customer satisfaction levels, and reducing employee absenteeism rates

- ✔ Focus on core competencies translates into improvements in your value streams and the potential outsourcing of non-core systems or processes

These sometimes financially intangible measures translate into the value they create for your customers and shareholders, such as revenues from new services and products, retained customers, and profits. Translated strategies provide a common language and framework for your entire company to use. Instead of one function speaking English, one speaking Chinese, and the others speaking who knows what, all your functions speak in the same language — one that's well understood and measurable.

Aligning your organization to the strategies

To align your organization to your scorecard strategies, you want to create synergies among your various business units and functions. The breaking down of functional silos and barriers and improved communication and coordination are the keys. To achieve this, your executive team should set a consistent message and priorities, linking business units and shared services within the company.

Making strategies everyone's daily job

Incorporating the strategies into your employees' everyday work means ensuring that all your employees understand the strategies and how they can contribute to attaining and sustaining the strategic goals and measures. An executive's job becomes one of communication, education, and eventually empowerment of the workforce to continually improve and work toward achievement of the strategies.

Strategies should be deployed downward to the operational and tactical levels of the company, and the various levels should be allowed to individualize their scorecard measures and to go beyond functional boundaries and silos. Team-based and corporate-gain rewards and recognition incentives should be established to motivate scorecard knowledge and achievement. You don't want your people walking around like a bunch of mind-numbed zombies; take the blinders off and allow them to view the organization as a whole.

Turning strategic deployment into a continual process

You must take three basic actions to make strategic deployment a continual process:

- ✔ Link your strategies to your budget.
- ✔ Call on management to hold regular reviews of the strategies during their normal meetings and reviews.
- ✔ Develop a process for learning and adapting the strategies.

Rather than the once-or-twice-a-year, half-hour review of strategic goals and performance, with the associated variance analysis where everyone gets two minutes (or less) to explain why they're not achieving goals as planned and what they think they can do to get back on track, strategic deployment becomes a topic for discussion on a regular basis. By regular we mean once or twice a month, not once or twice a year. And, oh by the way, the meeting may take a few hours—or even more—if necessary.

Mobilizing change through your executive leadership team

You must strive for the active involvement, support, and ownership of the process by your executive team. It comes down to walking the walk and not delegating the strategic deployment and balanced-scorecard approach to other staff members. If your executive team sends the message that Balanced Scorecards and strategies are important but they're too busy to get involved, your company will hear the real message loud and clear. And if it isn't important to the executives, it won't be important to them. Every person has the same 24 hours in a day, and we all seem to make time for the things we consider to be priorities.

You're looking at a changed management approach, not just another tried-and-failed, go-out-and-measure-everything-and-keep-score exercises. It comes down to making a fundamental change in how your managers and executives view the management of your business and its culture. Remember, keeping score by itself doesn't tell you a darn thing about how to win the game. If you try to manage solely by the score on the scoreboard, you'll win only by the luck of the draw. In order to win consistently, you need to have

- ✔ Good team players who get actively involved in the scorecard game.

- ✔ A sound strategy and gameplan for winning based on your team's knowledge, skills, and abilities.

- ✔ A good understanding of your competition and their strengths and weaknesses .

- ✔ A willingness and ability to change in the face of new and unforeseen developments.

What if the four legs of the scorecard — customer, financial, internal processes, and learning and growth — aren't enough? What if your executive team thinks they need more than four legs to truly achieve organizational balance? Perhaps they want some additional scorecards that handle research and development, your supply chain, or your company's leadership. Well, go ahead and add them! The four legs create a template for you to use, but they aren't written on stone tablets. You can be versatile and use scorecards in whatever ways you find necessary to cover all your bases. The four legs are just the bare minimum.

Developing Your Strategy Map: A Balancing Act

Developing your scorecard strategies and making the strategies the core of your business objectives are the main goals of the balanced-scorecard approach. To meet your goals and to achieve balance among the four legs of the scorecard, you need to develop strategy maps. These maps are typically (and best!) developed by senior executives and their direct reports, and they form the basis for the operational and tactical level plans, projects, and scorecards.

Strategy maps are the vehicles by which you ensure that your scorecards have balance. Strategy maps also allow you to see how your operational and tactical plans and initiatives are linked and work toward achieving your strategic objectives.

It takes some work on your part and the part of your management team to create strategy maps, but the effort is really worth it. So, call a meeting with all your management peers, lock the door when everyone enters the room, and don't leave until your strategy map is done (make sure you order some coffee, doughnuts, and bagels — and don't forget the cream-cheese spread!).

Doing your mapping homework

Before you gather the faithful and lock the meeting-room door to get your strategy map done, you need to do some strategy homework. Gather and review the following information:

- Your annual reports
- Your mission statement (if you don't have one, get it done!)
- Your corporate and organizational values and guiding principles
- Your vision for the future
- Your project plans and initiatives
- Consultant studies, reviews, and reports
- Performance reports for the past 12 months
- Competitive data and analysis
- Your organizational history (to get in touch with what the founders of your company valued and wanted to achieve)

✔ Stock-market analysts' reports (if available)

✔ Trade journals and news articles on your company

✔ Benchmarking reports and information

Be cautious not to play follow-the-leader and just do what other companies have done — especially when it comes to competitive and benchmark analysis. These have to be *your* strategies and scorecards, not just carbon copies of what other companies have done. And, while you're at it, look for a consistent thread regarding your vision, mission, values, and guiding principles. If these statements aren't consistent, revise them to make them so.

Drafting the strategy map

If you've done your strategy homework (see the previous section), you should be ready to develop your strategy map. The strategy map in Figure 2-3 gives you a good idea of what the end result may be. Your strategy map will undoubtedly be more complex than this example.

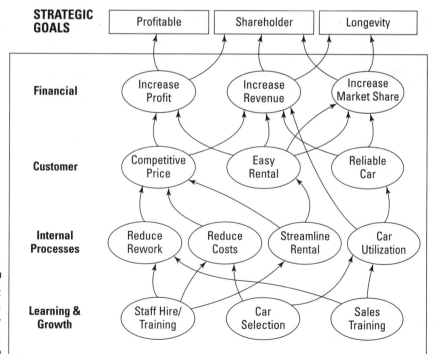

Figure 2-3: A simple strategy map.

To create a strategy map, follow these basic steps:

1. **Gather and analyze the necessary information: Market studies, industry reviews, SWOT (Strengths, Weaknesses, Opportunities, and Threats) analysis, financial statements, etc.**

2. **Develop business strategies, such as: Grow the business by 50 percent, or increase customer retention rate by 15 percent within three years.**

3. **Develop the objectives and goals for each leg of the scorecard.**

4. **Ensure that all of the interactions and linkages are defined among the four legs.**

 Some companies want to start with the financial leg first by setting financial goals before working on the other three legs. Others may start with the customer leg first, assessing customers, markets, and customer trends and forecasts for the future before getting into the financial leg. It may be one of those "Which came first: the chicken or the egg?" discussions. Your executive team must make the call, but we'll say this: There's some logic behind starting with your customer and market studies. Many companies set unrealistic financial goals and then try to force them upon their organizations, only to find out that their customer bases and markets won't support them. Starting with the customer leg and then moving to the financial leg based on a realistic assessment of your customers and markets helps you avoid this issue, which prevents some potential rework in the long run.

 Using strategic-planning tools such as SWOT analysis, Delphi analysis (futurists' view of likely trends in markets), best practice and competitive benchmarking can be invaluable when developing your long-term strategies. For more information on these topics, simply do a web search and you'll find tons of information at your fingertips, both for free and for a price.

Ensuring a Balanced Scorecard (And What to Do When Yours Isn't)

Making sure that you have balance within the various legs of your scorecard comes down to a close examination of your strategy map (see the previous section). Did you miss anything? In other words, can you identify any holes in the map? Get your people back together to review the strategy map. Though you will constantly be reviewing and revising your strategy map while it's being developed, you should do one final check before blasting it to the world and issuing your marching orders, just to make sure nothing slipped through the cracks. You should also have a continual review and revision process in place to make sure no unanticipated problems develop as things change (don't you hate it when that happens?).

The reviewing process of your strategy map gives you a great opportunity to communicate your strategies to your people. Take full advantage of it. As you make changes to your strategy map, review it with your people to get their ideas; check it for any holes or omissions; and communicate with them about your strategies. The balanced-scorecard approach is, after all, a continual process.

When reviewing your strategy map, check for holes or omissions, such as:

- ✔ Obvious holes made by ignoring one or more of the four legs in your strategy map
- ✔ Failing to link strategies between the four legs, such as: Not taking into account the potential technological ramifications of a decision to enter a new market (impacting upon all four legs of the Balanced Scorecard through potential impacts to customers, increased financial needs, new or revised internal business systems and processes, and needs for new employee knowledge and skills)
- ✔ Undefined ownership, responsibility, and authority for each element identified on the strategy map
- ✔ A lack of defined and measurable goals for each element of the strategy map

Figure 2-4 is a diagram of a nifty tool, originally developed by Walter Shewhart and W. Edwards Deming, called the *Shewhart Cycle* (though some know it by the name of The Deming Cycle, PDSA, or PDCA Cycle).

Figure 2-4: The Shewhart Cycle is a tool that helps you maintain scorecard balance.

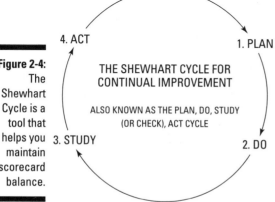

4. ACT

1. PLAN

THE SHEWHART CYCLE FOR
CONTINUAL IMPROVEMENT

ALSO KNOWN AS THE PLAN, DO, STUDY
(OR CHECK), ACT CYCLE

3. STUDY

2. DO

Getting more than lip service

One company that we worked for (in a distant galaxy, far, far away) adopted a once-every-three-or-four-months — whenever the urge hit the senior executives — strategy map and scorecard review style. Well, it eventually became apparent that the process was broken because during each review, the people presenting would have to get up in front of the executives to explain why they weren't hitting their marks, why they had variances, and what they planned to do to get back on track. This went on for about two years until someone decided that the reviews were only giving lip service to the entire process and no one, including the executives, was taking the process seriously.

Fortunately, the executives were learning about some guy named Dr. Deming and a thing called the Plan, Do, Study, Act Cycle and how it drives continual improvement. In one of those famous (or infamous) closed-door meetings that executives love to have (especially when things get interesting), our executives resolved to make strategy maps and Balanced Scorecards important parts of how they ran the business. They went back to square one, starting over and taking the steps we discuss in this chapter. They began to hold frequent reviews — once a week at first and then every other week — and as the message was heard loud and clear throughout the organization and people started to achieve and report progress rather than recovery plans, they went to once-a-month reviews. By applying the PDSA Cycle, the executives got the business back on track — and kept it there.

By using the Shewhart Cycle and applying it to your strategy map and Balanced Scorecards, you put your organization in a continual process of

Plan

Do

Study

Act

After you *plan* for and select the strategies, projects, initiatives, and measures, you implement them *do*. After implementation, you *study* them to ensure that they do what you intended them to do and measure what needs to be measured. Once they are just right and on the mark, you *act* to make sure that you sustain and control them. Then you start the cycle all over again, when appropriate.

By following the Shewhart Cycle, you ensure that you'll never lose your balance with your strategy map or Balanced Scorecards. Continual improvement is a wonderful thing, indeed!

Adapting to Changes in Your Markets or Business

"Change is constant" is one of those universal laws of life, and it never rang so true as in the business world. When it comes to change, you have only two options: manage it as best you can, or bury your head in the sand and get run over by the steamroller that is your competition. We recommend the former option; it's far less painful!

Here's our no-money-back guarantee: Change will affect your strategy map and your Balanced Scorecards. You can do nothing but be prepared for it and manage it. Accepting the need to roll with the changing tides of your markets and business will put you far ahead of companies that take the steamroller approach. That's the good news. The not-so-good news is that it requires time, effort, and due diligence to make sure you see the signs of change coming before they run you over. The sections that follow give you some good direction to ensure you're prepared for and can anticipate changes that will affect your scorecard.

Spotlighting external influences and their effect on your business

So many external influences can force change upon your organization, and it may become a little overwhelming at times. Fortunately, you can do some things to stay ahead of the curve and remain prepared for change. We discuss how to prepare for changes that affect each of the four legs of the Balanced Scorecard in the following sections.

Customer-leg influences and their effects

You better believe it: Your customers change over time. Their expectations can change for any number of reasons:

- ✔ Higher expectation levels
- ✔ The effects of your competition driving ever-increasing demands for better quality and service
- ✔ Always faster and maybe cheaper products/services
- ✔ New technologies and ways of doing things

A chilling look at customer expectations

One need only take a trip to the refrigerator to see how The Kano Model is true. In the dark beginnings of time, people didn't have frost-free freezers; layers and layers of ice were the norm. These layers of ice invariably grew thicker over the course of a month, eventually choking off the freezer and encasing its contents in an arctic prison. The cure? Users had to unplug the freezer for a few days to let the ice melt. The invention of frost-free freezers was understandably a real delight to customers. They didn't have the product before, and they were tickled pink to have this new innovation in their kitchens. Customers would even pay a little extra just to have the luxury.

Try to go out now to any appliance store to find a refrigerator that doesn't have a frost-free system. Good luck — you'll be looking for a while. Would you even consider buying one? Heck no! You see, the innovation that was a real delighter has become a basic level of expected performance. If a refrigerator manufacturer doesn't provide it, the company isn't even close to being in the game as far as the customer is concerned.

Whatever the reasons, the customer expectations placed upon your products/services will constantly be changing, so you need to forge very close relationships with your customers. Listen to what they have to say about your company.

Just because customers are happy with you today doesn't mean that they'll be happy with you tomorrow. A wise fellow from Japan named Kano understood this and developed what's called *The Kano Model*. In the model, he describes how a company's performance that satisfied the customer at one time won't even come close as time goes on. Why? Because the customer comes to expect more from you and your company. Kano went on to say that the things that delight the customer now will be expected performance in the future.

The Kano Model forces you to continuously look for new innovations and ways of delighting your customers while you work on delivering what they already expect at the basic levels of performance. You can't rest on your laurels when it comes to the customer leg of the scorecard! Not when it comes to what customers expect from you.

To stay ahead of the ever-changing customer-demand curve, you also need to look outside your organization:

- ✔ Keep your competition in your sights — especially what they're doing and how they're doing it.

- ✔ Examine your competitors' best practices, and find out if a company that isn't your competitor may have some practices that you can benchmark and make your own.

- Look into developing your own latest-and-greatest innovation or new technology (this can get expensive and risky, but if you hit a home run, it really pays off).

- Make it a habit to rummage through business and industry journals to see what's out there and in the pipeline for future developments in your markets.

While you're at it, find out if you can borrow some ideas from outside your industry and markets. Many of the so-called "inventions" and "innovations" in the marketplace were actually adopted from unrelated industries! Do the proverbial "thinking outside the box" and see what you can borrow from others.

Financial-leg influences and their effects

Let's hear it for Wall Street! So, do you think the dot-com businesses felt the influence of any external financial changes forced upon them? Maybe just a little? How about a lot! And the thing is, for companies that really paid attention to what was going on, they saw the changes coming. Almost every day, some newspaper or radio talk show was saying how overpriced the dot-com market had become. Yet, when the crash came, plenty of companies got caught flat footed and really felt the pain.

Always watch the markets and read the reports about what's going on in your business and industry — especially within your market segment and their stocks. Read the analysts who review your market segment, watch the cost of capital, and track investment dollars. See where the smart money is going.

Some of the common financial influences include

- The effects upon costs of goods sold resulting from a change in the price of a commodity or raw material (for example, consider the ramifications of the changes in the price of oil, especially on airlines and transportation and the markets they serve).

- Unexpected shifts in the cost of capital

- The emergence of a new competitive product that eats into your market share

- Mergers and acquisitions within your industry

The one thing you may be powerless to predict is a global political happening. Sadly, the attacks of 9/11 falls into this category. The influence of that day on business was profound. Travel was curtailed because nobody wanted to fly anywhere. Plans for new products and services were put on hold. Almost everyone went into a wait-and-see-what-happens mode, and some of these modes lasted more than a year. Some companies never recovered from the hit.

For more on the financial leg, see Part III.

Internal-process-leg influences and their effects

The internal-process-leg influences are much the same as your customer-leg influences. Your internal processes are heavily influenced by the following:

- ✔ Your customers
- ✔ The competition
- ✔ Innovation
- ✔ Best practices

The financial side also influences internal processes, in terms of cost of capital and investments in new or upgraded plants and equipments.

When looking at ways to understand the effects of external influences on your internal processes, take a long look at the things that influence your organization both from the customer and financial arenas.

Learning-and-growth-leg influences and their effects

The effects of your need for employee knowledge, skills, and abilities can be just as profound for your organization as the other legs — maybe even more. When new technologies, systems, and processes come into the market, that knowledge comes at a very high premium. Just take a look at what happened with the Six Sigma quality move (see the upcoming sidebar). Seeing the huge salaries available, Six Sigma experts flooded into the experience vacuum to take advantage of the market conditions for their knowledge.

For this leg, you should keep a close eye on universities, colleges, trade schools, new technologies, and consultants. You need to see what's in the pipeline in the education system and what influences new technologies are exerting that require new knowledge, skills, and abilities.

Can supply and demand for new knowledge and skills have an impact on your company? You bet it can! Therefore, some companies will wait out the new technologies and the knowledge requirements that go along with them until the situations stabilize. This is a strategic and tactical decision on the part of your company that has to be balanced with what your customers want and need and what you're willing to pay in order to deliver it (versus the costs if you don't).

Keep your eyes on the places where new knowledge is being introduced and see what's coming down the pike. Based on your observations, weigh your options and make your decisions on the best course of action: jump on the bandwagon or sit out for a while and wait for things to cool down on the supply and demand curves.

Dealing with the supply and demand of knowledge

When Six Sigma first became the latest-and-greatest thing, a trained and experienced Black Belt could easily get a salary of over $150,000 a year. Why? Because these experts were hard to come by, and it was a simple matter of supply and demand — demand was high and supply was low. Master Black Belts could get even higher salaries.

Now try to find out what Black Belts are making today. If you check the papers or do an Internet search, you'll find that they get much less than $100,000 a year. Sure, some companies pay more, but they tend to target Black Belts who also have some managerial abilities (like directors and managers of quality or supply-chain managers). Again, it comes down to supply and demand. The demand is still there, but the supply is now fat, dumb, and happy.

Recognizing early warning signals

Early warnings of potential issues, concerns, and problems are worth their weight in gold (or platinum or diamonds, for that matter). The good news is that you can use Balanced Scorecards to do just that: give you some early warning signals, particularly at the tactical level.

At the tactical level, you measure and report on the key indicators at the project and process levels of detail. Your tactical-level scorecards and dashboards—when they measure the right things with timely information—will provide early warning signals that things will soon go wrong at the operational and strategic levels. You can catch those things before they become problems at the higher levels.

What are some of the things you can catch at the tactical level before they hit the executive suites?

- ✔ Quality of products/services that are going wrong
- ✔ Process issues that affect delivery
- ✔ Revenues that aren't quite performing as needed
- ✔ Rising costs of goods sold

Almost anything and everything you measure at the tactical level should provide an early warning signal that, if you don't fix an issue, it will hit the operational and strategic scorecards and dashboards in a negative way. Isn't that neat?

Balancing in today's environment — a moving platform

It bears repeating and keeping in mind: You have to be ready for change. You have to prepare for it. No matter what your plans are, you should have some contingency plans ready for when things don't go the way you want them to. Trust us, your organization will have to change them from time to time.

One way to make sure your business is prepared is to do some what-if scenarios. It's a simple process, asking the question, "what if this happens?" or "what if that happens?" Conduct some good brainstorming sessions and be open to many possibilities. Questions can be far reaching and varied:

What if the competition does this or that?

What if a new technology on the horizon comes along faster than anticipated?

What if one of your suppliers goes in the tank?

What if . . . well, you get the idea.

In some organizations, what-if people are looked upon as nay-sayers. They seem more than willing to throw a wrench into the works with their visions of potential doom and gloom. Just as people are getting ready for the first chorus of Kumbaya, the what-if types pop up and put a halt to the celebration, and everyone groans and moans. Well, you need to encourage everyone to embrace the what-if people because they can save your bacon. They help you keep your feet firmly planted when your platform moves on you so that you're ready and prepared to deal with the situation. You'll have your contingency plans in pocket; all you have to do is pull them out, dust them off, and get going.

Chapter 3

Planning For the Balanced Scorecard

....

In This Chapter

▶ Mapping out the basic planning process

▶ Acquiring the necessary resources and support

▶ Setting the foundation for your Balanced Scorecard

▶ Giving your plans a final inspection before implementation

....

So, you've decided to try a Balanced Scorecard approach for your organization (or are at least considering the possibility). First, congratulations! But before you head straight to the meat of this book to get started, we need to talk. You have a few things to put in place before you can start establishing and using a Balanced Scorecard. Planning is an unnatural thing to do; it's a lot more fun to just start doing an activity so you feel like you're accomplishing something. But, before you jump into an activity — especially in the business world — it makes sense to lay out a roadmap so you can be certain of where you are now and where you want to go.

You may be surprised at how similar a company is to a house. The foundation of a house must be sound in order to safely support the rest of the house. A company is no different — the foundation of a business defines the success of its structure and systems. In this chapter, we explore the critical elements and framework necessary for Balanced Scorecard implementation and sustained success. In this chapter, we introduce several key planning considerations, explain how to ensure that the foundation is solid, and review ways for both sustaining and communicating your scorecards for a continued competitive advantage in your marketplace.

Getting Your Planning in Order

Getting started in planning your Balanced Scorecards means following a simple, standardized multi-step roadmap to first confirm what you want to do and how you intend to do it, then defining how you intend to measure doing it, and finally outlining what specifically you will do better than your competitors. And you'll do this all while taking changes in your market, customers, employees, suppliers, components, data and many other factors into account.

When planning your Balanced Scorecard, you should go through the following steps in the order shown to achieve the best results:

1. **Design your Balanced Scorecard strategy.** The Balanced Scorecard should align with the overall business strategy of your company. Elements of consideration should include key company or organizational achievements, goals, and objectives. One of the best tools to use in this step is the Strategy Map (see Chapter 2).

2. **Plan the framework of your scorecard.** The framework should be customized to your business and your industry, and consist of the four legs of your scorecard, and include key elements such as risk and variation indication, and interrelationships between the legs as well. It is here that you will build the foundation and structure of your Balanced Scorecard process. Elements of consideration should include how each leg of your scorecard will provide insights into how the company is doing now, and how it will do in the future. Also include feedback/flexible loops that can both enable detection and response to key changes which may affect business performance.

3. **Plan how you'll put your scorecard together.** This includes all of the key metrics identified in the earlier steps, interlinking them in such a way that they are directly related to each other. Elements to consider should include how well the metrics relate to the direction and mission of the company, how well they show what you need to see, and their ability to indicate change or variation quickly and effectively.

4. **Set up support for the scorecards.** You'll need support throughout the organization, but especially with its leaders and managers. Elements to consider here must include their input, from design to metric selection to how performance will be assessed, as participants, not just onlookers.

5. **Plan the implementation and tracking of your Balanced Scorecard.** Link the scorecard to every activity and event, and to the key performance indicators for your department and your business. Elements of consideration will include how your managers and employees will perceive and successfully implement and communicate their scorecards, the effectiveness of the feedback loops, and flexibility to changing conditions, among other things.

6. **Plan a self-assessment process.** As mistakes are occasionally made, your organization can learn quickly and effectively from them and make adjustments along the way. This enables a continuous improvement and refinement capability, which is critical to the long term success and sustainability of your scorecards. Elements of consideration should include designing a good "lessons learned" process, and integrating the study and understanding of the results of this process into new project and scorecard implementation processes.

Planning Your Work and Working Your Plan

The plan for your Balanced Scorecard involves some complexity in both width (across your company) and depth (within each department or function). In this section, we introduce you to the initial key actions you need to take before developing your scorecards and dashboards (for the basics on dashboards, see Chapter 1).

Planning for the resources you will need

To understand and apply your company's resources when and where you need them most in the planning stages of scorecard implementation, you must consider these vital five points:

✔ **Resources are constrained.** We never have enough people, money, time, space for everything we want to do. For planning, we need to tailor our approach to the level of available resources we can dedicate, in terms of level of effort, timing, and response—both in funds and people.

✔ **Successful scorecards are collaborative.** This can be a force multiplier when planning your scorecard resourcing, because everything in a company is related to everything else. Utilizing this characteristic in planning means aligning the different available resources to support more than one leg or scorecard component, in order to gain advantage with fewer resources.

✔ **Priorities can and will change.** Plan for this, especially as different priorities can and do impact resource allocation. Build processes into your planning for shifts in direction, so that you are prepared with contingencies.

✔ **The future is important, but so is the present.** It's easy to get caught up in the future, but you have to be careful not to compromise the present. Watch your key risks regarding planning for resources in the current state situation, and where they need to be allocated best for scorecard support. Then, plan for an effective transition for your resources toward supporting future initiatives.

✔ What to do when you don't have what you need. Options include, but are not limited to:

- Paring down what you want to do

- Stretching the time period for action

- Planning for some of the resource responsibilities to be shared with management and key leaders, to free up key resources

- Reconsidering how you were planning to use the resources, and seeing if there is another way that might prove more effective.

- Narrowing the task to a specific area, division, product line, or function first, and then to the other ones in turn.

Garnering support from management and others

Planning for, designing, implementing, and sustaining a Balanced Scorecard system requires support, encouragement, and involvement from just about everyone in your organization — especially key leaders and managers, since they are the decision makers within your organization, and they have the power to enact change in the work environment. Imagine planning a deployment strategy for a new product line, or to break into a new market, and then attempting to execute the plan all by yourself. It is highly unlikely to happen. The reason is that you need to work with and depend on a variety of key people who are needed to bring such a plan to fruition. Implementing your Balanced Scorecards is no different, because your leaders and managers likewise have to feel the same level of ownership and commitment, since their scorecards (and even dashboards) will work together in enabling the overall organization to accomplish its mission. Enlisting their support must happen early and often, and include the design, development, and implementation of the scorecards as well as their support structure.

Within your group or organization, you need to contract for Balanced Scorecard support. All your leaders need to integrate their different actions to manage the Balanced Scorecard so that your company can minimize duplicity and enhance its skill and knowledge leverage.

If you've ever implemented any kind of change program, you know that you have to spend a fair amount of your time selling the concept — idea, the roadmap, the benefits, the WIIFM ("What's in it for me?"), and many other aspects of the program. Here are several tactics you can use to get everyone on the Balanced Scorecard bus:

- ✔ From the beginning, especially during the planning period (see the first section of this chapter), include fellow managers, and invite critics to participate as well. As these people participate in the planning process, they'll commit to the overall implementation, too.

- ✔ Publish as many of your scorecard submittals and ideas as you can, giving credit where possible. This has a good chance of motivating people to provide input and get involved — especially the "the wait and see" folks.

✔ Conduct reviews with different groups before scorecard implementation to get their feedback.

Involve many people, and invite different perspectives to get innovative, new ideas about Balanced Scorecards, from planning concepts to expectations, and be genuinely interested in every submittal. You'll come across as a leader who's interested in the feedback and ideas of others, and you'll benefit from the collaborative, diverse thinking of many people.

✔ Set up a phone number for folks to call and ask questions. Put a policy in place to return answers within 24 hours. And make sure you get it done!

✔ Don't assign one person to always give answers to scorecard questions. Solicit ideas from multiple managers whom you'll count on to develop and implement their own Balanced Scorecards and dashboards.

✔ Set up a list of standard questions or FAQs (frequently asked questions) on your company Web site about Balanced Scorecards, dashboards, your deployment plans, and your roadmap. Include some text about why your company is doing this and the benefits of scorecards. Express your need to have people involved and committed, and encourage employees to share their thoughts, ideas, and experiences.

Building the Foundation and the Structure of a Scorecard

When everyone in your company is on board with scorecard implementation, supporting your vision and concepts of what needs to be done, you can start laying the foundation for your scorecard. (If you don't have everyone on board, just skip back to the section, "Planning Your Work and Working Your Plan" for info on how to get them aboard.) A good foundation has

✔ Key involvement across the company

✔ A sound understanding of customer/supplier relationships through the product and service value streams

✔ Systems and processes in place to support the implementation and sustaining of a Balanced Scorecard approach

✔ Dashboards set up for measurement tracking

In this section, we look at what it takes to establish your scorecard's foundation and structure. You need to put the building blocks in place, make room for adjustments as needed, and consider contingency plans if your assumptions are inaccurate.

Check in with your employees frequently to renew their support and build their faith in themselves as they move forward in the planning steps. This will also ensure that the people who are planning the scorecard deployment have an opportunity to share their thoughts with you, and gives you the chance to correct any misperceptions or make adjustments along the way in real time.

Stacking the building blocks for implementing a scorecard

One of the critical aspects during the initial planning stages is to ensure that all four legs of the Balanced Scorecard are included, as well as considering the concepts, benefits, general steps, and key indicators of success and return expected of scorecard implementation. You may not want to go to the detailed level of a blueprint, but perhaps paint an overall picture in order to give folks some idea of what you have in mind and to indicate distinctive differences in the approach from how things are done now, to help assure success. If we compare the process to building a house, it would be like a diagram to highlight several floors, vaulted ceilings, and innovations in bedroom, bathroom, and other areas.

Planning building blocks are critical to ensure that you build the right systems that work best with the structures in place. You wouldn't build a skyscraper on a garage foundation; it wouldn't have the proper support. A foundation must provide the necessary attributes to allow Balanced Scorecards to work well and enable dashboards to be effective tools in managing your business. You need to put the following specific building blocks in place to be sure that you have a good foundation:

✔ Make sure your approach is clear, complete, and simple to explain. Management depends on others to make scorecard implementation work, so be clear and concise about what it is that you want to do so that everyone understands your concept of how to deploy Balanced Scorecards.

✔ Review your company's strategies for growth, development, performance, and understanding and meeting customer needs to ensure that they're sound and concrete. Update any missing or incomplete information based on the latest market, customer, technology, or environment findings.

Make sure your strategies contain no contradictions. In other words, if you want your company to grow, make sure your predictions for growth don't contradict your margin-achievement actions. Likewise, you can discuss cost-cutting measures, but be consistent when combining them with increasing headcount to create competencies in new areas.

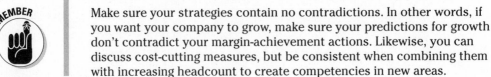

✔ You need to have some initial degree of agreement amongst your leaders regarding your overall scorecard approach. This means setting up structures for discussion, review, and adjustment in Balanced Scorecard deployment strategies against your plan. Companies often achieve this through an executive steering team that oversees deployment and determines any changes to the plan for maximum effectiveness.

✔ You need to comb through your company's results/analysis systems and structures. You need to

- Make sure information is readily available to **you.**

- Check out the current systems with which **your company** analyzes information and makes decisions.

- Find out how your company evaluates decisions regarding operational and strategic performance.

You need to integrate the results/analysis systems and structures into the Balanced Scorecards and especially the dashboards developed and utilized throughout your company. Use any strengths of these systems to your advantage, and understand and take into account any weaknesses or limitations.

✔ You may have to install certain process measurement capabilities before you can implement Balanced Scorecards. You need basic information about financial performance and other operational measures, and if these measures aren't available or aren't current, you need to fix this problem first.

Adding flexibility so you can adjust a scorecard for effectiveness

Famous leaders have always alluded to the fact that after you implement a plan, you often need to make adjustments after the fact — sometimes within the first several moments. So, you need to plan not only the scorecard implementation well, but also your methods for tracking progress and leaving room for the possibility of change. After you implement, you may need to adjust actions, observe the results, and change again.

Some people want to plan immaculately, taking months to make sure they take everything into account. Others realize that they just need sufficient planning and communication to get going; they recognize that things will change, and they build in systems that allow them to make adjustments quickly and effectively. The latter groups are the folks who are getting things done; the others are busy talking about changes or trying to decide why they can't be done.

The key is to strike the best balance of advance planning and flexibility possible, to enable quick, decisive action when the current environment requires it. In other words, plan enough to get started—realizing that the plans will change anyway—and begin.

With all the changes that occur in markets and with customer demands, technology, and environment — not to mention changes due to people moving and changing careers and goals — you need to be sure to include a flexible structure to allow for changes in your Balanced Scorecards and dashboard deployment. The key is to build in processes to a enable quick, responsive assessment capability of your current business situation, along with a decision process that can take this information and process it to give you options regarding what has to change and when. For example, if your primary supplier of a key component was to go belly-up, then having such an assessment and decision process in place would enable early detection of this problem, and enable quick consideration of various contingencies for the best solution.

The following list presents some more things to consider when building flexibility for change into your scorecard plan. The next section explains in detail which tools or methods are best for this approach:

- **List your assumptions in your plan, and put a process in place to regularly assess them.** You want to see if they still hold, and you want to be alerted when they're no longer valid. For example, a truck transport company would need to regularly check assumptions around driver skills, driver and truck availability, diesel fuel pricing, and changing traffic construction conditions. If options and contingencies are planned well in advance, then when changes are detected early, adjustments can be made to minimize the impact on performance.

- **Build in a way to assess the risks associated with specific actions taken when implementing your Balanced Scorecards and dashboards.** You could do a "what-if" for each action to see cause-and-effect relationships and to see if you've planned for each effect adequately. This way, you can trade-off risks to decide the best course of action for a given situation.

- **Build in a periodic self-assessment process so each manager can look at his or her scorecard and dashboard objectively.** To ensure objectivity, you could have different managers look at each other's scorecards and offer suggestions or ideas for improvement.

- **Put change processes in place that enable fast adjustment and have good measurement capability.** You want to be able to detect mistakes early and allow for re-adjustment. Deploy all changes to the appropriate level, favoring distributed rather than centralized decision support.

Most people are visual learners by nature, so pictures and graphs go a lot further in providing clarity and understanding in trend analysis. You want your employees to easily see key indicators of performance.

Contingency planning methods

Now it's time get into the meat of your friend and ours: contingency planning'. Contingency planning isn't risk management; risk management needs to occur at all levels, but contingency planning is about planning for alternatives on the basis of potential changes in market conditions, customer behavior, or other external influences to your business. Contingency planning means looking at what would happen if some of your assumptions about the market, customers, and environment turn out to be untrue. You can also plan for regulations that may change or customer demands that could shift. For instance, in the music industry, iPod digital-music technology has completely altered the future market of CD-based businesses.

Some companies have devised very effective ways to plan for contingencies. Most have not. A common problem is the only people attempting to plan for alternatives are the same people who set up the strategy in the first place. People have a natural bias toward believing that their plans are going to work; basic assumptions about the world in which your plan exists couldn't possibly be wrong, could they? You need a method to ask that question and ask it effectively so that you can include options and alternatives for possible eventualities.

The best example of a successful contingency planning process is the Wargaming portion of the U.S. Army's Military Decision Making Process, or MDMP. There we find the staff split up into role players, each determined to challenge the planning of his or her colleagues in a simulated battlefield environment, to see what would happen if events did not occur as expected. The success of our armed forces is proof that this tried-and-true process works well. For businesses, it can be no less demanding to plan effectively for contingencies and alternatives, so that if and when things change in the marketplace, they are ready.

You need to have "new eyes" on your plan — both in the planning and the execution — so that you don't become susceptible to groupthink or other self-convincing traits common in groups or teams. Involve outsiders who don't have a vested interest in making the plan work. The cost of not considering possibilities may be your customers, your market, and even your company.

Here are some key elements instrumental in planning for contingencies in your operations:

- **Systems in the planning process that allows you to challenge the plan.** You can use force-field analysis, devil's advocate role playing, or Ed de-Bono's 6-Hat Thinking methodologies. Many other methods would work, too; you should design a system that works best for you and your team.

- **Call in an outside expert to assess your plan regarding risk and contingency planning.** Even if you are sure you know best, install an "outside eyes" process check within your contingency planning process, and be sure to bring in the best, so that your planning can ultimately take the right perspectives into account.

✔ **Require managers who plan for their Balanced Scorecards to also set up contingency planning processes.** Require deliberate, standardized methods that require managers to critically assess their plans and actions based on possible changes, and make this a pass/fail gate to plan authorization and implementation.

✔ **If possible, compare contingency plans from similar organizations, departments, or functions.** Set up a benchmarking process to look for the best planning practices both in and out of your industry, and enable sharing so that each team can benefit from other planning methods.

✔ **Design triggers in your Balanced Scorecard implementation plan that will warn you and others when certain conditions change.** Once you have planned effectively, run a Failure Mode and Effects Analysis (FMEA)-based risk assessment tool, and ensure you have designed effective detection and warning signals into your scorecards, and especially your daily dashboards.

Adding the Final Touches

After you've tested and proven your plan and have shared it with other managers and groups to get their feedback, you have another task to accomplish before execution: You need to add the details — the small yet significant items so necessary for a plan to enjoy success. The following sections help you focus on the final touches that might be easily overlooked.

Taking care of the details

The following list outlines some details that allow you to put the final touches on your scorecard foundation:

✔ Clearly identify roles and responsibilities for the people who will play a part in your plan to deploy Balanced Scorecards. Make sure you have their commitment to these roles and responsibilities prior to execution.

✔ Identify the milestones by which you'll evaluate your plan and make them clear on your scorecard. Also include the measurements on your dashboards so that you can see and report progress quickly and efficiently.

✔ Establish configuration control on the final version of your plan.

✔ Start the clock rolling after you put your plan into motion, not before.

✔ Put specific review dates on the calendar to review progress, performance, and any other meetings or key activities regarding Balanced Scorecards and dashboards. Get commitments from key participants for these reviews.

✔ Track and adjust your plans/scorecards openly and honestly. Search **for** help and advice from teams and other managers, and communicate frequently with supervisors so that they know what you're doing and why.

Ensuring that your scorecard is fireproof

For whatever business you're in, you need to plan a direct relationship between what you need to measure with your Balanced Scorecard and your dashboards. Whether you work in retail, wholesale, manufacturing, engineering, consulting, or even banking, your managers have to make sure that their scorecards balance all four legs and that their dashboards appropriately indicate relevant factors for change.

For example, a clothing retailer would balance between existing inventory and new models and financial performance against growth rates, and it would devise a dashboard to indicate how these would relate in simple terms. The company would also establish threshold alarms to detect any variation in the balance that needs immediate attention and adjustment. Such a retailer would want to make sure that its measurements and dashboard truly indicate potential risk factors. It wouldn't make sense, therefore, for the retailer to measure thread or button consumption, phone calls per day, or perhaps garments mis-racked per day, because these measures wouldn't relate directly to the *key performance indicators* (KPIs) relevant to the business — such as margin, profit, volume, inventory levels, and style changes. We will cover this connectivity throughout this book specifically through each of the scorecard legs, since dashboards are the daily barometers of our company's performance planned for in our Balanced Scorecards.

Performing a final inspection

So, you're ready to implement your plan. The last question you must answer is, "Can I live with our Balanced Scorecard system, our dashboards, and the methods we'll use to monitor, update, adjust, and respond to the performance of our department, operation, or business? In other words, will this system be something beneficial to me and my peers and other managers?"

This question is very important. People often get caught up in the excitement of all the action around them and forget to stop and reflect on what they're doing. Sometimes, what kicks us off in certain a direction isn't enough by itself to keep us going, and we wonder what we were thinking in the first place.

When it comes to Balanced Scorecard planning, you need to feel like you can commit to the program, from the very start until the end, and that the program will indeed bring your group to the level of performance and continuous improvement you've always wanted to achieve.

If the answer is no or if you aren't sure, go back and review your plan again, and look for where it begins to come apart. Many times, a reality check by the author or program manager of an initiative will uncover a fatal flaw that went undetected in the planning process. The flaw may be small yet absolutely key to the success of the plan or initiative.

Chapter 4

Putting Your Balanced Scorecard into Action

In This Chapter

▶ Launching your Balanced Scorecard

▶ Making sure your scorecard passes the test of time

▶ Spreading the word of scorecard throughout your business

As you know with any change or improvement, sustaining power is the key. So is it the same for scorecards. In this chapter, we will talk about when to put your scorecard into action, and how to ensure it sustains, in order to best support your initiatives toward competitive advantage.

Deciding When to Launch Your Balanced Scorecard

After much hard work and preparation, it's finally time to launch your scorecard! The key people are in place, metrics are selected and allocated to the appropriate leg, and measurement systems are working to sustain the scorecard. But wait: there are two things that must first be in place when you launch your scorecard.

The Scorecard passed the pilot, and everyone knows it!

The *pilot* is where you prove the value, worth, and effectiveness of your scorecard. By implementing your scorecard in a controlled pilot environment, you can seen how it works, adjust as you go, and ensure that the goals and objectives are successfully met — and perhaps even exceeded.

When your scorecard passes the pilot, be sure to share the success with everyone, every day, at every level — whenever you get the chance. You want word to spread about the success of the pilot, and about how getting workers involved with the development and implementation of the scorecard was instrumental in this success. Also, you need to share the results in terms of key performance impacts on the business. By getting the word out, you are setting up for general acceptance and agreement as to the overall value added of your scorecard. When you have completed this, you are ready to go to the second step:

The Scorecard is seen as genuinely adding value

Getting employees to see the scorecard as adding value to your company is a critical step in the ultimate success of your scorecard efforts. For scorecards to have lasting power, people have to believe they will work, that they add value to the organization, and that it is worth their while to participate in their success. You have to be sure that most of the folks believe that the scorecard will actually help them in their achievement of their goals and objectives, and that this will work without appreciable added work involved. You know this to be true. But you need to be confident in this shared belief.

Once you have confidence that most of the people are willing to work with their scorecard, and feel comfortable with the success of the Pilot, you are ready to launch!

Sustaining the Balanced Scorecard

The Balanced Scorecard has to become second nature to your company and your managers. For this to happen, you need to make sure that the process of managing with Balanced Scorecards is sustainable and flexible (so you can adjust it to better fit current needs).

Having your Balanced Scorecard in place is one thing. How many times have you seen a newly initiated system or process last only until the next full moon, never to be seen again? This often happens, as you may know, because the change was supported by a memo or maybe even some training, but not much else. Common flameouts include policy changes, changes in shift schedules, new travel process changes, and other administrative actions.

Another important concept to remember is that the planning and execution of your Balanced Scorecards and dashboards have to happen in concert, if the scorecards are to be effective. Think of it like this: If a symphony was played one instrument at a time, first a flute, then horn, then violin, there would be something that might be able to be labeled as noise, but nothing remotely resembling music. Only when all instruments play together and support each other does harmony happen. So the same is true when making business decisions for the company.

Indeed, even the name "Balanced Scorecard" implies a need for balance, harmony, and symphony, especially in its implementation and while you sustain it. Managers and leaders need to listen to each other and adjust their activities as they support each other and the company while they move toward achieving long term goals and objectives.

In this section, we talk about the fundamentals of implementation and sustainability as they relate to Balanced Scorecard and dashboard use, communication, and contingencies.

Promoting the scorecard concept

An effective way to help sustain your Balanced Scorecard initiative is to make it part of the very fabric of your company. In other words, treat it like it was part of the program all along, no different than any other process. However, you should make it seem promising, as if it will be very important to your organization's future success. So, how do you do this? Take the following actions:

- ✔ **Make the scorecard part of your strategic planning.** Refer to balancing your business through scorecards and utilizing dashboards to support your business decisions every day.

- ✔ **Promote Balanced Scorecards in a very positive light.** Refer to successful examples where companies with similar products and services implemented the Balanced Scorecard approach.

- ✔ **Encourage your staff, subordinates, and others to read about Balanced Scorecards.** Ask them to talk about the topic amongst themselves and consider how they may apply the concept and practice to their businesses, departments, or sections (for more on the basics of scorecards, see Chapter 1).

- ✔ **Recognize others in your company who are considering Balanced Scorecards and how they can help, and recognize and support scorecard applications, regardless of the outcome.** The important thing is to encourage experimentation and consideration, in spite of the perceived risks or unfamiliarity that may come with these ideas.

> ✔ **Be quick to recognize and adopt business practices that use Balanced Scorecards, and encourage others to do the same.** Look for ways to standardize as well, and make the practice an integral part of management policy and practices within the company.

For more on communicating these thoughts and ideals to your coworkers, see the following section.

You must manage expectations on the part of your employees. A Balanced Scorecard program allows for better decision making, more real-time data management, and greater flexibility and decisiveness. However, your employees shouldn't expect and demand immediate and significant change. Reminding everyone that although the Balanced Scorecard is a critical tool in successful business management, it doesn't guarantee success in and of itself. Your company must implement the scorecard in an environment that's open to self-evaluation and to potential changes necessary for better performance, which may require fundamental changes to the structure and systems currently in place.

Making scorecard the talk of the town

You know the guy who talks and talks about a particular sport, obsessed with this player or that key maneuver, to the point where you want to tell him in no uncertain terms that you've had enough? Are you that person? If so, good news: When it comes to sustaining the Balanced Scorecards, your people can never get enough. Of course, you must become the obsessed manager who can talk of nothing else in every form of communication — be it at meetings, during discussions, through memos, on references, and even when conversation is light and unrelated to work.

To sustain the scorecard through communication, you need to take a look at the different ways you communicate — be it through conversation, all-hands gatherings, e-mails, phone discussions, and meetings, and integrate them to create a sustained, regularly re-invigorated, continuous conversation about the scorecard and how we are doing. The following list covers the ways you can make scorecard the talk of the town:

> ✔ Work some reference to Balanced Scorecard into pretty much every business conversation you have, regardless of whether the topic seems related to the discussion or not. For example, during a conversation about a potential new client, ask how we will measure success. Another example would be if you are reviewing today's performance with the foreman, ask how he or she is measuring process performance and where improvements are being made, and how does he or she know? There are hundreds of opportunities to link activities with scorecard elements in a relevant and meaningful way.

✔ Adopt some special phrase to stick at the end of your sign off on all e-mails and correspondences. For instance, many people include quotes, or a famous saying, or a fond wish for a safe future. .

✔ Insert a set of coach questions into key discussions surrounding performance and relating to measures, scoring, visibility, and flexibility in responding to changing conditions. For instance, when discussing performance of a business unit, ask about customer and process metrics, how they know they are doing well, and how that ties to financial measures as well.

Offer ideas on how to measure, track performance, and link processes to knowledge or financial performance (see Part III for more). Ask your employees how they make key decisions and why, and prompt them to think about using scorecards and dashboards to help manage their areas better.

✔ Challenge processes that have stayed the same for a while. Old habits die hard, as they say, but with the world changing as fast as it is, we need to ask why we are doing things today the same way we did them five years ago. This has be done everywhere, especially in the finance, HR and legal departments.

✔ Set up management discussions with your peers to discuss integrating operations and functions. Use these times to talk about balance in your business and ways to better integrate skills development with operational and financial performance. Again, suggest in these discussions how scorecards and dashboards can help.

✔ If your business has a Web site, consider adding content that introduces how you're balancing your business or department. Include discussions that focus on each leg of the Balanced Scorecard and how scorecard helps performance, and insert some helpful hints on how to implement each leg. Direct your employees to this site to spread the word.

✔ Consider your company's guiding principles, and look for ways to integrate a balanced-scorecard approach to support them in conducting business.

✔ Highlight examples of companies that have planned and executed their scorecards with success, and mention new and innovative dashboards as well.

If possible, you should c solicit ideas and guidance from a company communications or PR specialist for these and other ideas. Also, make sure your scorecard plans integrate well with your organization's communications plans and activities to reinforce synergy and coalition. The upcoming section "Mastering the Art of Communicating Your Balanced Scorecards" discusses the topic of communication even more.

Cooking up the best time to launch

Most chili experts say that it takes many hours — even days — to create the perfect pot of chili; they scoff at the idea that a good chili can be prepared in only an hour or two. They believe the chili has to cook slowly so you can let the ingredients blend together at very low temperatures to allow for the best flavor, simmering, and mixing.

Balanced scorecards are launched and sustained well because, just like chili, the ingredients of the mix or blend are founded on your company's blend of factors such as market and customer changes, product mix, internal politics, and the internal workings of your organization,, all come together in just the right way. The foundation is in place as well, to ensure the measures are consistent with the measures used in key decisions.

For you, creating the right environment to launch and sustain means patience as well as perseverance. The pace may seem incredibly slow, but you have to hang in there. Here's how you can get through and help others get through the waiting — patiently:

✔ **Talk to and highlight progress with leaders and managers.** The key is to talk about how Balanced Scorecards will provide key advantages to your organization, and consistently use every opportunity to encourage and highlight progress in your company.

✔ **Be there for your employees.** For your employees, scorecard launch means change. You need to be with them and help them when they have doubts, encourage them when they try, and coach them when they fail.

✔ **Support learning from mistakes, rethinking, and adjustment.** In other words, taste the chili as you go. For sure, the first set of scorecards will probably be wrong, and the dashboards may be completely unrelated. However, you will learn, and your people will learn, and they may even surprise you after a while with possibilities in dashboards and scorecard elements you did not think of or consider.

Mastering the Art of Communicating Your Balanced Scorecards

Communicating with your organization about Balanced Scorecards is an art. Yes, we said *art,* and we mean it. Communication is a huge factor in planning and executing Balanced Scorecards; whether you do it well can and does determine to a large degree the success you achieve. In business, companies have to focus energy on delivering customer value and achieving market share while providing good (and even great) return on investment. We like to think of communication as the lubricant that makes your company successful in these areas.

When planning your Balanced Scorecard strategies and actions, you need to consider and design your communications strategies as well. You want communication to support your plans and to enable employees at all levels to understand the whys, hows, whens, whos, and whats of your scorecard and dashboard implementation. With this understanding, your managers can design and implement scorecards throughout the company.

In this section, we look at communication at the different levels within your organization and how powerful it is in shaping and defining your balanced-scorecard approach.

The view from the top: Senior executives

If you're a senior executive, you've led a significant change within an organization before. The difference is, with Balanced Scorecards, you must decide what's necessary to communicate in order to convince and motivate your managers and employees about the benefits. How can you help them manage their areas and support the decisions needed as things change, which they often do?

With Balanced Scorecards and integrated dashboards, your managers can detect and correct deviations from your strategic and operating plans. What you communicate sets the stage for how well this happens and for what direction their decisions will take your company going forward.

The following list presents some key communication considerations for senior executives implementing the scorecard approach

> ✔ **Above all, share your vision and long-term strategy for the company.** Present your vision in a way that includes implementing Balanced Scorecards and dashboards throughout the company. Talk about how employees can use scorecards and dashboards to see how well they're working toward achieving the goals of the organization. Also, talk about how they can use dashboards to make and support better decisions.

> Employees look to you for vision, direction, and consistent leadership, all of which benefit from the successful deployment of Balanced Score-cards throughout your organization. What you say, do, write, and sup-port says volumes about what you believe to be important. Sharing your strategies and expectations about Balanced Scorecards sets everyone

on a common path and ensures that your workforce works hard to support your vision for the long term. (For more on communicating to the company, see the section "Making scorecard the talk of the town".)

✔ **Discuss the importance of knowledge sharing.** Knowledge sharing is a key strategy for today's companies — especially those that want to stay ahead of the competition in terms of new products, services, and capabilities. Communicate that Balanced Scorecards will enable greater sharing of knowledge, skills, and capabilities within your company through integrated measurements and scoring. Also be sure to remind how they can use dashboards to quickly detect and correct potential inconsistencies.

✔ **Stress the need for long-term thinking.** Help your people understand that Balanced Scorecards don't resolve short-term performance; they're an investment in providing for a better working environment. Over time, information will be shared, not controlled, and informed management and workforce teams will make better decisions about process improvements.

✔ **Reinforce that Balanced Scorecards are here to stay.** You aren't just running a new activity or program to "save the day."

Surviving scorecards as a middle manager

Middle managers have the most difficult job as far as communicating scorecard knowledge and strategies is concerned. Why? Because of the following responsibilities:

✔ They must communicate in the interest of doing the right things right and motivate their sections, departments, or function to deliver products and/or services as required

✔ They must be cautious about what gets communicated in their areas and consider the repercussions to them, their teams, and their management. Managers need to know what to communicate and what to withhold as well as how to protect the company's interests.

✔ They must manage expectations because they're the front-line leaders who work with the teams responsible for delivery of goods and services.

✔ They have to work within ever-changing environments, deal with increasing demands from both senior management and their workforces, and constantly face newer tasks with fewer resources.

Alas, the middle manager has the most *important* role in ensuring the successful implementation of Balanced Scorecards. While the senior managers are busy forming strategy and direction and the workforce members are

executing the critical actions that deliver value to customers, the middle managers have to juggle implementing the strategic actions occurring across the company with managing the hundreds of daily activities that provide products and services to your customers.

When it comes to Balanced Scorecards, middle managers form the backbone of any organization:

- ✔ Leading their groups through performance challenges on a daily basis
- ✔ Working to achieve their goals and objectives
- ✔ Integrating their actions with other departments to form a well-oiled and operating company
- ✔ Sharing with other managers how well the company is doing
- ✔ Integrating all four legs of the scorecard so that executives and managers can make decisions quickly and effectively

Supervisor involvement will ensure greater communication, skill development, and practice, and help integrate the different levels of management with the reality of the operating teams environment.

Spreading the word from the front line

The front line — the people manning your workforce — is where the action is. Employees make, assemble, pack, and ship parts and products/service. They buy, transfer, and consume components. They execute services every day and plan, schedule, conduct, complete, and record countless transactions.

Because supervisors and line leaders can most directly relate production with performance, they must understand the advantages and gains to be had from communicating a balanced-scorecard approach on the front lines.

Some of the key advantages you can gain from the front lines include the following:

- ✔ Process workers are closest to your business reality (satisfying the customer), so they can help a lot in the communication department by verifying your measures and your performance.
- ✔ After members of the workforce come to understand the idea behind balancing a business with scorecards, managers can include them in the assessment and improvement of processes toward better performance against the scorecard.

✔ Involving the workforce in scorecard communication can improve the design of dashboards and reinforce the importance of self-development within teams and overall departments.

✔ Supervisor involvement will ensure greater communication skill development and practice, and help integrate the different levels of management with the reality of the operating teams environment.

Involvement = commitment, so by bringing your supervisors and their workforces into the Balanced Scorecard world, your company fosters an environment of commitment toward using scorecards and dashboards for possible performance improvement. Your company also demonstrates that its business decisions will take all four perspectives (or legs of the scorecard) into account and go beyond the previous short-term, near-sighted financial goals

Avoiding communication pitfalls

All businesspeople have made communication mistakes in the past. When some people think they're communicating, they may be just confusing, and if they don't check back occasionally, you can bet they'll leave the people hearing their messages room for interpretation. Interpretations of messages may come close or be very far away from the intended meanings.

The following list presents some communication pitfalls you must avoid when putting your Balanced Scorecard into action:

✔ **Touting scorecard as the big, be-all, end-all program:** Be careful with this. Be honest about what Balanced Scorecard will do for your company — how it will help you coordinate and integrate your activities better — but also include the implementation and sustaining challenges as well.

✔ **Making up a reason to change:** You don't want to send the message that you're changing the organization just because you want to install a scorecard. You first must have and communicate a need to change — regarding market or customer penetration or performance improvement — and explain how the balanced-scorecard approach will help you achieve this change.

✔ **Not being aligned with one message:** When senior managers talk about synergy, integration, and collaboration, but lower-level managers talk about internal competition where one shift, line, or department beats another in performance, you don't have alignment with a common message. Giving mixed messages will destroy any scorecard progress you make, so guard against sending out conflicting or contradicting statements or actions. Work to focus all leaders and managers in a collaborative way (see the earlier section "Making scorecard the talk of the town").

When your company commits to Balanced Scorecard and what you plan to do, stick to the message, even though it may not work well in the beginning. Whenever people try something new and it doesn't work so well, they want to fall back to what's familiar, no matter the consequence. You need to be consistent and persistent in your message, having patience all the while. Be unwavering in your resolve to say and do the same things toward successfully bringing Balanced Scorecards to your business.

✔ **Communicating in a vacuum:** You don't want to rely on one-direction communication, where you send messages but have no way to know if people hear, receive, understand, or comprehend what you're trying to say. This happens when managers conduct large, all-hands meetings to communicate a message and then expect everyone to know what's going on. Half the people may not have understood, and the other half think they understood, but most heard only what they wanted to hear.

Large group announcements don't work, and never really have — unless you want to announce the company picnic or pizza party. To make sure all people understand your messages, you need to communicate in small groups and allow for feedback in multiple ways.

✔ **Portraying insincerity:** You can't hide insincerity. People communicating about scorecard must believe in the Balanced Scorecard and come across in a sincere way. You want employees to trust you and actually try out the concepts, even with the risk of failure, because you truly believe it will work in the end.

✔ **Trying to tell everyone all by yourself:** Face it, you don't have enough hours in the day to sing the praises of scorecard by yourself, nor do you really want to try. Part of successfully deploying Balanced Scorecards is delegating the responsibilities to lead, develop, and implement scorecards at different levels. You'll realize that it's often better to learn by doing than by being told what to do.

✔ **Dispensing inadequate communication:** Believing in and implementing Balanced Scorecards takes not only considerable planning and timing, but also constant nurturing, attention, and advocacy by you, your management, and workforce teams. Most folks find managing four legs of the scorecard simultaneously within a complex business environment scary, so they need constant reminders that it will work.

Part II

The Customer — The Critical Leg

The 5th Wave

By Rich Tennant

"Our customer survey indicates 30% of our customers think our service is inconsistent, 40% would like a change in procedures, and 50% think it would be real cute if we all wore matching colored vests."

In this part . . .

No business exists without their customers, including yours. To be successful with your Customer Leg of the Balanced Scorecard Strategy, you must first understand your role with customers and how to measure what they want and need. You then need to know how to build your customer scorecards and dashboards and figure out what they are telling you — and the pitfalls to avoid so that you consistently hit the mark with your customers.

Chapter 5

Understanding Your Role with Customers

*U*nderstanding customers is difficult for many businesspeople. Heck, many customers don't even understand themselves. Delivering what customers want, when they want it — and then giving them just a bit more to "delight" them — often seems like an overwhelming task in many organizations. But it is a necessary task. Your workers need to understand how their jobs directly impact your customers instead of focusing solely on day to day tasks, crises, and deliveries. Establishing the customer leg of the balanced scorecard will help you focus your employees on the customer.

"What do our customers value, and what are they willing to pay for?" "How do we know if we're truly delivering value to our customers?" "How do we know if we're hitting the mark and dealing with problems before they become customer complaints?" These are just some of the questions your company must answer if you hope to gain as much as possible from your balanced scorecard and, ultimately, from your business.

So, how do you get in touch with your customers to find out what they really value so you can play your role in their lives? And how do you translate that understanding into tangible measures that you can examine on a day-by-day basis so that you *know* you're consistently delivering value to them? Glad you asked, because that's what this chapter is all about! Here I discuss the things you must know about your customers, how you can gather customer information, and how you can link that information to your company's strategies and goals in the balanced scorecard.

Five Things You Must Know about Customers

Getting to know your customers isn't rocket science. They want what they want — faster, better, and cheaper. And they want to feel like you really care about them. Pretty simple, huh? Coming to grips with how your customers view your company and its products and services — and why they have their views — can be a mind-numbing experience, though. But it doesn't have to be. Your balanced scorecard's customer leg should provide you with the information you need to track what your customers think and how they feel about your products and services.

Not all customers are created equal

This may surprise you, but it's true: Not all customers are created equal. Sure, you should treat all your customers fairly, with dignity, and with respect — but you shouldn't treat them equally.

Consider the following: Do you treat your biggest, most loyal repeat customers the same as customers who don't buy from you very often and contribute very little to your overall revenues? Do you give some special concessions to your top-level customers that you don't give to other customers? If you don't, you should. If you treat your repeat, top-spending customers the same as all your customers, you could end up losing your cash cows.

Allow us to make this point a little more personal, because it's very important. Say, for example, that you're in the market to buy a new car. You want to buy a very high-end car, one that costs more than $80,000. When you go to the dealership, don't you expect to be treated differently — like you're really special — than you would be at a dealership that sells $12,000 cars? Wouldn't it upset you if the salesperson brushed off your price demands and hurried you so he or she could go to lunch? ? Of course it would. And rightfully so.

When reviewing and creating your balanced scorecard's customer leg, you have to define your customer strategies by understanding who your top customers are and determining the level of service you need to provide to go the extra mile for them. The policies and procedures you put in place for customer service must be well-thought-out and detailed so that all your customer-service reps know how to treat customers in the ways that they deserve.

Figure 5-1 gives you a chart that will help you track the customer strategies, policies, and procedures placed in the customer leg of the scorecard.

Figure 5-1:
Tracking the
customer
leg of the
scorecard.

Customer Segment	Level	Product/Service
Customer Segment A	High End	Product Line X
Customer Segment B	Middle	Product Line Y
Customer Segment C	Low End	Product Line Z

Customers can go away

In business, you can't sit back and assume that your customers will be "customers for life." Customers can and do go elsewhere to find the products and services they desire. Why do customers go away, never to return? Price? Could be, but studies have shown that price isn't as big a factor as some may think. Price is important but isn't the primary reason customers flee to the competition. The fact is, studies have shown that 68 percent of customers leave because they're treated with indifference. They don't feel like anyone cares about them. They want to be appreciated and treated with dignity and respect, and they didn't get that.

Loyal customers actually spend *more* when doing repeat business with you. A well-accepted rule of thumb says that for every lost loyal customer, a company has to find between eight and ten new customers to make up the difference. It's a lot easier to keep the customers you have than to find so many new customers. And here's something to keep in mind: The customers who make purchasing decisions based on price alone rarely, if ever, develop a loyalty to any one company. After all, price is everything to these customers, and unless you always have the lowest price, they'll take their business elsewhere.

The main key to keeping customers is to improve the overall customer experience — how you treat them and how they feel about the relationship they have with you. If you treat customers with indifference, you'll be replaced, and losing customers gets to be very costly. When building your balanced scorecard's customer leg, you should keep track of your percentage of repeat customers and customer losses, along with the reasons why they stay or leave (see Figure 5-2).

Figure 5-2:
Tracking
customer
losses and
the reasons
for them.

Customer Segment	Level	Product/Service	Gain/Loss	Reason
Customer Segment A	High End	Product Line X	+5%	Service
Customer Segment B	Middle	Product Line Y	–2%	Quality
Customer Segment C	Low End	Product Line Z	No Change	

Aside from leaving due to unacceptable treatment, customers will take their business elsewhere because

- ✔ **They no longer need what you sell.**

- ✔ **They move to another purchasing category.** They go upscale or down-scale with their buying.

- ✔ **They're unhappy with what you're selling them.**

- ✔ **They pass away.** This is very sad, but you can't do much about that.

You must master the art of customer service

Customer service isn't just the job of your customer service department and representatives, it's the job of every employee in your company. And service starts at the highest levels of a company. To that end, creating the balanced scorecard customer leg is a great way to keep customer service in the minds of every worker in your company.

The following list presents the four key elements of good customer service:

- ✔ A high level of trust in your company and in the people customers deal with

- ✔ Knowledgeable employees who understand what customers are talking about

- ✔ The company and its employees not wasting customers' time

- ✔ Friendly employees who will go the extra mile for customers

The question is: "How does my company get to a high level of customer service, where the key elements become second nature to my employees?" Here are four steps you must take to achieve great customer service:

- ✔ **Make sure that everyone in your company understands and measures the customer experience.** Employees must know how their jobs impact the customer, and they must become obsessed with providing satisfaction to the customer.

- ✔ **Educate your people about how they should act and treat customers.** They must realize the importance of good customer service and what you expect from them.

- ✔ **Communicate examples of good customer service to your employees.**

✔ **Make sure that potential and new employees have the kind of customer-service mindset that you want.**

✔ **Deal with employees who can't or won't deliver the customer service you need.** You can move them to other areas of business or let them go, but you have to take action quickly.

Not dealing with the employees who don't have a customer-service mindset can be deadly to your company. Bad apples can spoil your efforts to deliver satisfactory levels of service to your customers.

Customers watch you closely

The modern customer is a pretty savvy consumer. He or she hears what you say and promise and then watches closely to see if you deliver. You've probably had some experiences as a customer where a company's walk didn't match its talk, and you probably took your business elsewhere. In your business, you have to continually find out if you're delivering the things you promise to your customers. It's natural to want to promise your customers the world, but you can't do so unless you know that you can deliver the world — or at least a sizable piece of it!

So, how can you find out how you're doing in the promise-delivery department?

✔ **Ask your customers for feedback.**

✔ **Keep in close contact with your employees and get their feedback, too.** Ask them how they're doing and solicit ideas about how you could help them do better.

Do right by your customer

Some wise person once said that managers are more concerned with doing things right, while leaders are more concerned with doing the right things. We believe that you should do the right things right, no matter your position. Although you should set out to accomplish both goals, doing the right thing should be your first goal. After you identify the right thing to do, you can then make sure that you do it right.

When setting your policies and procedures for satisfying customers in the customer leg of the balanced scorecard, make sure they'll achieve the desired results — that they'll "do the right things," in other words. Then make sure that the policies are carried out correctly, by everyone, time after time. By working with the customer leg of the balanced scorecard, you'll be able to identify the right things and figure out how to measure doing them correctly.

Some companies seem to fall in love with policies and procedures. Putting too many policies and procedures in place tends to restrict the ability of your people to deliver outstanding customer service. For instance, you shouldn't set policies and procedures to take care of a rare exception; you don't want to set a rule that's inflexible and will end up losing you customers. When setting your policies, be sure to evaluate whether they're necessary. Will they help or hinder your ability to deliver what the customer needs and wants? What do your employees think?

When in doubt, maintain flexibility and trust your employees to know the right thing to do. If they understand the importance of customer service and how their jobs impact customers, they'll know what to do and how to do it.

Using Customer Info to Keep Your Customers Happy

If you have a good understanding of your customers, (if not, see the section earlier in this chapter, "Five Things You Must Know about Customers") you're ready to acquire the information you need to create your balanced scorecard customer leg. Using info from your customers helps you create goals and measures that fall in line with your customers' needs and desires. In the following sections, we not only show you how to find out what you need to know about your customers, but we also show you how to use that info to create customer measures that can help you reach your goals in servicing your customers.

Gathering info about your customers' satisfaction levels

You have many ways to gather customer information about their satisfaction. One common way is to troll your customer service inbox for letters and e-mails. If a customer is dissatisfied with what you've provided in terms of quality or service, he or she is likely to send a letter or e-mail to let you know about the issues (after chewing out some managers, of course). No doubt, you have a method for dealing with customer complaints and the issues that arise from time to time within your company. The balanced scorecard customer leg is ideal for tracking these issues.

Solving problems rather than spinning wheels

While working on customer returns with a company, co-author Charles noted that its Corrective Action Team (the guys and gals who look at the problems customers are having and try to solve them) was reviewing customer returns only every two weeks. Charles observed that the number of customer returns was increasing and that the team was overwhelmed with data every two weeks. Management was all over the team because it didn't seem like the team was getting anywhere in its problem-solving efforts, and it wasn't — the members were spinning their wheels.

Charles recommended that the team meet more regularly and advised them to use the balanced scorecard approach to track customer issues and solve problems. The team started meeting for one hour each day. The members soon noted that they could actually identify problematic issues and solve the problems quickly, and they reduced the overall number of customer complaints significantly by doing so. After they got the number of complaints down, they continued collecting customer data and information in the balanced scorecard customer leg so that the members could anticipate problems before they reached the customers.

Here are other common ways you can gather information from customers:

- ✔ Evaluate communication at call centers and help desks
- ✔ Check out product-return centers
- ✔ Interview field service reps and technicians
- ✔ Conduct surveys and send out questionnaires
- ✔ Hire a third party (consultants, Web sites)
- ✔ Hold discussions with focus groups

The problem with most of the ways of measuring customer satisfaction is that it's too late in the game to prevent dissatisfied customers. In fact, the methods in the previous list typically measure how many customers are mad at you and how mad they are. These measures usually involve measures of quality, time, and cost.

Because the event has already happened, all you can do now is react to it. Hopefully you didn't make the customer too mad at you so you can salvage something from the relationship.

Are we saying that you shouldn't use these kinds of measures? Not at all. It must be done. The thing you need from this information is speed: The faster you can get it, the better. Waiting for a yearly, quarterly, monthly, or even weekly report isn't good enough. Why is fast necessary? Because you'll greatly reduce the impact to other customers by fixing a problem sooner, and you'll save yourself a bunch of headaches and money. The customer leg of the balanced scorecard will help you get the information.

Being proactive to find out what your customers desire

Knowing what your customers want before you provide something they don't is a key to keeping your customers happy. So, where can you turn to get some ideas about what your customers think and what they want? Where do you get information that's actually "before the fact" — not reactionary information that puts you behind the 8-ball (see the previous section)? Here are a few places for you to look:

- **Futurists:** Guys and gals who look into their crystal balls and see things in the future based on trends and their in-depth knowledge of such things.

- **Conferences and seminars**

- **Surveys and focus groups:** You can send out surveys and bring together focus groups of your customers and probe them about their desires and what they don't want. Ask about the following, in particular:

  - What they want in terms of basic/expected performance

  - What would be some neat stuff they'd like to get but don't expect

  - Who the guys are that you compete with and how you stack up against them

What are your customers telling others about you? What are they telling your competition? Customer surveys and focus groups can tell you the answers to these questions. It's a tough, dog-eat-dog world out there, and you need to be prepared for the good news and the bad. When using surveys to obtain customer information, don't forget to find out how your competition is doing stacked up against you. Have your customers rate you and your competitors (and find out who they are!) on a scale of 1 to 5. You'll either read 'em and weep or celebrate. Either way, you have work to do- no time for resting on your laurels!

Focus groups can take time and cost some money, but they're worth the effort when done well. The key to focus groups is to stay hands-on throughout the process. You have two options: You can conduct the focus groups yourself or hire a third party to help you. We generally recommend that you use an experienced third party. Customer research is too important to make errors with your own trial and error efforts.

Just make sure you don't let the third party to do it all. They can help you create the questions and the format, but make sure you stay intimately involved. Participate in the focus group sessions so you can ask insightful questions that only you know need to be asked, and follow any threads that may develop during the focus group.

✔ **Industry experts and consultants:** For a little bit of money, you can hire an experienced consultant to help you create surveys and hold focus groups. It will be well worth the effort. You can find a variety of free online survey and questionnaire services, but they typically limit the amount of questions and the number of surveys you can send out. They also invariably use standard "boiler plate" questions. Although these surveys may be good enough to get you some preliminary data, they're very limited in their ability to satisfy your thirst for customer knowledge.

✔ **Journals and periodicals**

✔ **Market studies by third parties:** You can search the Internet for studies done on your types of customers to find out what they think and want. In some places, you can get free information; accessing other studies can cost from less than $100 to over $3,000. You can even commission your own study — for a price!

Your customer leg of the balanced scorecard is a great place to keep track of these sources of information. Use it, and don't lose it!

Making sure your reputation precedes you

Co-author Rick Buchman once witnessed an interesting situation that may be familiar to you: A company's sales weren't good and, naturally, management was worried (imagine that). Something had to be done, and it had to be done *now.* The management team thought it had the answer: "Who needs all these studies, anyway?" The managers thought the reason for the bad sales was that the company had a bad reputation with the customer. Fix the reputation and sales would go up.

But before rushing out and acting on these assumptions, the managers did something smart: They validated their assumptions with data by doing a study (another one!) of customer satisfaction - in other words, they got up close and personal with customers. When the study results came in and they crunched the data, what a surprise! Their assumptions were wrong. Their "customers" didn't have any real opinions one way or the other about the company or its products. Why not? Because the "customers" they were trying to reach had never heard of the company before! Imagine management's surprise! Not only that, but the actions the company needed to take were very different than those they may have taken based on their "bad reputation" assumption.

By going to their customers for information, the company saved a bundle of money and determined what to do to gain recognition in the industry. Had the managers been using the balanced scorecard customer leg, they would've avoided the whole problem and saved even more time, money, and effort!

Walking miles (and miles) in your customers' shoes

A trick to getting to know your customers so that you know what satisfies them and what they value is to put yourself in their shoes. Putting yourself in your customers' shoes means more than just walking a mile in their shoes. You must go on a never-ending journey, where you follow them everywhere they go. You want to see firsthand how, why, where, and when they use your products and services. You talk with them face to face. You visit your customers' locations from time to time. You *listen* to them - what they want, what you give them, what others give them. You take notes and brief your coworkers. Are you beginning to see why so many organizations don't have a very good understanding of what their customers really want? It takes time, effort, and relationship building. You have to be persistent; managing your customer relationships is one place where persistence really pays off.

Managing your customer relationships becomes much easier when you take the time to do a thorough job of developing your balanced scorecard's customer leg. It doesn't matter if you make products or provide services; you have to ask a basic but important question: "Why do our customers choose to buy from us and not from the competition?"

Setting customer-based strategic measures

When you know what's critical to your customers' satisfaction (see the previous sections of this chapter), you can start the process of measuring the things *you do* that affect the things the customers want. By measuring, you ensure that you hit the mark, time after time, and that you know you're hitting the right mark!

When translating the customer's voice into the things that you can measure within your company, you can — you guessed it — look at and measure certain basic things. Some of the more common measures you have for measuring customer satisfaction are as follows:

- ✔ **Faster:** Examine your speed of service or product delivery. For instance, look at time from order to delivery, on-time delivery, the time a single process takes in order to make a product or provide a service, and so on.

- ✔ **Better:** Examine how you set and meet customer specifications and measures for quality.

- ✔ **Cheaper:** Examine product/service costs - both purchase costs and total lifecycle costs.

And, of course, always measure how you stack up against the competition on all the previous measures.

Linking Customer Measures to Your Strategies, Policies, and Plans

The time has come to develop the customer leg of the balanced scorecard. When developing your balanced scorecard customer leg, you should center your work on the following questions:

Where do you want to be in the market?

Do you want to be an industry leader, far ahead of the competition, or a follower, willing to let others set the direction and lead the way?

Within your market(s), do you want to target the high end, the middle, or the low end? All the above?

The answers to these questions, as well as the following sections, can help determine what your customers can expect from you, and they're absolutely necessary in developing your balanced scorecard customer leg.

Developing customer strategies

Generally speaking, your balanced scorecard customer leg calls for five basic core strategic goals. According to Robert Kaplan and David Norton in their book *The Balanced Scorecard* (Harvard Business School Press), they are as follows:

- ✔ **Increase market share:** How much of the overall market do you have?

- ✔ **Maintain a high customer retention:** Keep your eyes on the number of repeat customers you have.

- ✔ **Increase customer acquisition:** How many new customer can you attract?

- ✔ **Keep a high level of satisfaction:** Your customers need to stay happy with you.

- ✔ **Strive for high profitability:** How much do particular customers contribute to your overall profits?

Figure 5-3 takes another look at the chart you've used for your scorecard strategies and uses it to link your plans and tactics.

	Customer Segment	3 Year Strategy	Product/Service	Annual Plan	Tactic	Measure
Figure 5-3: Linking customers and strategies.	Customer Segment A	Grow 15%	Product Line X	+5%	Service Quality	SP 0107-2
	Customer Segment B	Maintain	Product Line Y	No Change		QP18-2
	Customer Segment C	Maintain	Product Line Z	No Change		

Creating customer plans and tactics

You have several things to consider when setting up customer-based plans and tactics for the customer leg of the balanced scorecard. The following list presents some of the more critical things you must do:

✔ Develop and implement a measurement and benchmarking (best practices and competitive) program to improve customer service processes.

✔ Leverage your metrics results to develop new customer strategies.

✔ Measure and enhance the customer experience.

✔ Improve customer satisfaction by responding to quantified customer data.

✔ Align your customer-service department and workforce with corporate strategies.

✔ Utilize Six Sigma and other business-process-improvement tools to continually improve customer interactions and service.

✔ Measure your multi-channel, contact-center, and online customer service.

✔ Utilize metrics and benchmarks to increase responsiveness and drive customer retention.

✔ Develop metrics to manage any outsourced and/or offshore customer service.

Taking action when your customers don't get what they want

Nothing is more frustrating when you're working on the customer leg of the scorecard than thinking you know what your customers want and need and then finding out you've missed the mark. Trying to recover is not only costly in terms of time and effort, but also can kill your product or service in the marketplace. Some companies never recover from such a fatal error. You need to get on top of the situation and do it fast if this occurs. This is one reason why the balanced scorecard is so critical: It lets you know when you're on track and when you're missing the mark, and it enables you to get back on track — fast.

When what your customers want and what they get don't link, you need to go back and review your customer research strategies and your plans and tactics for the customer leg to find where the disconnects occurred. Ask the following questions:

✔ Is the information from your surveys and focus groups accurate?

✔ Are you dealing with real or perceived information (in other words, does the information come straight from customers)?

✔ Are your relationships with your customers satisfactory? Are you close enough to your customers?

✔ Are you communicating customer information to your employees, and do they know what to measure and how?

The key to success in the customer leg of the scorecard is getting your workforce obsessed with customer satisfaction and giving them the tools and measures that allow them to focus on customer satisfaction. Your employees have to know what your customers want and how their jobs impact the customer experience. They have to know how they add value to the customer experience, how to measure the experience, and what to do when they're not hitting the mark. Customer survey and focus group data — and your balanced scorecard customer leg — have to be communicated and made available to all employees.

✔ Is your system for measuring accurate and capable?

The answers to these questions should pave the way to fixing any disconnects you have between the strategies, plans, and tactics within your scorecard.

Following Up with Your Customers for Adjustments

Unfortunately, rather than *follow* up with customers, many companies will *foul* up with their customers. That's good news for you, especially if the ones who are fouling up with them are your competition and you're the ones who are following up with them. It's a sad and sordid tale about the number of companies that don't validate the conclusions they reach about their customers and what they think they know. It's almost like they were marksmen who follow a process of ready, fire, and who cares about aiming. As any good marksman will tell you, you hit the target consistently only when you follow a process of ready, aim, fire. And we know you want to be one of those who are hitting the mark of customer satisfaction consistently.

In order to hit the bulls-eye like a true marksman, you have to validate your data and information with your customers. Doing so enables you to adjust your aim based upon new information, and finding out this new info is as easy as asking the following questions:

✔ Did we get this right?

✔ Is this what you're talking about?

✔ Is this what you want?

✔ Are we on the right track?

✔ Did we miss something?

And then, you need to keep your customers informed about what you've learned and the changes you make as a result of your new knowledge. If you do, you can manage the information they get and keep them thinking about you and your company. After all, they will think about you when it comes time to buy your service or product in the future. So keep your customers informed by:

✔ Putting out company newsletters or putting valuable information on your Web site are excellent ways to keep you customers informed about what you and your company are doing.

✔ Another way to keep customers informed is through newspapers and journals. You can use them to generate a buzz about new products and services and about how you're dealing with issues that are important to them. Let them know they matter to you and that you care about them.

✔ If a customer has a complaint, send them a personal letter, letting them know you are working the problem and you appreciate their business and will work hard to solve their issues. When solved, send them another letter, letting them know it's solved and what you've done to correct it.

Yes, we said a personal letter! Not one of those boilerplate, cookie-cutter kind of letters that get printed out en masse that has all of the personality of a pet rock. We know, it takes time to do this, but put yourself in their shoes. Getting a personal letter makes you feel special, and isn't that how you want your customers to feel — special?

Chapter 6

Creating a Customer Scorecard

In This Chapter

▶ Taking the proper customer measures

▶ Creating customer scorecards at the strategic, operational, and tactical levels

▶ Reviewing your customer scorecards

*D*iscovering the key measures you can use for your customers is the critical first step in building the customer leg of your balanced scorecard (for basic info on the scorecard setup, see Chapter 1). As a manager, you have to work with members of senior management to help them establish the strategies your company will pursue (and their strategic scorecards), and you have to work with the levels of management that report to you to develop the tactics and scorecards they'll use to achieve your organization's operational goals and to keep your scorecards on track. The following diagram in Figure 6-1 shows how you're at the center of the scorecard process.

After you zero in on the customer measures you want to examine, you need to put them into a system for tracking and communicating them so that you'll never lose sight of how you're meeting (or not meeting) customer requirements and so you can let your people know how they're doing in this regard. What kind of system? We're glad you asked: A balanced scorecard!

In this chapter, we explore the setup (the measures) and the creation of the customer leg of the balanced scorecard. We look at the measures that really matter to your business and your customers and at the common mistakes made in measuring customers. We also explain how to build your customer scorecards at the strategic, operational, and tactical levels so that you can see how they tie together and so that, no matter your position within the organization, you'll be able to measure and track how you're meeting customer needs. After you acquire this powerful information, you'll be able to determine not only how you're doing, but also what actions you need to take if you're not hitting the mark. Happy tracking!

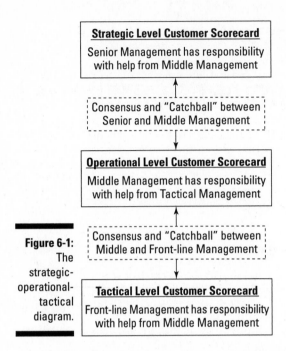

Strategic Level Customer Scorecard

Senior Management has responsibility
with help from Middle Management

Consensus and "Catchball" between
Senior and Middle Management

Operational Level Customer Scorecard

Middle Management has responsibility
with help from Tactical Management

Figure 6-1:
The
strategic-
operational-
tactical
diagram.

Consensus and "Catchball" between
Middle and Front-line Management

Tactical Level Customer Scorecard

Front-line Management has responsibility
with help from Middle Management

Zeroing In on the Right Customer Measures

How do you measure your customers? Do you get a ruler and size them up,
or do you count them out one by one? Most companies already have some
data and information on their customers, and we're sure you do, too. That's
well and good, but the first thing you need to ask when beginning the customer scorecard is if your data and information includes the *right* measures.
Do they really reflect what your customers think and how they feel about
your products/services? Do they focus on the critical few things that are truly
important to customers? In short, does your data measure what you really
need to measure?

You can take many different approaches to measure your customers, but the
key is to find the critical measures that are important to you and your company so that you can hit the right mark and avoid costly mistakes. The following sections work to help you identify these proper measures and weed out
the bad ones. We also assist you in implementing the tracking measures, and
we list the common mistakes you want to avoid at this stage of the process.

The measures you select depend on where you are in your organization. A strategic-level customer scorecard, for example, will have measures that comprise high-level objectives, such as customer retention and loss rates and profit and revenue per customer. Customer scorecard measures at the operational and tactical levels will be more specific. For example, you can measure what it is about your product or service that drives retention, profit and loss, or revenue measures at the strategic level. Such measures usually focus on things like quality, cost, and speed of delivery. For more on the specific scorecards, see the later section "Building the Customer Scorecard".

Weeding out the wrong measures

Your company (or department) almost certainly has some systems for tracking sales returns, late deliveries, and customer satisfaction. But are these the measures that really matter to your customers? You guessed it — the answer is no! Sure, these measures are important to you and your business, but they don't go far enough in giving you the information you need to satisfy your customers. Why? The measures for tracking such things as sales returns, late deliveries, and customer satisfaction

- ✔ Only measure how many customers you've potentially angered because of your failure to meet their needs.

- ✔ Are just too late in the game. With these measures, you're always behind the power curve, trying to play catch-up without the ability to ever get there. The measures put you into a mode of reaction rather than prevention.

Relying on these measures to satisfy customers is very much akin to trying to drive your car by always looking in the rearview mirror. Sooner or later, you'll miss something and cause a wreck that can be very costly. And you don't want that to happen, do you?

Discovering customer measures that matter

In trying to translate the customer's voice into things you can measure within your company (French? Spanish? Mandarin Chinese? English?), you have — you guessed it — certain basic factors you can look at and measure. The measures your customers are concerned with — and the things you should focus on in the customer leg of your balanced scorecard — include factors like the quality of your products and services, their cost, and the speed of delivery. Specifically, your customers want your products/services

✔ **Faster:** What's your time from order to delivery? Do you always have on-time delivery? What's the time a single process takes in order to make your product or provide your service?

✔ **Better:** How do you set and meet customer specifications and measures for product/service quality?

✔ **Cheaper:** What are your product and service costs (both purchase costs and total lifecycle costs)?

Customers also want to feel like you really care about them. They want to matter and not be treated with indifference when dealing with your company. That's not too much to ask, is it?

Understanding customer loyalty

One of your jobs when choosing measures to track customers is to gauge customer loyalty. Some customers find a company they like and stick with it. Others will make buying decisions based on lowest price alone; these customers don't develop a loyalty to any one company. Trying to keep these customers can be a waste of your time and effort, because they're always willing to go wherever they can get the bottom-line lowest cost.

If you want to better understand the kind of customer who's loyal to your company, ask why you think your customers buy from you — or your competition. Do customers base their decisions on

✔ Better features?

Do customers prefer what your product does, how it does what it does, how it looks, and so on?

✔ Higher performance?

Is your product/service better or faster than the competition?

✔ Longer-lasting and more durable products?

Are your products robust and withstand the environment and how they're used, or do they break or malfunction when used in ways that should be expected?

✔ How they're treated?

Do you act like your customers' business is very important to you? Do they receive products and service that go beyond what they expect?

You find the answers to these questions by — yep, asking more questions. The following sections cover more questions you must ask and different ways you can go about collecting customer information.

Asking the right questions

The best way to gauge customer loyalty is to ask the right questions. The following list presents some basic questions to ask of your customers when developing your balanced scorecard for them.

Many companies ask customers to answer on a scale of 1 to 5 for most of these questions, with 1 being the most negative answer and 5 being the most positive. These questions are typically asked in surveys (written or online surveys) or in face to face sessions (such as focus groups).

1. How often do you use our product or service?

2. When was the last time you purchased our product or service?

3. Overall, how satisfied are you

    a. With our product or service?

    b. In dealing with any complaints you had?

4. Did you get your product or service in a timely manner?

5. How would you rate the features of our product or service?

6. How would you rate the durability of our product or service?

7. How would you rate the reliability of our product or service?

8. Were the sales/service people you worked with helpful?

9. Were the sales/service people you worked with friendly?

One thing to keep in mind while you're presenting these questions: Your customers may base their answers on how you stack up against the competition. They'll give you their gut feelings and thoughts based on the choices they have when looking to spend their hard-earned money. When analyzing the answers with this in mind, you can get some good competitive benchmarking information from your customers.

With this in mind, you also may want to ask a couple important questions that require longer answers and some thought on the part of your customers:

10. What are the key considerations that help you decide whether to purchase from us or others?

11. What recommendations can you give us to help our organization improve?

   a. Quality

   b. Speed of delivery

   c. Cost

   d. Customer experience before the sale

   e. Customer experience during the sale

   f. Customer experience after the sale

Don't take any of their answers personally, and make no assumptions! The most negative answer could end up being the most beneficial for your company.

Collecting customer info

Companies must decide whether to gather customer information on their own or through third-party consultants. We suggest that you take the time to gather the customer information yourself — actually, through your employees who have day-to-day direct contact with your customers or other people who are closest to the customers (the so-called "customer-facing people" within your organization).

Some companies prefer to use third parties. If you want to use a third party to gather your customer information, try not to rely solely on that service. If you do, you'll lose your listening ability and eliminate all the wonderful possibilities that develop when you get up close and personal with your customers.

A good use for third party consultants is to have them validate your collected data. The best way to work with third parties, though, is to rely on their expertise in creating and conducting surveys and customer studies but counting on your people to lead the way and ask the questions.

Taking customer measurements

After you identify what's critical to your customers (if you don't know, check out the section earlier in this chapter, "Discovering customer measures that matter"), you can start figuring out how to measure the things *you do* that affect the things your *customers want*. And, believe us, what you do here has a huge impact on your customers! By measuring, you ensure that you hit the mark, time after time — in other words, you satisfy your customers on a consistent basis. Not only that, but you ensure that you hit the *right* mark!

The following list presents some examples of measures you can take for the customer leg of your balanced scorecard.

- Customer satisfaction and loyalty levels (which you can find out from surveys and focus-group data)
- Length of your customer relationships
- Repeat customer rate
- Number of customer complaints
- Product return/warranty rates (per 100 units, 1,000, 10,000, and so on)
- Number of complaints resolved the first time
- Customer response time
- Cost of complaints
- Customer loss and retention rates
- New customer acquisition numbers
- Total number of customers
- Price of your products/services
- Total product lifecycle costs
- Your price compared to the competition
- Revenue per customer
- Revenues from new customers
- Sales volume
- Sales per product/service line
- Sales per employee or per employee contact

Common mistakes made in customer measures

Measuring and tracking the wrong things in the customer leg of your balanced scorecard can not only waste your time, money, and effort, but also cost you customers. In the end, it can be fatal to your business. You need to avoid that deadly mistake and those in the following list and all the problems that come with them if you want your business to be the kind of success story that appears in all the leading business magazines:

- **Not getting help when obtaining customer data and information.** You should ask for the aid of outside consultants or a third party when you need it; don't always believe that you can do it all by yourself.

✔ **Not getting the cooperation on tracking the customer measures and objectives from the employees who are responsible and accountable for them.** Your employees don't want to have measures and objectives forced down their throats by higher ups or people outside of the processes and systems being measured.

✔ **Shoving old (and often flawed) customer measures and objectives into your balanced scorecard.** Do your customer measure homework and do it the right way.

✔ **Having a lack of data integrity.** You can't have people fudging or decorating numbers so that they can avoid changes, critical issues, and potential conflicts or confrontations.

✔ **Not taking measures often enough to get real-time or near real-time data.** Don't rely on bi-weekly, monthly, quarterly, semi-annual, or annual data reviews.

✔ **Not acting upon the data and information you gather.** Don't develop a sense of complacency or a "we'll worry about that tomorrow" type of attitude. Take the info you gather and use it to create your customer scorecards (see the following section).

✔ **Denying what your customer information is telling you or arguing over the validity of the data until it's too late to resolve the issues in a timely and cost-effective manner.**

✔ **No drill down from the high-level measures and objectives to the areas that drive those measures and objectives.** You need to pass information from the strategic level down through the operational- and tactical-level scorecards; see the following section for more on this topic.

✔ **Trying to measure everything.** Focus on the critical measures that really matter to your customers and your organization (see the earlier section "Discovering customer measures that matter").

Getting Dependable Data

Notice, we didn't give this section the title "Getting Data." We said, "Getting *Dependable* Data." There is a huge difference! Anyone can get data. That's never a problem, really. Getting *dependable* data can be.

In this section, you'll learn some of the more common pitfalls when dealing with data and their sources. You'll check out some of the pitfalls with data from customer focus groups, data mining, and surveys. Then, you'll delve into the pitfalls associated with the questions you might be asking your customers and the pitfalls of over complicating how you chart your data and information.

Hocus, pocus — the focus group

Conducting focus groups can be a fun and exciting experience. They can also be interesting, like a root canal can be interesting: get it wrong, and it can be very painful. Get it right, and you will find a wealth of information that will help you to better understand what your customers want and need from your company and its services and products.

Just as with any other form of direct contact with your customers, your focus groups need to be well thought out and planned before you conduct them. They are not to be left to the novices and first timers. You need people who know what they are doing throughout the process, or you may end up wishing you were having that root canal, instead of trying to figure out what your focus group data is telling you.

The following list of pitfalls will help you understand some danger signs that may indicate your focus group sessions will not be as effective as you might hope.

- ✔ Not getting experienced people involved in conducting the design, planning and execution of the focus group involved from the very beginning

- ✔ When meeting with a focus group for the first time, not informing the focus group who you are, why you are doing the focus group, what you want to achieve, how the information you obtain will be used, and that the information they give is confidential

- ✔ Making the group too small or too large — typically three to eight people is best

- ✔ Not getting a true representative sample of your customer base

- ✔ Cherry picking your focus group members to provide people who are likely to gives positive answers to the questions and topics being discussed

- ✔ Not maintaining a level of flexibility or staying to tight to a script, thus not allowing for follow through and a deeper discussion of emerging themes and issues that come up during the focus group

- ✔ Making audio or video recordings of the focus group (something you should do) makes people feel uncomfortable

- ✔ Allowing individuals to avoid contributing to the discussion or giving their opinions (a good and experienced focus group facilitator will ensure everyone participates — even those who are shy or afraid to speak up in a group)

- ✔ Too many outsiders – or people not involved in running the focus group — showing up and asking questions. Leave the running of the focus group to the experts and ensure they are the only ones who interact with group members.

By now, you should have a good feel for the fact that running a focus group of your customers can be very valuable, but it needs to be well managed and run by experts. Get the help you need so that you get the information you want!

Asking all the wrong questions

When using customer surveys and interviews, you will need to design a questionnaire to get answers to your questions and gather your customer data and facts. We've all been the user (and sometimes the victim) of questionnaires of some sort. Sometimes, you may have been left wondering what the whole thing is driving at and why they asked certain questions. Designing a questionnaire isn't all that difficult, if any old thing will do. Getting it right takes some planning.

Designing a good questionnaire, one that gives you the answers you're looking for — takes some thought and skill to accomplish. A poorly designed questionnaire will send you down the wrong path faster than you can say, "This questionnaire is messed up!" Well-designed questionnaires will minimize your sources of bias and will give you the accurate and relevant information that you need to gather from your customers. That said, questionnaires need to be as focused and as simple as you can make them.

The following is a list of the more common pitfalls made in designing and using questionnaires.

- ✔ They may provide only limited insight into problems because they typically allow for only a limited answer to the question being asked

- ✔ Many times, the wrong questions are asked

- ✔ The questions asked may be open to interpretation, resulting in responses that don't accurately answer the question asked

- ✔ Bias may enter into the picture by way of questions that lead the respondent into the kind of answers that don't reflect their true thoughts and feelings on the issues

- ✔ Questionnaire design is often left to those who have no understanding or background in how to create and implement a well thought out and planned questionnaire

- ✔ The questions asked may ask for personal information that respondents don't feel comfortable in answering, such as name, address, phone number, income level, or other information they don't want to — and may not — answer

- ✔ Poorly designed questionnaires will ask the most important questions at or near the end

✔ Designing the questions in no particular order, without a logical flow

✔ Not providing a cover letter that explains the what, how and why of the questionnaire

✔ Not running a pilot of the questionnaire to proof it and assist in its development before blasting it out to the whole world

✔ When using a Likert Scale for your questionnaire, respondents have a tendency to "be nice" and answer in a positive way or to answer in the neutral or middle of the road with no feelings expressed one way or the other, thus not allowing you to measure and analyze their true feelings

Remember that you will most likely get only one shot at getting your interview or survey right. Having a fast horse in a horse race is a good thing, but not if it goes off in the wrong direction and never crosses the finish line. Don't rush through the process of developing your questions and the design of your questionnaire. It needs to be well thought out and planned for. Take the time to do it right so that you get the data and information you need to keep you in touch with your customers. Make sure you cross that finish line!

Keeping data charts simple

Have you ever noticed that people sometimes overcomplicate things way beyond any needs they may have? It almost seems to be a condition of the human element. If we can make something harder than it needs to be, we invariably will. This is especially true when looking at data and information.

In today's world of powerful computers and software applications, with all the neat things they can do for us, there often seems that there are system capabilities just looking for a victim that it can be applied to. It's kind of like having a hotrod car and then always driving the posted speed limit — you just have to put the accelerator to the floor every now and then just to hear the engine growl — you just can't drive the speed limit! Like the old song says, you just can't drive 55!

Well, just because you have the capability to do all those fancy graphs and data analysis doesn't mean you should use it. In fact, if you do, you may end up creating a fuzzy picture and getting the analysis — and your decisions — wrong.

Take a look at some of the more common pitfalls you'll want to avoid so that you can keep your data and charts simple and easy to understand.

✔ Not providing the who (name), what (type of information) and when (date) details on the charts

✔ Not including a legend for comparative data shown on charts

✔ Cluttering the chart with too much information

✔ Listing a long line of data and expecting people to be able to interpret and understand what it is saying

✔ Trying to show too many comparisons on any one chart, making it hard to read and understand

✔ Using too many colors on the chart or fancy and confusing color schemes, especially as a background for the charts

✔ Not staying focused on the story the chart is trying to tell

✔ Using complicated analytical charts when they are not necessary to tell the story you're trying to convey — if you are using anything other than simple line, bar or pie charts, make sure you really need to use them

✔ Not proofreading the chart for information and grammatical errors

✔ Assuming people will understand any of the abbreviations used on the charts

✔ Not educating people on how to read and interpret your charts, especially those used for the first time or showing data in a new and different way

✔ Not cross checking with people to see if they understand what the chart is telling them

Charting is a powerful way to take data and make it tell a story that may be otherwise hidden. Avoid these common pitfalls, and you will get the power of charting.

Avoiding Interpretation Pitfalls

No matter what kind of company you work in, there are mountains of data available to you — it's all over the place. It's in this or that database, on the wall, in your emails, and on the internet. It's here, it's there — it's everywhere. Some might think it's like reading the tea leaves — there's some kind of magic required or it takes a special kind of potion to understand it all. Interpreting customer data and turning it into powerful information can be a tricky thing, indeed. But it doesn't *have* to be. Be sure to avoid the pitfalls described in the following sections.

Drawing wrong conclusions

Good data, the kind of data you can use to make good decisions, is a wonderful thing. That is, unless you're drawing the wrong conclusions from it and making the wrong decisions. Then, off you go to the Milky Way, chasing your tail by doing all the wrong things, though maybe for all the right reasons. Then, you're left with your head in your hands, wondering how this could have ever happened. Where did things go wrong? How could this be? Here are some things that are most likely to lead you to this sorry state of affairs so avoid them:

- Making incorrect assumptions about the data

- Introducing bias into your data — and its analysis

- Believing that a correlation means a cause-and-effect relationship. Would you believe that there is data that shows that storks deliver babies? It's true! A city in Germany has data showing a rise in the sightings of storks at the same time as there was a simultaneous rise in the number of children being born. Assigning a cause-and-effect relationship to this data might lead us to believe that storks are bringing the babies to this city, but we know that is just plain silly, don't we? Just because two things may be correlated doesn't mean there is a cause-and-effect relationship going on!

- Using sample data that is not representative of the population, thus giving you flawed information and conclusions from the analysis of the data

- Using the wrong measurement and analytical tools — in other words, the right data but the wrong approach, methods or tools are used to analyze it

- Using data taken with a flawed or faulty measurement system

- Trying to make the data fit a predetermined conclusion or solution

- "Cherry-picking" the data to fit your predetermined solution — often characterized by throwing out or ignoring certain data and outliers that don't support your solution

- Doubting what the data is telling you, based upon gut feel or personal — and often hidden — agendas by analysts and decision makers

- Using historical data without understanding any holes, problems or issues they might have

- Failing to understand the context and conditions under which the data was gathered and analyzed

- Using novices to apply analytical tools and methods without any coaching, mentoring and supervision by experienced analysts

- Failing to validate your data

Communicating timely with your customers

You should rarely, if ever, be surprised by customer-related problems. And, if you have a good system for measuring and monitoring how you're doing with your customers, you won't be. You'll know what's going on with them as soon as problems arise. This requires a system that is timely — as in *real time*. Not the once-a-year, quarterly, or monthly review of what your customers are doing, but an ongoing system — updated daily, hourly, or even minute to minute — to gather the information you need.

The key in being timely with customer information is in staying close and personal with your customers. Keep the avenues of communication open and two-way — especially with those customers who generate the highest revenues — your most important customers to your business.

Reading between the lines

When you get real-time customer information from your system, you may have to do some reading between the lines. This is especially true with survey, focus group, and interview data and information. After all, warranty, sales returns and similar types of hard data are pretty much cut and dried: they are what they are. But with interviews, surveys and focus groups, you can get deeper into the needs, wants and expectations your customers have of you, your services and your products, which is the sort of information you need to stay ahead of the game, keep problems from occurring, and to keep your customers satisfied.

With interviews, surveys, and focus groups you develop the questions and drive the interactions with your customers, leaving a lot of room for bias and interpretation on your part, so be extremely careful when setting up your interactions and in analyzing your data and information from these sources.

Quite frankly, if you don't have anyone who has good knowledge and experience with these kinds of information and data gathering, consider hiring someone to do it, either as an employee or as a contract consultant. This is not an area where you want to get it wrong. There have been far too many who have minimized the process of developing customer interview, survey, and focus-group questions and tried to do it on their own, and have regretted it in the worst way. Don't be one of them! Do it right the first time. You may not get a second chance.

Building the Customer Scorecard

If you know what to measure (see the previous sections of this chapter), building the customer leg for your balanced scorecard is pretty simple. The trick is using it effectively so that it leads you and your employees to take the right actions to stay on the right track. And that means constant measurement, review, and analysis. See the following section "Determining the Right Course of Action" for more on this important topic.

The following sections look at some examples of building scorecards for the customer leg at three different levels: strategic, operational, and tactical. By working on the different levels, you'll see that no matter where you are in your organization, the scorecards tie together and allow you to drill up or down through the organization. What we mean by *drill down* is this: If a measure at the tactical level is off-target, it will impact a measure at the operational level, which will in turn impact a measure at the strategic level — if you leave it unresolved.

Your measures at the tactical level should be early-warning signals for your measures at the operational and strategic levels. In this sense, they're leading indicators for trouble ahead in your efforts to achieve your annual operational and long-term strategic objectives. Without corrective action, off-target measures at the tactical level will cause the measures for your operational and strategic objectives to also go into the red zone. That's why it's so important to continually measure, review, and analyze your scorecards. You always want these measures to be in the green.

Strategic-level scorecards

To build your strategic-level customer scorecards, keep in mind that they should involve your long-term goals in at least three- to five-year timeframes. A simple scorecard matrix works well in helping you to construct with this in mind. As Figure 6-2 shows you, a matrix helps you tie this scorecard together with the short-term scorecards for your operational and tactical objectives, stringing the proverbial thread among them.

Customer Leg Scorecard with Strategic Measures	
	Three Year Strategic Goal
Increase Retention Rate	90%
Increase New Customers	25%
Reduce Cost of Complaints	75%
Reduce Response Time	**50%**
Reduce Lifecycle Costs	12%
Increase Revenue / Customer	5%
Increase Sales Volume	**10%**
Increase Satisfaction Rating	**90**

Figure 6-2:
Strategic-
level
scorecard
example.

In developing your strategic level scorecard for the customer leg, you need to be able to determine what your strategies are. These strategies will relate to the markets you serve and the position your company will take within those markets (leader, fast follower, late entrant). With that in mind, you have to do the following to create the strategic-level scorecard for your customer leg:

✔ **Take a look at your markets.** Looking at the markets you serve will help you to develop your market strategies, Is your market for a product/ service in a rapid growth period, a period of stability, or in decline? Answering this question will help you in determining your strategies for your product/service and thus the appropriate measures for that strategy and your scorecard. For instance, you determine your market is in a declining stage, but the market strategies you were following were for a growth market. For a true story about this part of the process, see the upcoming sidebar.

✔ **Answer the basic question of where you want to be as a company.** Do you want to be an industry leader, far ahead of the competition? Perhaps you'd rather be a fast follower in the market, letting others do the expensive research and development work and then jumping in after the products and services are developed and proven? Or maybe you prefer to enter mature markets and exploit the mistakes that others have made with your own innovative solutions so that you can take customers away from your competition.

Doing your homework, not jumping the gun

While we were working for one company (which shall remain nameless to protect the guilty), members of senior management for our division projected sales volume increases of greater than 50 percent for the next year. Everyone in our division went to work, setting their plans for the increased volume. People contacted suppliers; procurement personnel worked overtime to figure out how to get the added materials, parts, and subassemblies delivered; and managers signed contracts for the additional goods and services. Human resources spent time deciding how many more people needed to be hired. Manufacturing wanted to figure out how to get the additional volume through its existing processes or, if the existing processes weren't enough, what new equipment it needed to make it happen. Engineers went crazy to design new features and get them ready for the additional sales. Everyone was working very hard and, as you may imagine, people were very excited. The next year was going to be great!

That is, until word of the plans hit corporate headquarters. During a presentation of the good news at headquarters, one corporate executive went to the viewgraph (this was back in the transparency days), took the chart that showed the projected 50-percent growth, and flipped it upside down on the projector. As members of division management looked on in amazement, the senior exec said, "The customer will be reducing the need for our product by 50 percent, not increasing it." You see, we were working in the defense industry, and the Berlin Wall had just come down. As a result, defense spending would be cut drastically, meaning our product was no longer needed; therefore, our projections for growth were nothing more than a dream — one that would never be realized!

The moral of the story: Do your homework on your markets before setting your customer leg strategic goals.

- ✔ **Relate the answer of the previous question to your products, services, and customer base.** Determine what impact the answers you develop will have on your strategies and strategic goals and measures for your products, services and customer base.

- ✔ **Compare how you stack up against the competition.** What strategies are your competition following and where do you need to be related to them? What your competition is doing will influence and impact your strategic decisions (the strategies you select and measure) and your scorecard measures.

Operational-level scorecards

The scorecards you build for the operational level should typically cover a one-year timeframe and contain your annual operating plan goals and objectives.

These goals and objectives must tie directly to your strategic-level scorecard (see the previous section). Often, you'll have more than one operational-level initiative to support your higher-level strategic scorecard; knowing how much each operational objective will contribute to your higher-level objectives is essential. In Figure 6-3, an example of an operational-level scorecard for the customer leg shows you how this works.

Tactical-level scorecards

Just like the operational-level scorecard (see the previous section), the tactical-level scorecard dives deeper into your customer measures and initiatives. The tactical-level scorecard should feature a day-to-day view of your progress on the things you do — you guessed it — on a daily basis. The tactical level scorecard should measure the work you do to achieve your scorecard objectives and measures. These scorecard measures need to be real-time or as near real-time as you can get them. Figure 6-4 gives an example of the tactical-level scorecard.

The tactical level scorecards and their measures are your early-warning signals for the strategic and operational scorecards. If work isn't going well at the tactical level, these measures and results are sure to have a negative impact on the higher-level scorecards. You want to catch the bad news as early as possible and take action to fix the problems pronto!

Customer Leg Scorecard with Operational Measures		
	Three Year Strategic Goal	Annual Operational Goal
Increase Retention Rate	90%	75%
Increase New Customers	25%	15%
Reduce Cost of Complaints	75%	50%
Reduce Response Time	50%	30%
Reduce Lifecycle Costs	12%	8%
Increase Revenue / Customer	5%	3%
Increase Sales Volume	10%	7%
Increase Satisfaction Rating	90	80

Figure 6-3: Operational-level scorecard example.

Customer Leg Scorecard with Tactical Measures, Performance and Trends					
	Three Year Strategic Goal	Annual Operational Goal	First Quarter Tactical Goal	January Q1 Performance	Trend
Increase Retention Rate	90%	75%	72%	70%	↑
Increase New Customers	25%	15%	12%	10%	→
Reduce Cost of Complaints	75%	50%	30%	28%	↓
Reduce Response Time	**50%**	**30%**	**20%**	**10%**	⊕
Reduce Lifecycle Costs	12%	8%	4%	5%	↓
Increase Revenue / Customer	5%	3%	1%	0.75%	↑
Increase Sales Volume	**10%**	**7%**	**2.5%**	**−2%**	⊕
Increase Satisfaction Rating	**90**	**80**	**75**	**62**	⊕

Figure 6-4: Tactical-level scorecard example.

Analyzing a Scorecard and Determining a Course of Action

After you've created your balanced scorecard for the customer leg, you need to analyze it and understand what it's telling you and what actions you need to take going forward. If your scorecard review brings good news and you're on target, great! Please pat yourself on the back for all your hard work and keep doing more of the same. If the news is bad, though, and you're not hitting the mark (or don't think you'll be able to), now's the time to figure out the corrective actions necessary to get back on track. After all, if you don't take action when you're not hitting the mark, why bother creating scorecards at all?

The following sections give you tips on how to figure out the direction you should take in analyzing your results as well give you strategies for making sure you stay on course.

Knowing which way to go

To analyze your scorecards, you have to start asking questions — sometimes, a bunch of questions. You have to go back to the very beginning and make sure that all the dots connect. The following list is a checklist you can use for the review process.

When determining which way to go by analyzing your customer scorecards, you have to be collaborative. You have to work with your people and teams, and you may also want to include your customers in the conversation. After all, they're the ones you're trying to satisfy. Don't do this by yourself in your office or cubicle. Get your team involved!

1. **Do the mission and vision make sense?**

   Yes_____ No_____

2. **Do our customer strategies tie in to the mission and vision?**

   Yes_____ No_____

3. **Can our customer leg strategies be achieved as stated?**

   Yes_____ No_____

4. **Do we have the right measures and objectives for our customer strategies?**

   Yes_____ No_____

5. **Do our operational-level customer measures and objectives directly influence and connect to the strategic-level measures and objectives?**

   Yes_____ No_____

6. **Are our operational-level customer measures and objectives achievable?**

   Yes_____ No_____

7. **Do we have the right operational-level customer measures and objectives?**

   Yes_____ No_____

8. **Do our tactical-level customer measures and objectives directly influence and connect to the operational-level measures and objectives?**

   Yes_____ No_____

9. **Are our tactical-level customer measures and objectives achievable?**

   Yes_____ No_____

10. **Do we have the right tactical-level customer measures and objectives?**

    Yes_____ No_____

Did you answer "No" to any of these questions? If so, those points are where you need to begin your corrective actions. Actually, you need to review and possibly revise each question below the point where you answered No to get back on track, because a change may influence the questions and answers below that point in the checklist. For example, if you answer No to Number 4, you may have to revise your operational and tactical measures and objectives to ensure proper alignment after you take care of your strategic-level issues. Indeed, you may need to go through this checklist a few times and then a few times more. But we're confident that you'll think the time you spend on this will be worth the extra effort in the end.

Making sure you stay on course

Staying on the right course is the bottom line of the customer scorecard — or of any scorecard, for that matter. It's why you use them to manage and lead your organization on a daily basis. You have to make your scorecard a living document — one that you use to get the real-time or near real-time information you need to stay on track and hit the marks you've set for your organization or department.

If you find that you're consistently failing to hit the goals and objectives laid out in your scorecard, pull out the checklist from the previous section, ask the questions again, and review the answers. But what if you can still honestly say "Yes" to all the questions? Houston, you have a problem! You need to take some corrective action because you're missing something. Something within your process isn't working for you, and you have to find it and fix it. The sooner the better.

Here's an example of what we're talking about. Say that you want to retain 80 percent of your customers, and your customer scorecard shows that you're retaining only 65 percent. The obvious question is, why? Doing a little investigation, you determine that your scorecard measure for customer service is lower than you need it to be. Bingo! Maybe your customer service is causing you to lose customers, thus the low marks. Maybe your service people aren't following the policies and procedures you've put in place. Perhaps your service people are following them, but your policies and procedures need to be reviewed and changed so that your people can deliver the level of service you need. See how this works? When things go wrong, ask why!

You can use a well-known process for trying to get to the root cause of a problem called "The Five Why's." In short, the concept states that by the time you ask "Why?" five times, you should be able to get to the root cause. Now, asking the question five times isn't written in stone; it may only take three why's, or it may take six, seven, or even more. The key is to ask why enough times to get to the answer you need so you can solve the root of the problem, not one of its symptoms.

Always put processes and systems under the microscope first, not your people. Usually, when people are making errors, the systems or processes they have to work within are causing the problems, so be careful when assigning blame to people. After all, most people do the best they can, trying to do the right thing. No one comes to work hoping to do a bad job! Trust your people to do the best they can, and they may surprise you with their performances.

Chapter 7

Building the Customer Leg Dashboard

*Y*our customer leg dashboards and scorecards are probably the most important ones you'll ever work with. Your customers are your reason for being and doing what you do and how you do it. They create your profits — or losses — and they determine whether your business thrives, or dies. Now, that's not to say that you can ignore the other legs of the scorecard strategy. To do so would be — well — unbalanced, and that just wouldn't be right. But it does let you know that your customer dashboards and scorecards are pretty important and can't be taken lightly.

When it comes to your customer dashboards — or any of the dashboards, for that matter — there are some fundamental things you need to know and understand, so in this chapter, you first get a good dose of what those basics are. Then, you see how to build your dashboards, from the basic keep-it-simple style, to the more complex, and you see how keeping it simple is the best option — not only for the ease of creating and updating them, but for the ease of reading and understanding, too. And finally, you get a good understanding of how to analyze and update your dashboards.

Customer Dashboard Fundamentals

The customer dashboard you build depends upon

- ✔ The markets you serve
- ✔ The customers you have
- ✔ The critical few key process indicators that you identify to measure your customers

The most basic measurements for your customer dashboard will be your customer satisfaction measures (see Chapters 5 and 6). Your measures may also involve indicators like revenues per customer or market segment.

Once you've identified those critical few measures for your customer dashboard, you need to get them into a single page dashboard. Remember, the objective of the dashboard is to keep it simple, yet display the data and information in a way that is easy to read and understand. It tells a story that is read at a quick glance.

Dashboard basics

You have a lot of choices when it comes to creating your dashboards. Software for dashboards is cropping up like dandelions in an open field on a mid-summer's day. Good products are all over the place and spreading faster than a wildfire in dry brush. The good news in this is that you have a lot of choices, out there. The not-so-good news is you have to choose carefully, or you just might end up with something that doesn't work for you. Then you're stuck with something that is like a nagging relative that moved in, full of promises to be no bother at all, but then does nothing but bother you, from sunrise to sunset.

The dashboard has, at its core, one simple function: to present the information you choose in some form that makes it available for you to see in a format that is easily read and understood. Beyond that basic function, software providers have crammed a lot of functionality and options into their products. Knowing what functions and options to get — well, that's the job you're faced with when selecting your dashboard software. It's not a decision to be taken lightly. Choose carefully, and choose well, because you will be living with that choice everyday for quite some time.

At its core, a dashboard needs to have the following key attributes:

- ✔ Quickly communicate information to show performance and trends — easy to read at a glance
- ✔ Easy to use and update — user friendly
- ✔ Good visualization - no fancy graphics and backgrounds that distract one's eyes and requires time to filter through to get the message and information being conveyed
- ✔ Charting and graphing capability
- ✔ Ability to link and drill-down to key process and metrics drivers

Determining ownership and responsibility

Ask the question in some companies about who owns data and information you'll either get a shrug of the shoulders and raised eyebrows, or you'll hear that, if it's data and information, the Information Technology people must own it. Well, when it comes to a dashboard, that's the wrong answer!

So, who does own the customer leg dashboards? Are you ready for the classic business school answer? Here it comes. The answer is: It depends.

Depends on what?, you ask. Well, it depends on who generates and uses the data. Sure, the information technology staff will most likely have some responsibility in the process, like helping to capture and distribute the data and information, and working the software and systems issues, but they don't *own* the data and information. If they own anything, it's the systems and technologies used to manage the dashboards — and that may be a very big if, indeed.

Ownership of the data and information comes down to one simple word: management. Yes, management owns the data and is ultimately responsible for it. Try as you might, you can't delegate this important responsibility to someone at a lower place in the organization. Each manager is responsible for ensuring the data and information they use are reliable, well managed, kept up to date, and used effectively.

So, guess who has ownership and responsibility for the dashboards? You guessed it: management!

When you think about it, it makes sense. Managers are the people who need the dashboards to run the business. They are the ultimate users of the dashboards to track and steer the organization in ways that achieve the strategic aims they have set. They have deployed the scorecards, determined the goals and measures to be pursued, they lead the entire effort, so they have the ownership and responsibility for the dashboards. Enough said? Good!

Taking appropriate action: Who, when and how

If management has ownership and responsibility for the customer dashboards, can you guess who needs to take the appropriate action when using the dashboards? You got it, it's management, again. They are the decision makers or they are the ones ultimately held responsible for the decisions they delegate to empowered employees. Whether or not you choose to delegate is your call, based upon your company's culture and environment. But there is no escaping the fact that management has to take the actions dictated by what they see in the customer dashboard.

Regarding *when* to take action, one good approach is to use control charting to provide you with the answers you seek as they were designed with this specific issue in mind. Now, we're not going to go off on a long dissertation on how to do control charts, but we highly recommend you become familiar with them, if you aren't already. Specifically learn how they are used — they can be a little tricky if you're not careful — and the meaning of common and special cause variation. For more information on this topic, take a look at *Six Sigma for Dummies* and do some research on Walter Shewhart and W. Edwards Deming. These sources will give you all the help you need.

When it comes to the how to take action, that's pretty simple. Get your people together with the data and information in hand and work it out with them. Make sure that you have the right people involved — subject matter experts, people affected by the decisions that are likely to be made, maybe even the customers that are affected — and hammer it out. After all, when we're talking about customer dashboards, you'll often be dealing with customer satisfaction issues. Woe be unto those who leave the customer out of the discussion!

We cannot stress this enough: Do not leave your customer out of the process when making decisions and taking actions that will affect them. They are what the whole thing your working on is about, aren't they? Why would you want to leave them out of it? Sure, it takes a little extra effort to get them involved, but you'll find that rather than guessing at what they want and need (which means what you want and need to do), you'll know what needs to be done.

Building the Customer Dashboard

When building your customer dashboards, you need to consider what information they should display. You want them to give you the information you need, when you need it. You want them to be easy to read and understand at a glance. You want them to be easy to use. Not asking much, are we? And — oh, by the way — can you get all this information onto just one page?

Keeping-it-simple-style dashboards (KISS)

At the very lowest end of your dashboard options are the home-grown and standard off-the-shelf software packages. These will be your least expensive alternative, but they will also have the lowest levels of options and connectivity to your company's databases and other information systems for automatic updating of your scorecards and dashboards.

For the do-it-yourselfers that want to go with the bare-bones, no frills approach, you have the ubiquitous Microsoft Excel software. The beauty of Excel it is that you most likely already have it on your computers and people in your organization use it every day. It's probably on your computer, right now.

When getting started with your scorecards and dashboards, this is probably where you want to start learning and gaining your experience — at the low end, using these less expensive options. After you've gotten some knowledge about running your manual dashboards, you will be in a far better position to start looking around for some more advanced ways to create and run your dashboards. Then again, you may just find that what you already have works just fine and stick with it.

The fundamental purpose of a dashboard is to communicate. It is a visual tool designed to communicate your important business information. The visual techniques you use to communicate that information is one of the most critical elements of your dashboards. If you and your people cannot quickly and easily differentiate data and information, you have failed in designing a dashboard that successfully communicates that information.

When designing your dashboards, just ask these simple questions:

- ✔ Does my design enhance or inhibit visualization?
- ✔ Does it make it easier to read, or does it cloud the message behind a bunch of fancy presentation styles and a lot of useless bling, flash, fluff and confusing color schemes?

After all, you're not looking for dashboards that will win the prize for the use of the most colors and backgrounds or the greatest amount of graphic complexity. You're looking for simple — repeat simple — and easy to read and use dashboards.

If you're looking for prize-winning customer dashboards (or any dashboard, for that matter), follow the advice of Henry David Thoreau: Simplify, simplify, simplify! Keeping it simple will get you what you want: Dashboards that are effective by being easily read and understood. When you're successful, you can see relationships and trends in your key business information and that makes it a whole lot easier to make sound business decisions.

The example in Figure 7-1 details a keep-it-simple style dashboard. Note that it keeps it to one page, doesn't have a bunch of glitzy graphics and background color schemes that detract one's eyes from the key information, and it is easily read and understood.

High-end dashboards with all the fluff

There are some places where you want to have a whole lot of capability — and there are some places where it just gets in your way and becomes a distraction. When it comes to your dashboards, high-end software and its capability may just get in your way.

There, we said it! Be very careful when you go looking for software for your dashboards. If you want easy-to-create and understand dashboards, stick with the low-end software. Quite honestly, they work just fine, and probably have more capability than you'll ever need.

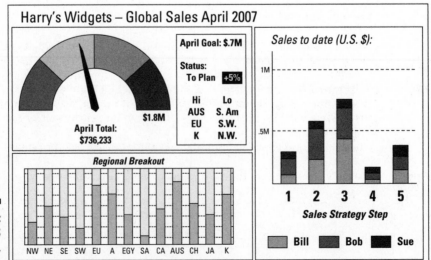

Figure 7-1: Basic KISS dashboard.

The whole key to your dashboards comes down to two things:

- ✔ Presenting the data and information you need with ease
- ✔ Presenting that data and information in a visual way that makes it easy to read and understand

You want to be able to quickly focus on the message being presented and you don't want to have to go looking and searching through a bunch of fancy, fluff-filled graphs and charts that detract you. 3D bar charts, with all sorts of shading effects, cone charts, and all the other options that you will have at your fingertips will distract the reader's eyes from the main message: the information you're presented with and the analysis of that information. Sure, they look nice and you can wow people with your ability to make very pretty and colorful charts and graphs, but in the end, it all detracts from what you want and need in your dashboards.

Resisting the temptation to go with higher-end dashboard software, and all the glitzy things they can do, may be tough. Some people in your organization may push you hard to use them. The recommendation is for you to resist that temptation and get yourself prepared to explain why it isn't a good idea to go with the glitz. If you want effective dashboards, stick with the keep-it-simple style dashboards and the software that will provide it for you.

Just one word of advice. Okay, maybe two or three:

- ✔ When looking at your dashboard options and making your decisions about which ones to use, you may feel a little like you're in the market for a new car, so be prepared.
- ✔ Know what you need from your dashboards, find those dashboard providers that have what you need, and then look around. Compare options and prices. Take them for a test drive.
- ✔ Steel yourself against any possible high-pressure sales tactics, and make your choice wisely. You may even have to convince some of your own people that the high end is not where you want to go.

In the end, you have to go with what works best for your and your organization. Benchmark best practices in dashboards? Sure thing. It's always a good idea to see what others are doing. But, don't jump on a particular presentation or dashboard style just because it works for the XYZ Company or some other organization. Do what is best for you and the people you work with and for.

For more information on how to create effective dashboards, you might want to take a look at a book by Stephen Few, *Information Dashboard Design: The Effective Visual Communication of Data* (O'Reilly Media).

Figures 7-2 and 7-3 are some examples of more complex customer dashboards. You will note that there are two examples: one using higher-end software and one — well, it shows an example of the sort of things you really want to avoid in your dashboards. Things like too many colors, too much confusion caused by fancy graphics. When looking at them, try to figure out what they are trying to tell you with a quick glance. Do you have to look at them and take some time to figure it out? If so, they are not what would be considered a good dashboard, even though the data and information maybe on point and accurate.

Just-in-time versus just-too-late dashboards

There are a couple of elements involved with just-in-time dashboards. The obvious one is how often you update the dashboard itself. You want your dashboards to be updated as often as necessary to give you the hands-on information that you need for measuring and monitoring your key indicators. Depending on your business and your information needs, this could be anywhere from real-time updates, to once an hour, daily, weekly . . . whatever is needed for you and your organization. And again, the real power is how you use that information to not only monitor your organizational performance, but to make timely decisions. That's where you gain a strong competitive edge: making timely decisions — and the right decisions!

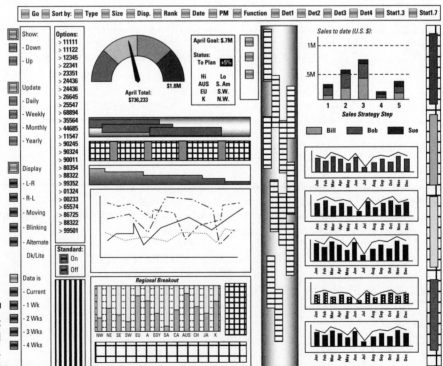

Figure 7-2:
Higher end
dashboard.

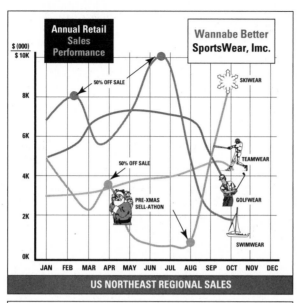

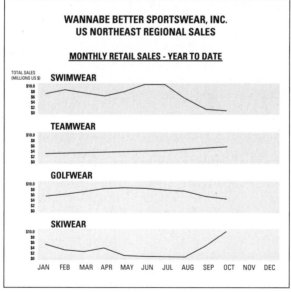

Figure 7-3: Dashboard to avoid with too much junk.

The other element of just-in-time versus just-too-late dashboards is in the information itself. What we call lagging and leading indicators.

> ✔ *Lagging indicators* provide performance, output or outcome information: they are just too late for prevention of major problems and issues.

✔ *Leading indicators* are used to predict future performance: they are just-in-time and help you to prevent problems and issues from becoming a major catastrophic event.

Both types of indicators are needed for your Balanced Scorecards and dashboards. Lagging indicators are used for holding people accountable, while leading indicators are used for internal management. For example, many financial performance measures are lagging indicators since they report past performance, or measure things that have already happened. Customer loyalty and employee willingness to learn and change are more likely to be leading indicators. They often lead your customer measures for satisfaction and performance. These performance drivers may vary, depending on how you're using them. For example, one company found that employee satisfaction was a leading indicator for customer satisfaction, which in turn was a leading indicator for their company's profitability.

You need both types of indicators. But which type do you think is harder to develop and measure? Of course, it's the leading indicators. That's why they are often ignored. Well, just because they're harder to come up with doesn't give you a get-out-of-jail-free card for ignoring them. They are necessary if you want to stay ahead of the game and to be just-in-time with your business decisions. If you rely solely on lagging indicators, you will always be just-too-late with your decision making and you will always be placed into the no-win game of playing catch-up. No, we didn't say playing *ketchup*, where you sprinkle some tomato type substance all over the place (though playing ketchup may be fun as on off-site team building exercise, playing catch-up is not only very messy, it's extremely painful and costly, too).

Another thing that drives your just-in-time versus just-too-late dashboard is how often they're updated. For now, we'll just say that you want them to be updated often enough to make sure you can take timely action when things go wrong. This is especially true at the tactical levels. Get your information updates at the tactical levels right, and you'll avoid problems at the operational and strategic level dashboards. If you have just too late tactical level dashboards, you'll have nothing but trouble at the operational and strategic levels.

Tracking and Analyzing the Customer Dashboard

When it comes to your tracking and analysis of your customer dashboard, don't put it off until the elusive time for it comes around the bend. When it comes to dashboards, there's no time like *now*.

Diligence is the name of the game when it comes to tracking and analyzing your customer dashboard — or any other dashboard, for that matter. If you put it off and procrastinate, you're well on your way to a lot of very serious problems. It's something you have to stay on top of. Just like riding a horse, you have to stay in the saddle, or you won't get anywhere and the old horse will just go wherever it wants.

Once you get your customer dashboard set up, you then have to figure out who is going to use them and keep them up to date. You will also need to understand how your dashboards at the strategic, operational and tactical levels integrate and what day-to-day processes they link to. If you don't' understand the integration and linkages, there is no way you will be able to drill down, or up, when problems occur. Without this drill-down capability, you lose one of the key aspects of the Balanced Scorecard and dashboards: early warning signals of problems that will impact your overall functional and corporate performance before they become major issues.

Figuring out who needs to know

If you're going make any mistakes in communicating your customer dashboards, it's much better to err on the side of communicating more, rather than less. Just because someone isn't responsible for updating or analyzing the dashboard and taking action, doesn't mean they wouldn't find value in knowing what's going on. Especially when it comes to your customers.

Very often, companies treat employees like mushrooms. They are kept in the dark and fed a bunch of garbage. This is a very risky prospect when dealing with information about your customers. Employees need to know what their customers are thinking about your services and products. Employees need to know how the things they do, day in and day out, affect the customer and your organization's ability to achieve what customers want. And it's up to you to communicate that information and to make sure your employees understand how what they do impacts the customer.

Customer dashboards must be communicated to those who have decision-making responsibilities. Executives, managers, and supervisors who are responsible for making decisions must have customer dashboards for their respective functions:

> ✔ At the strategic level, executives need to see how the operational plans are helping to achieve their strategic goals for the customer scorecard. If everything at the operational and tactical levels are linked properly, with the right measures identified and all is well, the executives should snug as a bug in a rug because they should never see any issues or problems arising on their dashboards. How can that be said, you ask? Because the operational and tactical level scorecards and dashboards are the early warning signals for the strategic level scorecards and dashboards. When

properly linked and measured, your operational and tactical level measures will catch issues and problems before they hit the strategic level. It's as simple as that.

✔ The same holds true for your operational level. Your directors and mid-level managers need to know what's going on with the customers. How's marketing going after new customers and how the new products will affect their areas of responsibility and how existing customers feel about their current mix of products and services.

✔ Your tactical-level measures, dashboards and scorecards are the early warning signal for the operational level. Any problems or issues that show at the tactical level, with timely and effective decisions and corrective action, will prevent the warning signals from going off at the operational level.

So, in answering the question of who needs to know about the customer dashboards, the answer is that pretty much everyone. Even though an employee may not be a decision maker, he or she needs to have a customer focus and understand how their job impacts upon the customer.

Updating the customer dashboard

When it comes to updating the customer dashboard, it's the same story as with communicating: if you're going to make a mistake, it's better to update more, rather than less. It's always easier to adjust to a less frequently if necessary, than it is to ramp up to a more frequent update scheme.

How often you update your dashboards depends upon their target audience:

✔ At the strategic level, you may only need to update them weekly or bi-weekly. It just wouldn't make sense to update strategic level dashboards on a real-time, hourly or daily level, now would it?

✔ At the operational level you dashboards may need to be updated once, twice a day, or weekly.

✔ At the tactical level, you will probably find that real time, once or twice a day updates are the best option.

You have a couple of ways to update your dashboards. One way is to do the manual approach. It's time intensive and may have some opportunities for things to slip through the cracks if someone becomes ill, or just doesn't have the time to get to it.

Another option is to set up some automatic updating capabilities, with automatic access to your databases and information technology systems. In the end, you'll most likely find out that you will need to have some of both types. You may find that this is particularly true at the tactical level. Information and data gathered at the tactical level may have to be gathered and your dashboards updated manually, but that the drill up to the operational and strategic levels can then occur automatically as the tactical dashboards are updated.

Now you come to the question of who should do the updating. The simple answer is the people who own the data. This is especially true if using a manual updating process. Basically, the processes and process workers that generate the data, own the data. It's all theirs and no one else's.

Your Information Technology (IT) department and the systems they use do not own the data! This is a problem often found with automatic updating systems that make use of IT professionals and systems. Do not fall prey to this fallacy. You and your workers own the data and information. IT is just a set of systems and tools that help you and your people to manage, communicate and analyze your data.

Drilling down to root causes

Dashboards should be linked between the strategic, operational and tactical levels. Information from the dashboards are linked so that the tactical level dashboards feed up to operational the level and the operational level feeds up to the strategic level. This is why you need to ensure they link. It enables your drill-down and up capabilities.

As you drill down, the levels of data and information become more actionable. Let's take a look at a simple example in Figure 7-4.

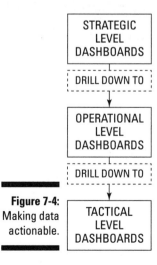

Figure 7-4: Making data actionable.

Let's say that a strategic level measure has gotten into some trouble. Customer satisfaction is in trouble. It's trending in the wrong direction because the product or service quality is in the tank. Senior executives are getting a little nervous (they tend to be that way when things aren't going according to plan). They should be able to drill down and find the things at the operational level that are driving the issue: the things that aren't going right at the operational level. Maybe it's a certain customer service policy that isn't being properly followed, or the quality of a product has gone south due to some equipment or supplied materials problem.

The executives, being the take-charge-and-find-out-what's-going-on types they are, call in the operational level manager(s) responsible for this travesty. The thing they'll want to know from the responsible operational level manager(s) is what's driving this travesty and what are the root causes. The operational manager(s), being on top of their game and having their dashboard drill-downs in hand, will be able to answer these questions by quickly showing the executives the specific tactical level processes and measures that are the culprits and let them know what they've been doing to solve it.

The whole beauty of the drill-down-and-up capability of scorecards and dashboards is that the executives should never have to get nervous because there is a problem on their strategic dashboards and scorecards. Why? Because, if your on top of things at your level, their dashboards should always be green and trouble-free. If there are problems at the tactical level, and you're doing things right, the issues will be dealt with long before they become an issue on the operational and strategic dashboards.

Now, when you do your drill down to find those little culprits that have caused you trouble, don't go on a witch hunt of who to blame and hang for the problem. Very rarely are people to blame. Look to the systems and processes. Just like the people own the data and information they generate, the management team owns the processes and systems. When mistakes are made or things are going wrong, look in the mirror and repeat this saying: I own the systems and process. And believe it! Yes you — management — are the ones who make the decisions on what systems and processes are used. You — management — determine the course of action and makes decisions regarding the work and how it's done. Even if you have an empowered workforce, you own it. If you want your dashboards and scorecards to fail, there is no quicker way to make that happen than to start using them as a means to beat people over the head and to point the finger of blame. If you're going to point the finger, point it in your direction — and then get busy fixing the systems and processes that are the real problems.

Part III
Financial Measurement — The Foundation Leg

The 5th Wave   By Rich Tennant

"We're using just-in-time inventory and just-in-time material flows which have saved us from implementing our just-in-time bankruptcy plan."

In this part . . .

As the cornerstone of the business, it is the financial leg of the balanced scorecard that lays the groundwork for determining the health and performance of the business, and even its solvency. In this part, we introduce financial measurement, first discussing management's role in financial metrics, then outlining how the scorecard and dashboards are developed and support each other, and finishing by providing some insight into pitfalls to avoid.

Chapter 8

Understanding Your Role in Financial Measurement

*F*inancial measures have been the backbone of companies for decades, consistently reporting on balance sheets, income statements, and cash flow. We see them in every industry, in every form of business — large and small. Financial measures are used by business leaders to make key decisions, and to determine the financial status of a company or business.

When we ask CEOs and COOs what plans they are making for the long-term future, we get great answers, about having a shared vision, compelling missions, clear direction — everything a growing company would need to succeed. However, when we ask mid-level managers the same question — and especially when we ask the folks who make, buy, assemble and produce the products shipped to customers — we get answers more along the lines of "We don't know what the company has in mind for the future," or "I've got no idea, I just work here."

Startups never have this problem. They always know exactly where they are going, and they can't wait to get there. Everyone is involved, and everyone has the same razor-sharp focus on where they are going, how they will get there, weaknesses they have to overcome, and a plan for their own path for the future. Such cohesiveness is indicative of shared clarity in direction, and a common understanding of the road it will take to achieve the organization's goals, both by overcoming weaknesses, and by learning from others who have already been there.

As you might guess, there are countless considerations, criteria, and reasons for selecting specific financial measures. To be effective in planning and achieving your goals and objectives, we must determine what we need from this sea of financial confusion. In this chapter, we start by identifying key aspects of financial measurement, the opportunities available, and how you ensure your measures align with the company's strategy and direction.

Five Things You Must Know About Financial Measurement

Financial measurement—just those two (not so little) words can give us the chills, and even make some people break out in a cold sweat. Others simply run away in fear, or ignore them—hoping they will go away. But, we need not fear financial measures, and if we can learn not to fear them, we can discover their power, and use them to help us make crucial, strategic and tactical decisions for our business, and for the future.

Here's the good news: Most of the financial measures we need involve only simple addition and subtraction, with some minor division thrown in every once in awhile to keep you on your toes. In fact, if the financials are *too* complicated, they are probably not helpful to you anyway.

Your financial measures must be accurate and highly dependable

Well, duh! But, you would be surprised how often we have found actual financial measures in use by companies that are not only inaccurate and even inconsistent, but calculated differently, and with wide variations in rules and assumptions about the numbers and what they are supposed to do.

For example, we have seen:

- Different assumptions in different countries and regions about what to include in gross profit calculations, and what determines a variable cost.
- Within a region, different definitions for the same terms, such as date of invoice, cost of capital, and even what constitutes a receivable or payable.
- Different operational assumptions region to region regarding cost of goods sold, and where to put accruals and depreciation, and what constitutes a capital asset.

This often happens when we acquire different companies and expect them to integrate seamlessly. It can also happen when we employ different leaders and managers with widely different backgrounds, and do not indoctrinate them into our financial measurement system. If you don't teach what your system is all about, most employees will default to whatever they used at a previous employer — which may or may not resemble your company's approach. The result? Disparate systems, incongruent data, and an inability to make clear, meaningful decisions. Not exactly the outcome most of us would prefer.

For you to be able to make clear, unambiguous decisions based on dependable data, you will need to first ensure your measures are accurate and highly dependable. If they are not, then you must resolve this issue first — before any other issue you might have. Without clean consistent measures, you will not be able to make key decisions about the business accurately or effectively. You can do this through several ways:

- ✔ You can ask each business unit leader to do this too, within his/her business unit, with each department, again for the same reason and desire to have consistent measures.

- ✔ Once the business unit leaders have provided assurances that their financial measures are consistent across their units, you can get the general managers together — with their financial advisors — and conduct a workshop to sort out what the standard way to calculate each financial measure should be. Have them convert to this new standard right then and there — together with their financial managers — documenting the changes they will need to make to ensure consistency across the business units.

- ✔ If there is huge time pressure, you can also ask for an explanation of the calculation of each of the business financial measures you are using, and with the aid of a financial expert, run a comparison to see where differences are, how different they are, and the adjustment required to make them all consistent with what you need. If you do this, you will need to send it back out for agreement and approval from the business units, to ensure they will buy into and support and work with the standard financial measures.

If you want the buy-in, support, and even the ownership by your company's top management team, you will need to be sure to include them in the process of selecting financial measures. Many companies make the mistake here, defining the measures for the company without input or involvement of members of management, usually resulting in disconnects in measuring performance, and finger pointing, blame, back stabbing, and other nasty behaviors all meant to justify why objectives were not met. Take our advice: It's much better to get management involvement and engaged in developing the key financial measures you want everyone to use.

Your financial measures must truly reflect the value of your business

The ultimate goal is to make sure that the financial measures you are using reflect the total value your company is providing, in terms of speed, quality, and delivery, to result in higher sales, margin, and cash. It is easy to get off track, what with the different ways we can define revenue (usually at time of delivery, not necessarily when we get paid), cost (usually amortized instead of when actually incurred), and cash flow (easy to mistake for accounts receivable less accounts payable, cash management incorporates investments as well as payments schedules.). Fortunately, there are some things you can do to help ensure your financial measures reflect the value your company is providing:

✔ First, be consistent in defining your assumptions and calculations. For example, date/time of delivery, invoice date, gross and net profit, and working capital. This does not preclude you from taking advantage of legal variations, just pick one and be consistent across your business.

✔ Demystify and simplify your financial measures, by selecting simple, effective and easy to understand terms.

✔ Be clear about what is included above and below the line, or the gross profit number. "Above" usually are sales, cost of goods sold (COGS) numbers. "Below" are the operating expenses, and interest and taxes. Remember: Being consistent is key to managing those factors above the line, which usually vary a bit more than the others.

✔ Be clear about just what sales, COGS, cost of services (COS), and operating expenses are. For example, operating expenses are those costs not directly related to making the product or delivering your services.

Clearing up calculations

Working with a large international firm, we attacked the issue of parts and components made and shipped from three separate plants in three different countries to a final assembly plant located in a fourth country. So far so good, but costs of final assembly in the fourth country were climbing out of control, and nobody knew why. When we took a close look at the financials for all four plants, we soon discovered the problem: Two of the three component plants were charging a surcharge above the normal price to cover shipping to the final assembly plant and, ultimately, to make sure they would achieve their budget performance for the year.

The problem had gotten so bad that the final assembly plant was starting to buy, under the table of course, less expensive components from competitors in order to meet their margin goals and objectives. Once we got the company to convert to a Balanced Scorecard, they saw the devastating impact from this structure, and changed it immediately, eliminated the surcharge, and worked to improve the entire value stream to the customer, and the costs as well. Within three months, we saw an immediate turnaround in performance, and by year's end, all plants were hitting on all cylinders.

Your financial measures must cascade easily from top to bottom

Don't worry: For results type measures such as sales, costs, and expenses, chances are you're probably already cascading your financial measures. What do we mean by *cascading*? We mean that financial measures roll down from corporate to division, from division to region, to plant or function, down to lines or departments. Most companies do this. However, we need to go beyond cascading basic financial measures and be sure that key process measures cascade as well, especially as they are directly related to performance of the value stream in how well and consistently products and services are delivered. This must include measures for specific periods, such as hourly, daily or weekly.

Where most companies drop the ball, and do not realize it, is in asking this important question: If all lower-level objectives are all met, does this assure — with near 100-percent certainty — that every goal at the next level up will be achieved? If the answer to this question is not "yes," then we may be surprised when goals at the department level are all completed, but goals at the regional or divisional goal are not. What happened? What happened is that we did not check back up the ladder, to make sure that 100 percent of the goals at the higher level were covered by 100 percent of the actions at the lower level.

Once you start asking these questions, you force a two-way dialogue between different levels in your business, and they become the quality check for performance. They also act to track and adjust the appropriate financial measures that cascade both up and down the different hierarchy levels of the organization, helping to ensure that goals at all levels are completed as originally planned.

Many businesses generate financial measures once a month. If something changes in the market during the month, however, these businesses will not be able to adjust. The result? Financial loss, lost opportunities, and even lost customers. Not the results we typically hope for in our businesses. A critical point here is to implement a system to not only check back up the chain for 100 percent coverage, but also that allows regular review and adjustment of the measures, so that if something should shift — for example, if the acceptable performance cycle time is cut in half, or standard cost expectations drop 45 percent, or volume level expectations double — that you can respond by adjusting or changing the measures within a very short period of time, in order to stay ahead of issues and resolve them before they become problems. By implementing a more real-time focus with appropriate financial measures focusing on all four legs of the Balanced Scorecard, you will be able to respond much more rapidly, perhaps within days or a week maximum. This will in turn allow you to minimize the impact of the change on your performance and ultimately on the financial results measures for the month.

Your financial measures must be easy to use and explain

You know what we mean. Using magnifying glasses to see the numbers on a spread sheet has gone out of style. Receiving a financial report for the month that is about half an inch thick is also old fashioned. And sitting through hours and hours of financial reports — with most of the sheets looking almost identical from one to the next, and someone presenting the information line by line — is also out.

Certainly, we need to have the data. No question. However, we need to make our financial measures as visual as possible to help us understand important information quickly and efficiently. The solution at many companies is to develop dashboards that depict trend information using graphs or charts instead of lists or tables of data. The key is to make the presentation useful by providing the data in a way to helps users analyze and understand what they need to look at and how to view it. Here are some ways you can make your financial measures communicate much more than numbers:

- In general, provide graphs that help users see trends in performance. Trend charts are useful — and control charts are even better — to help understand the mean and degree of variation of a particular measure. Figure 8-1 shows how we can use such a line chart to focus on key issues (in this case, why the costs would suddenly fluctuate in Q4 for example).

- Analog data are often more useful than digital data. By this, we mean that, where percentage of error is useful to determine failure rates, it does nothing to help you understand the nature of these failures. Yet, if we have the raw data, we can see swings or clusters around specific aspects of performance, such as failures in first pass yield (first time right, no rework, through a process step).

- For specific financial measures pertaining to each of the other three legs, you can be inquisitive in both selecting the measure and deciding the best way to depict it. For example, you might compare *takt time* (a six sigma term for the time it takes to do a specific value added step) to total time in bar charts. Or you might show weekly rework by area on a trend chart, to see if it is predictable and stable, to best determine corrective action. (If it varies a lot, that suggests the process needs to be brought under control before it can be improved.)

- For customer metrics, clearly you want to focus on what the customer is interested in. And, by measuring more frequently, issues will be detected sooner and can be corrected while still relatively small, rather than having a great, big problem.

> ✔ Behavior of data can often lead to understanding and setting priorities. A pareto (or bar chart) diagram is often useful in this way, to accrue value, or occurrence, or average time needed per data point, and display by the largest bar where the greatest opportunity is. Figure 8-2 clearly demonstrates how we can use this graphic tool to help us decide where to further investigate performance problems in first-pass yield failures.

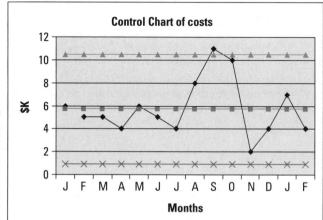

Figure 8-1:
SPC (Control Chart) on financial cost control.

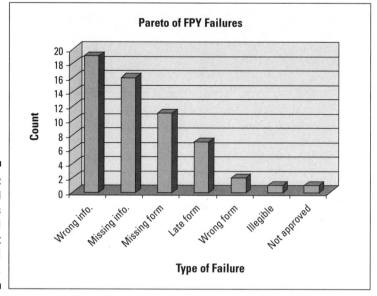

Figure 8-2:
Financial measures correlated to key first pass yield failures.

It's all about deciding what you need to know, and how best to get the information simply and effectively. Select those financial measures that tell a story relating to all four legs of the scorecard, not just financial performance. And be sure the financial measures show how well the value stream is performing — to support current as well as future growth and development requirements, as well as revenue trends.

Your financial measures must adhere to current regulatory and tax laws

You would think that this one is a no-brainer. Well, it isn't. Every day we see more and more companies veering into questionable business practices. These same companies are surprisingly not aware of their walk on the criminal side of life until after they have already broken a law, resulting in hefty fines and penalties.

We can't emphasize this enough. With the advent in the United States of Sarbanes-Oxley and other financial accounting laws and regulations, more than ever you need to have financial measures that are not just useful, but also legitimate and lawful. With companies globally distributed, this is a huge challenge, given different regional, country, and even state or district laws regarding taxation, environmental and labor law compliance.

Here's the good news: There are a variety of techniques you can use to ensure you are compliant:

- Pass financial measures and their assumptions through your legal department to have them reviewed for potential legal implications.

- Have all financial measures reviewed by the governing board of directors, which should consist of both officers of the company and other chief executives and prominent business leaders who do not have a vested interest in the particular company. Having such a body involved eliminates possible collusion, and ensures objective selection is made.

- Enlist a team of legal and financial eagles to develop and publish guidelines to all management, outlining what would and would not be acceptable according to generally accepted accounting principles (GAAP), with lots of examples, so as to help middle managers in selecting appropriate financial measures consistent with regulatory and legal requirements. Of course, audits would need to ensure continued compliance. One thing: remember that GAAP is different for different countries — what works in the U.S. may not work in the U.K.

- Tracking and publishing compliance problems to determine chronic repeatable issues while providing feedback to management can ensure that legitimate policies and procedures are practices by well-informed management.

Finding The Financial Data Gold Mines

Understanding a company's finances, and how these finances impact a company's operations, is one of the most important indicators of success for today's business leaders. Successful leaders use real-time updated information pertinent to their business in order to leverage actions toward a competitive advantage, balancing growth with results, and customer satisfaction with financial performance. In the sections that follow, we explore these and other aspects of competitive leverage.

Scratching the surface of a goldmine

When successful leaders make the kinds of decisions that will shape the destiny of their companies, they almost universally rely on a few extremely powerful — but simple — considerations.

A number of these business gold nuggets relate directly to financial measures. The following basics get you started in using financial measures to their fullest:

- **Understanding the fundamentals of your business and its products and services is critical to success:** This includes how products and services come together, what they consist of, and how they are provided to your customers.

- **Understanding how your customers use your products and services, and where it adds value to their lives, their operations and how they meet their customers needs:** Knowing this enables an understanding of how to leverage key advantages such as quick delivery, technology or even packaging.

- **Keeping it simple is also important, as this means keeping the number of measures down to a significant few, to better credibly compare performance in a reasonable period of time:** This works too, because ratios transcend specific products or services conditions, such as revenue per employee, or product development cycle time, or even trends in

- **Real-time information update is fundamental to their success as well:** This means they had a dashboard approach, with ways to get updates at least daily, in order to see trends, and make timely adjustments.

Knowing your business equals leveraging your financial data

Learn your business. The more you know how your business works, and more importantly, how your competitors' business runs, the better prepared you will be to take advantage of any opportunity. These days, opportunities come and go quickly, so you must be ready to act quickly, too. So, what kinds of things should you be looking at?

- ✔ **As you pursue cost control, learn how your direct competitors control similar costs.** Also, seek information on how companies in other industries control similar costs, to see if you can capitalize on better practices.

- ✔ **See how your products and services are used by your customers, and learn lessons about how you can help your customers improve their performance.** You can then leverage what you learn to offer to add value to your customer's business processes, and ultimately his bottom line.

- ✔ **Collaborate with colleagues in other functions, and discuss key aspects of each as they contribute to the overall company profitability.** Then, investigate how you as a group can use the Balanced Scorecard to integrate your actions and interrelate your departments' financial measures.

- ✔ **Tend toward analog or actual performance data information, and away from digital or "yes/no" type of information.** Granted, you may need to see go/no-go results to determine where to dive into further detail, but you will need raw data to determine how best to analyze performance and determine best application. For example, percent on-time delivery will tell you what it is. But, actual delivery time of each step can help you understand which step takes the longest, and therefore identify time targets for improvement.

Knowing your business can enable your financial measures to tell you how well you are taking advantage of any market or technology advantage, as well as help you determine possible expansion opportunities, into other markets, with other customers, or to cross over to completely different applications.

The key is to use a combination of lean applications with fundamental technology applications in your business, to enable you to see leverage opportunities, to either add value to current customers or engage new customers and thereby increase market share.

Using key measures to gain a significant competitive edge

Return on investment, often simply known as ROI, is a fundamental financial measure to help you understand and decide on investment opportunities. Using this financial measure can give your business a definite competitive edge in a number of different ways. First, you can determine the potential return of an investment as a function of its magnitude and the level of increase in sales and profitability over a specific period of time, to decide if it is an investment worth making. Second, when you make the investment, as you assess progress through your scorecard, you can make adjustments to key actions to control costs and/or increase revenue.

The simplest system to calculate ROI is payback: Just divide the total investment by expected revenue per year. The result is an estimate of how long it will take to break zero, and begin to achieve positive ROI. To show this as a calculation, we should first look at an example investment:

Investment: $25,000

Expected revenue per year: $7,000

ROI = $25,000/$7,000 =3.5 years

For someone who has to decide if the investment is worthwhile, it would be important to know the payback time period toward profitability. So, the question to ask is: Is this soon enough? The answer might be different based on current strategy, key market and technology penetration plans, and possible competitive advantage gained.

Even as most managers do not need detailed, calculated financial measures in order to do their job, the pitfall to avoid here is to assume you don't need any measures at all. As a manager, you need to understand the basics of what financial measures tell you to make good decisions using this important data. This doesn't mean, however, that you need to know and understand financial measures as well as your controller or chief financial officer. Call on experienced professionals as you need them to help you make your decisions. See the section, "Making sure the right people do your measuring," for more information on finding professional help.

Turning difficulties to your advantage

Given certain data trends or partial information, managers will often make assumptions about things. Sometimes these assumptions are good ones, and sometimes they are not. They make assumptions even though it involves some risk — especially when considering decisions involving whether and where to invest, make capital expenditures, or institute cost-cutting measures.

By using financial measures linked to a Balanced Scorecard instead of making assumptions or using your gut feelings, you can make better decisions, by taking the whole business perspective into consideration. This is especially important when you are faced with less-than-stellar performance, a downturn in the market, or unexpected costs. When difficulties arise, we are sometimes forced to make difficult choices quickly about costs, investments, or those actions related to future growth and development. With a Balanced Scorecard approach, the right decision is much more likely.

Let's say you see a dip in sales this month, and your data projects the dip to continue for the next three months. Traditional financial management would lead you to immediately cut costs, reduce investments, and consolidate operations wherever possible in the short term, to preserve margin levels. With limited financial information available, this looks on the surface to be a reasonable and even prudent strategy. However, there may be any number of reasons why this approach is a very bad idea, and they become apparent when you look take a total business perspective:

- **Cutting costs and consolidating operations may negatively impact internal process costs beyond just the income statement.** Cost cutting might include buying cheaper parts, shipping bulk, or increasing consignment. However, cheaper parts may affect quality, resulting in rework or additional purchases or expediting costs. Bulk purchasing might increase inventory, work in process (WIP), and if errors occur, greater levels of rework and expediting. Increasing consignment can also increase costs, and compound other issues as well. To avoid these risks, you will need to know more about the ramifications of such cost cutting measures, and see if other ways can achieve the desired results without such risks.

- **Reducing investments may also seem reasonable.** Yet, if the investment is for key operational improvements, or technology, then you could mortgage the future for the present. Avoiding such risks will necessitate trade offs, to assure we do not compromise improvements and technological advantage for present, short term perceived savings.

- **Consolidating operations, or more likely, transferring activities to lower cost countries, will not solve key cost issues.** Transferring broken processes to a lower cost area will only continued enable poor performance to impact not only operations, but increase delivery cycle times as well, and will most likely increase costs. In fact, the right approach — looking at it from a combined perspective of internal processes coupled with customer focus — would dictate using a lean approach, enhancing value added, and eliminating non-value added activities related specifically to delivering products and services to customers.

- **Other measures, such as layoffs, for example, also put the company at risk, much more beyond just determining potential labor savings.** See the example in the sidebar " Weighing labor savings against risk . . . or not."

How can you avoid making wrong or costly decisions when times are tough? The answer is in the application of the Balanced Scorecard, and looking for the right mix approach to yield the best financial return for the whole company, both in the short term and the future. Here are several ideas to consider:

- **Price is not just what you charge — it should be compared to competitor pricing.** Look for trends in seasonality, or even during the week (gas prices always go up Friday, and come back down Monday or Tuesday morning.).

✔ **Look at your costs, and make sure you are taking the *total cost* idea into account.** Total cost means the complete cost incurred along the entire product chain, from order to creation to delivery to payment. Cheaper parts may result in lower quality or higher inventory.

✔ **Look to other valued aspects of your products or services, such as breadth of selection, timeliness of availability (Wal-Mart's availability averages less than two hours), service, and reliability.** Do you offer added services such as training, assistance, or explanation with your products.

✔ **Customer loyalty is also very important to consider, and should not be underestimated.** Return customers often define the livelihood of many companies, not just in service industries such as U-Haul or fast food, but also with larger firms needing specific products or services on a regular basis (Frank Allen and Associates provides comprehensive hiring and staffing services, above and beyond normal search activities. They have one of the highest client return ratios of any search firm.

✔ **Finally, not all ratios are bad, and some are better when seen with other ratios.** For example, a trend of decreasing margins taken by itself is a red flag for improvement. However, when seen against acquisition investments, decreasing margins may not be a problem at all. And rising travel costs alone may tend to indicate loss of control. Yet, coupled with an increase in sales and expanding customer base, we rising travel costs might indicate positive position development. The point is, look at your ratios with an attitude to the whole business, not just one part.

Measuring and Interpreting with Accuracy

You would think that obtaining consistent and dependable financials would be easy — a piece of cake. Guess what? They're not! Very often, companies make decisions based on financial measures and key financial indicators developed with assumptions that are inaccurate, and that depend on conditions that change quickly and unexpectedly.

We know that there are certain assumptions about the rules by which financial measures are established. Revenue is declared at some point, either where products or services are provided, or perhaps when such deliverables are qualified and acknowledged as received by a customer. On-time delivery has a specific definition, otherwise, it could be just about anytime, as early as in-plant verification to as late as final tic-list completion. Given such potential variation, it becomes clear why we would need to establish consistency of definitions right away, to avoid erroneous assumption, which could result in mistakes in revenue, earnings, cost and delivery values. It also becomes clear how dependable our assumptions need to be in order to ensure they don't change too often or without good reason.

In the sections that follow, we show you how to find the right people to measure the right things, all of which builds a better scorecard (see Chapter 9).

Making sure the right people do your measuring

When people take responsibility for financial measures, but are not responsible for their assessment and utility, the inevitable result is errors, disconnects, and a clear disregard of discipline in maintaining these measures, or understanding which ones are key. This problem keeps compounding when decisions are then made based on these errors and disconnects. The results can be simply bad or completely devastating.

Financial measures must be captured and assessed in detail by the manager whose performance is most closely linked with them. Anyone else, and you're setting yourself up for failure.

You may sometimes encounter the automatic acceptance in a corporation to any idea or suggestion from higher up. But deference to status and authority has caused more inept, unusable, and irrelevant data collection than any other cause, often resulting in the creation of entire departments to track, manage, and create the data and its collection. Guard against this tendency whenever you see it rear its ugly head. See the sidebar, "Status doesn't imply better," for an example of the problems such deference to status can cause.

Sources for assistance in applying and interpreting financial measures are usually found in different places, depending on the measure and its application on the dashboard.

- ✔ **Basic information:** Common to most businesses, such as the type of results measures found in financial reports (for example, Return on Net Assets (RONA), Net Profit, Earnings Before Interest and Taxes (EBIT), Cost of goods or services sold (COGS, COS), Cash flow, and others). Resources for help with this information will consist of your average accounting manager or analyst. These individuals can provide all the necessary background on these figures, and then some.

- ✔ **Process financial information:** This comprises the information related to the process performance from a financial perspective, such as cost of first pass yield failure, on-time and off-time delivery costs including expediting costs, investment levels for growth, and process competency capability modeling and costs. Resources for help with this information will most likely come from controllers, and financial planning and analysts dedicated to specific product or service lines.

> ✔ **Strategic elements of financial risk assessments regarding failure severity, probability and detect-ability, to include long term capital, total product or service family risks, applications of alternatives in shop floor layout or alternative process flow analysis:** Resources for help with this perspective might be your strategy planning chief, or the DFO, or even in the legal department as well.

Identify who you want to talk with, quickly articulate what it is you want to know, and listen carefully to the discussion.

Using consistent and dependable measures

You can't measure everything, although many keep trying to. When you try to measure everything, and link everything, it starts to get a little crazy.

Here's an example: a retail clothing boutique wanted to improve its profit margin. Clearly, this is a financial measure, yet of course it also links to the growth (increased profits means higher revenues), operations (how will my inventory be affected?), and customer (buying trends) legs of the Balanced Scorecard as well. The temptation was to measure not only cost against sales price, but also sales levels as a ratio of sales price, to try to get the highest price possible, and to measure sales and sales costs by product type, region and other market characteristics. They also tried to connect key market and strategic decisions to financial performance.

The way to avoid this problem is to do a simple test: Ask if the specific goal is directly or indirectly related to delivering value products and services to the customer. If direct, the measure is probably ok, although we need to monitor closely. If indirect, we will need to determine a link, if any real link exists, and what level of importance we will need to attach. If we can't find a link, then the metric may best be set aside, or identified as a supporting measure.

The general rule for financial measures is no more than five to eight core measures, with perhaps another three to six supporting measures. This allows between nine and fourteen total financial measures, which is more than enough for most companies. If you are tracking dozens of measures, then you're not focusing on what is most important in your organization. The cure? You should reduce your key financial measures to those five to eight ones that are truly core to what your company does.

Avoiding measurement pitfalls

Not a bad idea, at least on the surface. But, the pitfalls begin to appear when key strategic decisions are made based on these comparisons. There are several reasons:

✔ To determine the best price, instead of testing the market (easy way), you try to set the best price through calculated sales levels ratios (very difficult). This results in forecasting, ordering, styling, and shipping based on mathematical models, which are less than dependable in a number of industries, including retail clothing, food, and personal hygiene and health products.

✔ You may overlook critical non-financial information, such as recent legal issues for a prospective acquisition, or high management turnover, or core competency weaknesses with no development plan, all of which could indicate a more appropriate course of action other than that suggested by financial measures alone.

✔ You may find you can't even measure some critical aspects of your business, such as successful leadership, how we treat our employees, or ethics practices. Some companies attempt to measure these in the hopes to improve them, which is laudable. But direct links are sketchy at best, and any really important decisions based on such information is risky indeed.

Turning Numbers into Information

Have you ever had this happen? You're sitting in a meeting going over all of the business related information, and then the financial types get up and it seems like the lights got turned out and everyone went home? And, even though you listened intently, it seemed like they were speaking some foreign language that nobody understood? If not, you're fortunate. It happens more often than many of us may like to admit. These sections give you ways to and not to report data so everyone leaves the room with an understanding of what you just showed them

Examining reporting pitfalls

Avoid the following pitfalls of reporting numbers and financial information, and you'll be well ahead of the game when trying to turn numbers into information.

✔ Numbers are listed as just that – tabular lists of numbers – and not in some form of graphical or visual presentation that is quickly and easily understandable

✔ Not varying the graphics and visualization techniques used to find the best method to display the numbers

✔ The numbers are presented in the language of the presenter and not in the language of the audience they are presenting to

✔ Ineffective use of fonts and color schemes to present the number - using too many or too few colors so that the critical information gets lost in the background

✔ Use of acronyms that go unexplained and assuming everyone knows what they mean and not talking in plain language that everyone understands

✔ Throwing in data and information that isn't on point or that doesn't lead to an understanding of the point being conveyed to the audience

✔ Not knowing what it is you're really trying to communicate to the audience

✔ Presenting numbers from only one viewpoint or perspective

✔ Not using stories or analogies to try and create a better understanding of the numbers (not always possible, but very effective if you can pull it off)

Most people are visual in nature. This means that pictures and graphs go a lot further in gaining understanding, which leads to information and knowledge. Long lists of numbers are hard to visualize, interpret, and then apply critical thinking skills to gain understanding. They are hard, if not impossible, to determine trends, issues and problems. So get visual and avoid the pitfalls (see "Showing financial info simply").

Showing financial info simply

The best way to show financial information is to get graphical and use good visual presentation techniques. This will most often come down to presenting the numbers in some form of chart. Popular software programs such as Microsoft Excel make turning row after row of numbers into simple and compelling charts easier than ever. The most common forms for showing financial data are:

✔ **Line charts:** Best for showing trends over time types of data

✔ **Bar charts:** Best for showing comparisons (stacked bar charts, side-by-side bar charts)

✔ **Pie charts:** Best for showing relative comparisons such as percentages of total of the whole or size comparisons

The use of colors to show different graphical elements of financial information is also a good way to show or highlight comparative information, too. Just remember that too many colors can be just as confusing as not using any at all. And, just as with your dashboard and scorecard color schemes of red equals problem areas, yellow equals marginal or potential problem areas, and green means you're good to go, these colors can be used for the same things in your financial reporting. Once you pick a color scheme format, stick with it.

If you're stuck in a black-and-white world, the use of different gray scale shading or graphic textures will go a long way to helping you differentiate and show information.

Have you ever seen a line, bar or pie chart with so much junk crammed into it that you can't make heads or tails of what it's showing you? Take the lessons from it and don't try to shove too much information into any one chart. Your charts have to be easy to differentiate the lines and bars at a quick glance. If in doubt, go get someone to do the quick glance test — where you show it to someone who hasn't seen the chart before — and ask them to take a quick look at the chart and then have them tell you what the chart is telling them. If they get it wrong, you know you have some more work to do on improving the presentation of your financial information.

Use legends where appropriate. Yeah, it seems kind of basic, but you wouldn't believe the number of charts that don't' use them. After all, people need this sort of thing to help them remember what the various colors and visualization schemes are supposed to mean.

Linking Financial Measurements To Strategies, Plans And Tactics

You must always remember that a Balanced Scorecard is the bridge between strategy, planning, and the actions of execution. This is because Balanced Scorecards — as they define and track organization objectives, measures, targets and periodic performance — provide for key decisions and execution of the strategic plans. Of course, this means you should plan first, in order to enable everyone to align their scorecards with single focus and direction in mind. And while the scorecard will integrate all four legs, it is the financial measures we will focus on in this section, as they are the glue that binds all others to the strategy and the plan.

A key aspect of your role in financial measurement development is focus on the strategic perspective of your business, no matter the level within the company. One tool to help you in this is called the strategy map. The strategy map lays out the step-by-step road map in plain language regarding necessary actions to support the development and execution of your Balanced Scorecard.

The strategy map is quite simple, and introduces integrating your objectives and measures across your scorecard, such that they tell a story related both in context and sequence. In other words, the strategy map spells out how each objective is related to the others, and how, through achievement of your objectives in sequence, you will achieve your overall organizational goals. See Chapter 2 for an example of a strategy map as well as basic info on how to create one.

Financial measurement is dependant on strategic focus

Would you agree that, before embarking on a day-long shopping trip, it's a good idea to have some idea of what it is that you want to buy? Otherwise, how will you know what kind of stores you'll want to go to and, once you arrive, what it is that you'll purchase? This means you have a long-term strategy (having food in the house so that you and your family don't starve, for example) which drives your decisions on what you need, where to go, how much to buy, and even what conveyance you will need to carry your purchases. We formulate strategies routinely in our lives, and then take action to fulfill these plans. And of course, our financial measures are related to the actions we take to fulfill these strategies, whether we are shopping to stock, or for a special occasion, or for large purchases, where we also may take interest rates into account, payment schedules, and other factors.

In business, the strategies might be different, but we develop our plans according to whether we plan to maintain, sustain or grow our business. As you can imagine, your business financial measures will also be dictated to a large degree by the strategy or strategies you have, as defined by one or more of these perspectives.

- ✔ **Sell and get what you can, and manage your assets.** Appropriate financial measures would include return on assets, shareholder value added, and minimizing costs, to include some possible improvement in operations.

- ✔ **Milk the cash cow, with continuous improvement.** Financial measures here are more oriented to longer-term focus, enabling some integrated value stream mapping and continuous improvement programs, especially for long-term fixed-fee contracts.

- ✔ **Grow your business, revenue, and expand market share.** Financial measures center around ROI, longer term planning, technology innovation, and market expansion opportunity, and might include capital planning, earned value added (EVA), and value stream performance ratios.

The key is to ask where your business is going and where your focus should lie, and to talk with your peers, your boss, and even other department heads, before you select your financial measures, so that what you measure aligns with what you want to ultimately achieve.

What you do depends on what you want

So, how do we know what we want? A wise man once said, "Be careful what you reward, because chances are that's what you will get." We certainly see this all the time in business. If we reward our managers for cutting costs, our managers will cut costs. If we want to improve competency, we will train or hire more capable people. But, executed in isolation, these single points of improvement could prove disastrous for a business.

A Balanced Scorecard approach is the only way to ensure all elements of a business are taken into account. So, we need to define what we want from a complete, holistic perspective. For example, a complete picture of financial measures might include not just cost cutting, but cost cutting as a percent of internal process improved performance, linked to customer satisfaction in delivery and pricing. We can then define appropriate financial measures that relate all four legs of the scorecard.

So, it's not just about measuring financials. It is about deciding what you want as a function of all four of the scorecard legs, and then relating the appropriate financial measures to tell you how well you are doing, and what might need attention, and when.

Using Failure Mode Effects Analysis (FMEA) to assess risk

Selecting the right financial measures is certainly dependent on your strategy, but the bottom line is all about action. Measures themselves enable good decisions, but execution is the key to performance. Your financial measures, therefore, must enable not only assessment and decisions, but must also lead to action.

Risks are a key ingredient in the action stew. You assess, take, and manage your risks based upon a multitude of factors, at varying levels:

- ✔ Your strategic risks are linked to market forecast accuracy and timeliness, product design characteristics based on assumptions of customer desires, and acquiring technology according to our perceived future vision of where we want to be

- ✔ Your operational risks involve investments in equipment and improvement initiatives, optimizing purchase pricing and change management as we move toward a more lean enterprise approach

- ✔ Your tactical risks center around line performance, administrative task management, and cash collection and payment.

The best way to assess and manage risks at any level is to understand not only the level or impact and probability of risk, but also the potential visibility as well. A great tool to help in this assessment, and ultimately in deciding what to do, is a Failure Mode Effects Analysis, or FMEA. Most engineers have heard of this tool as they routinely use it to assess designs. Let's take a look at the tool, and what it does:

Figure 8-3 is an example of a FMEA. Notice that there are three distinct evaluative columns, listed as *severity*, *probability*, and *detectable*. Using this tool, you can evaluate each risk factor in terms of these three criteria:

✔ **How severe is the risk to the company and the project?** Highly severe would rate a 10, while minimally severe or no impact would rate a 1.

✔ **How probable is the risk to occur?** Highly probable would rate a 10, while highly improbable would rate a 1, with varying degrees in-between.

✔ **How detectable is the risk?** This is the one everyone misses, as they usually assume we will see it. Yet often something happens, and we do not see it at all, right away. Here, the scale is reversed. Highly undetectable, or not visible whatsoever would rate a 10, while highly detectable would rate a 1.

The risk priority number, or RPN, represents a total risk level, and is calculated by multiplying all three risk scores. For the most severe risks, then, we see that the RPN can be a maximum score of

$$10 \times 10 \times 10 = 1{,}000$$

The FMEA structure is very consistent — the risks are listed, and each one is evaluated against these three criteria. The management team looks at RPNs to see where the highest risks are, and they plan for contingencies against such risks, focusing each mitigating action toward reducing one of the three factors, and thus the RPN for that particular risk.

Risk	Severity	Impact	Probability	Detectable	RPN	Priority
Increased cost	8	Reduced Margin	6	3	144	4
Damage in transit	5	Increase Scrap, write offs	3	3	30	5
Slump in Sales	10	Higher Inventory	5	3	150	3
Building Problems	8	Inconvenient, affect sales	8	7	448	2
Interrupted Deliveries	9	Lost sales, no inventory	5	10	450	1

Figure 8-3:
Example of a FMEA.

Here are some ways you can use this tool to help your business:

- ✔ High severity can be mitigated by adding robustness to the product or service, or by finding alternate processes that don't rely so heavily on this risk.

- ✔ High probability can be mitigated by designing fail-safe systems, duplicate or backup processes or systems, or planning contingencies to be executed during implementation, as situations change.

- ✔ Highly undetectable risks can be mitigated by adding visual systems, alarm systems and processes, and making it difficult for such risks to materialize without some pre-visibility or warning., or through contingency planning and preventative measures.

- ✔ Mitigating high RPN scores would necessitate combining key factors as listed above, as they might work together. For example, adding robustness to products to resolve severity may also reduce probability of occurrence. Adding visual management systems such as alarms, visual aids and other factors may improve delectability while at the same time reduce probability of risk occurrence.

The bottom line is, we can use financial measures to help us mitigate risks of our business, through applying Balanced Scorecards at all levels and in every department and division, and in linking these measures to achieving our overall strategies, goals and objectives.

Chapter 9

Building the Financial Leg Scorecard

*T*his is it. The financial measurement chapter. This is where the rubber meets the road, as they say. We're going to go out on a limb and take a wild guess that you are probably looking in this chapter for one of three reasons:

> ✔ **Your company is doing ok, but just not making the numbers as well as you think it should.**
>
> ✔ **Your department can't make the budget this year, and you are thinking maybe it has something to do with the formulas, or the way things are calculated.**
>
> ✔ **Sales this year are doing great, but your margin is eroding, and you are looking for some way to explain why this is happening.**

Although this list isn't all-inclusive, the point is, you tend to first direct your attention to the financials when things are not working the way they should, or when you're not meeting your goals. Why? Because as rational, human beings (we know we're making a big assumption here) there must be a logical explanation for our current performance situation. And what better way to explain a business performance situation than numbers, right?

Well, guess what? You are in for a big surprise. Among other things, this chapter will dispel such erroneous beliefs, because performance is really a function of all four of the Balanced Scorecard legs, not just the financial one. We will get into the real world of financial measures, and discuss some ways to leverage financial measurement to be able to see across the company, and really understand how an organization works. And, we show you not just how to set up a scorecard, but also how to interpret what it tells you and what to do about it.

We would be remiss if we didn't caution about what you can and can't discover in this chapter:

- ✔ Be ready to have many of your beliefs about financial measures shattered, and some of your assumptions proven incorrect.

- ✔ Even as we will provide many examples of financial measurements for sound Balanced Scorecards, it is highly advisable not to take them verbatim, but use them instead as a framework for customizing your own scorecards and dashboards.

- ✔ Sorry, but this chapter will not make you a financial expert — not for the relatively small amount of money you paid for this book! But this book will help you make key operational and business decisions without focusing too much on financial performance.

Key Aspects of Financial Measures

There are a number of tips and considerations you may want to take into account as you create financial measures for your Balanced Scorecard. Again, lest we forget, these apply regardless of whether you are an executive, middle manager or supervisor, and you should find them helpful in different ways, depending on how much you know about your business and where you want to improve.

Focusing on the right things

Remember, it is not about being the best manager, or the best team in the office. If the Balanced Scorecard gives us anything, it is the ability to synergize with every group, section or department member on the critical vision, mission and goals of the organization. Financial measures for the Balanced Scorecard can ensure we are all aligned, working in the same direction, and sharing a common vision and focus for the company.

Some of the things we need to focus on include:

- ✔ Strategic and growth goals of the company
- ✔ Good environmental and community citizenship
- ✔ Value added focused, for all stakeholders
- ✔ Industry recognition for expertise in your industry
- ✔ Providing the best value in your industry in the world
- ✔ Being an ethical company

. . . and many others.

One key aspect of focus is the need to communicate effectively. Whatever your level and role in the organization, you will need to share and communicate your vision, your sense of purpose and your direction for your organization

Managers as leaders can define reality by providing clear and unambiguous messages about the strategy, vision and direction of the organization, and reiterating and repeating this messages in every interaction we have. Through this method, they can ensure their financial measures are based on the right things as well, and are consistent, focused on the right things, and provide the information we need to make good decisions.

The WIIFM (What's in it for me?) station everyone tunes into

One thing we always hear in organizations is the simple question, "What's in it for me?" In other words, what do I get if I implement financial measures for a Balanced Scorecard? This is not uncommon for employees at all levels in any organization, and pops up a lot when a new initiative is introduced. How would *you* answer this question?

We need to first understand what the middle or upper manager sees as their role in the organization, and what their responsibilities are in managing their operation or department. When we ask such questions, we hear things like: "I manage my department budget", or "I am responsible for making the numbers." Most also agree that their current financial metrics lack any kind of in-process capability to correct or adjust before the end of the reporting period. When pressed, they also agree that it would be good to have a way to see a problem before it becomes a *big* problem, but they are not sure how to do it.

The Balanced Scorecard, and particularly, its financial measures, can provide such real-time readings of the pulse and heartbeat of an organization. Therefore, we only have to show that the current management systems and structures are designed to see problems and mistakes after they happen, building in error and waste into our business model, to help middle and upper managers see that they need a better way. So, how do we do that?

Well, for starters, let's take a look at how effectively we are currently managing our business. How well do our current financial management tools and techniques provide early detection and correction opportunities for changes in our business, such as increases in customer fees, changes in parts or components or shipping pricing from suppliers, or freight carrier route revisions? If we look at the things that 'came up' over the last year that impacted our sales, profitability or volume, we can see many instances where, had we known, we might have been able to mitigate their impact on overall performance, instead of just reacting to it once we found out.

How does this benefit the middle manager? When correction can be done quickly, and when adjustments can be made to avoid mistakes or critical failure to meet goals, then the manager and his or her team can work toward success through understanding their business, to the greater good of the company. Not bad for a day's work.

Timeliness is your competitive edge

Many financial measures also are only updated monthly, provided in monthly reports, where we get the information after the fact. In fact, most financial measures in traditional management provide after-the-fact information, usually so late that there is nothing you can do but react to a trend of performance a year old or more.

A good technique we have used in the past is to compare the update rate of your financial information with your ability to effect change. You will notice that, if your updates are monthly, you cannot effect change any faster than that. If you want to be able to adjust performance faster, say on a weekly basis, you will need to go after the financial measures that can be provided at least weekly. Many companies balk at this, saying their financial systems cannot report more often than on a monthly basis. We can change these things, once they are made visible and it becomes clear how limiting they are when it comes to needing to make timely, effective decisions based on up-to date financial measures.

Financial Measures That Matter

Standard financial measures — including sales, expenses, costs, and profit — have been used for millions of years to run companies,. Well, maybe thousands of years. Whatever the case, financial measures such as these have been the universal language of business for a long time, and do tell us some very general, basic information about the company. You can see if your company is healthy and making money by looking at its sales (also known as *revenue*) and its profitability.

However, to make key decisions, you need a bit more information than the simple measures mentioned above. The problem is that, for decisions, we need information that tells us how well we are doing, indicators that tell us things about our operations. We need to see when changes occur and why, and be able to make real-time decisions about our operations, and then adjust, re-balance, and exploit situations for our competitive advantage.

Key questions help you see what to measure

Let's start by asking, what is it you want to do with your business? Most of us would say (we hope), make money, of course! Fine. But for how long? One year? Five years? 25 years? And, what about growth? Do you want your company to stay about the same size, or double in size, or grow from 50 to 500 employees, maybe to 5,000 or more? And what about geography? Stay in one place, have multiple locations, or franchise within California? North America? Globally? And, lest we forget, what products or services do you want to sell or provide, and what will give you the edge, to generate customer interest? Is it patentable?

As we quickly see, these questions cannot be answered by just tracking revenue, costs and profit. For most of us who are in middle management, when it comes to performance and keeping customers satisfied, we already know exactly what things the boss looks for.

A key advantage to utilizing Balanced Scorecards is the fact that they provide real-time information related to all of the questions above, and more. Armed with this information, middle and upper managers can make real-time adjustments in initiatives, projects, staffing and performance to take advantage of market and business opportunities which would otherwise be invisible.

So, explore some of these questions, and briefly provide some hints to help you select the best measures to help you run our business well.

✔ The product or service questions relate to the value your company provides to customers. Some of the key questions might be:

- What is the product or service your business will provide? Helps to decide how the product or service is to be measured.

- To whom would you provide your products or services? Helps identify customer and market targets, and how to measure successful current and future penetration.

- Why should customers select your product or service over someone else's? Defines what is special about your products and/or services, and helps to determine how to measure this in terms of financial gain and long term benefits.

- Will they have a lasting effect, or require renewal, and how often? Can they become obsolete, and if so, how long will it take? Defines detailed information about your products or services, what value customers gain, and how this value can be financially measured.

- Are there any regional, national, legal, or specific limiting factors I need to know about regarding the product or service I am providing? Defines the legitimacy of your products and/or services, how reliable they are, and any other advantages they provide. Helps to determine how to measure such advantage financially

✔ Strategy questions:

- How long will you want the company to run? Will you keep it, or sell it after five years? Ten years? Twenty? Defines the approach, personal investment, and your ultimate long term objectives.

- What market do you want to focus on? Will it be a stable, cash cow or risky, new product/invention kind of business? How will you balance income with investment? Tells about your margin and profitability expectations, and your growth intentions for the future.

- As the company matures, how will you evaluate and adjust key strategies and actions, refine focus, and align resources? Tells how you will manage your business or department. This is a key aspect to selecting the right financial measurements for your scorecard.

✔ Resource, financing and deployment questions:

- How will you finance your business, both initially and ongoing? Public or private? For department managers, how will your budget be decided? Defines how you are starting up, as well as the financials regarding sustaining your business or department.

- How will you staff your company, particularly its key positions? Helps realize specific methods to manage resource costs, allocations.

- How will you deploy the business? Local, regional, national or global? How, how fast, and when will you decide? Financial measures can actually help here, especially regarding speed and direction for expansion. The answers here will frame the overall approach for tracking deployment financially, in terms of return on investment, and potential financial risks for certain locations.

✔ Long-term planning questions:

- When will I need to expand to keep up with demand? How will I know? How can I invest with confidence in a good return? What happens if I make a mistake? Helps define the type of financial measurement needed to track the expansion, and make good investment decisions.

- How do I keep up with and ensure flexibility with changing market, customer, environmental, regional conditions? Links directly with the growth and development leg of the Balanced Scorecard. Helps define how to detect, analyze and decide actions related to changes.

These are just some of the key questions we need to answer, in order to select the right indicators and measures that can help us manage our business. But, there is another piece that has to be added before we can select our financial measures. Even as we define our products and services and begin to understand and exploit our potential competitive advantage, we will need to define specific performance indicators — called Key Performance Indicators, or KPIs — that will tell us how we are doing.

Selecting key performance indicators (KPIs)

There are many options to selecting financial measurements, depending on whether you are growing the business or just sustaining performance. This means that the answers to several of the initial questions will help determine whether you are growing or sustaining, or both.

For example, if your focus is primarily on sustaining performance, you should focus on the measures that track cost reductions, budget compliance, product profitability, and performance against competitors. If, however, you are trying to grow the business, you should focus more on market share acquisition trends, profitability of new products, revenue/sales growth trends, investment and training percentages, and revenues proportion from new products and services. Of course, if you are focusing on sustaining current business while developing new markets, your measures will be some combination of all of these.

Tips for finding key measures

Use the following tips to help you decide what measures to pursue, based on the questions in the previous section, "Key questions help you see what to measure ":

- ✔ Answering key strategy and product or service questions about your business, such as what value you are offering, to whom, and what advantage they provide, will then enable you to select financial measures such as:

  - Actual value created for customers, possible financial advantage over competitors, and a comparison of your product or service value with other alternatives. Take the customer's metrics and how you are impacting them for their competitive advantage, and yours.

  - Percent of available market share, in terms of sales, margin, growth opportunity, and current and future demand

- Total customer product or service lifecycle costs, support systems investments and performance as profit centers to supporting these costs, and current margins generated.

- Measures to assess market and business environment changes, to enable adjustments to your Balanced Scorecard financial measures as appropriate.

✔ Answering resourcing, financing, and deployment questions will enable you to select financial measures to help you track and manage how you execute your business processes, and enable you to adjust in real time to changes in demand, supply, investment capital, and strategy.

- Estimates of the point of diminishing returns on this product/service line, and when we can expect the follow-on line to take over.

- Financing for your business, and where it comes from, especially current budgets for your product or service families, and investments in new products.

- Staffing, in terms of function and key positions, and utilization as well, not just per employee, but specifically for the different functional specialties that define your competitive advantage (such as design, or distribution or IT systems expertise).

- Deployment in financial performance, by organization, geography, product family, and customer mix. Financial measures can actually help here, regarding speed and direction for expansion. The answers here will frame the overall approach for tracking deployment financially, in terms of return on investment, and potential financial risks for certain locations.

It is critical to know where the overall company is going, whether it be sustaining or growing. Or driving straight for the ditch. The framework of your financial measures will be determined by this, as well as other factors such as where you will invest capital, or budget allocations within each department, or how you will track and manage progress.

How measures differ

The financial measures of importance are a subset of all of your performance indicators, and become the financial KPIs for your business. Of course, depending on your position within a company, these measures will be different. Let's see how that might work out:

For executives and senior managers

Strategic focus will influence you to define financial KPIs for the overall organization, totaling revenue, costs, expenses, interest, taxes, apportionment, depreciation, stock value, and free cash, and others as you might find on a profit and loss statement or a balance sheet. Most of these financial measures are results-type figures, meaning they are the end result of all of the collective efforts of the company. At the executive levels, the financial measures are summarized at the end of a reporting period, albeit they do form the financial leg of the Balanced Scorecard. Consequently, they have little if any effect on the reporting period itself, but are often used to try to influence future performance.

For middle and lower managers

Operational focus will influence you to define your financial KPIs at a much more budget and process level. This means including those measures described above. But there are additional KPIs at this level which can help a department or function actually improve performance during the reporting period. Examples of these include First Pass Yield (sometimes known as Rolled Throughput Yield), or FPY, and cycle times of specific functions such as product development, procurement, recruiting, and product and/or service delivery. There is also model mix, supplier performance trends and behavior, and asset management. There is tremendous strength in the financial measures of the Balanced Scorecard at this level, therefore, because managers can use the scorecard to review performance and adjust accordingly throughout the reporting period, and especially as they support the process (for sustaining strategies) and growth (for growth) legs of the scorecard.

For line managers

Tactical focus will influence you to look to very specific financial measures, related to your daily/weekly/monthly goals and objectives. A *sustaining* strategy, for example, will mean selecting KPIs focusing on cost reduction and management, budget control, and employee efficiency and expense control. A *growth* strategy, on the other hand, will mean selecting KPIs focusing on new technology development, investment percentages, new product/service development cycle time, and prototyping. Of course, a combination of these two overall strategies would see KPIs selected which integrate and focus on one or the other or both, depending on participation support to one or the other. This works well for the Balanced Scorecard, in enabling the financial measures that are pertinent to relate to the department's focus across all four legs, and to each leg as it support the line or task performance tracking and adjustment.

The key for middle and line managers is to select KPIs that are linked to your overall company strategy, but that represent the participative part your department, function or line plays in supporting this strategy.

Don't worry too much about getting your KPIs right the first time (but if you value your job, you'd better get it right by the second or third time!). Especially where financial measures are concerned, it can take several attempts to get consistent, standard financial measures, especially as they relate to the other three legs of your Balanced Scorecard. This is because you should not take for granted that every business entity tracks costs and other financial measures the same way, or with the same measuring stick. In fact, as a company gets more globally focused, it gets harder to get everyone on a consistent definition of the KPIs to be used, and especially when different countries and cultures are involved. The key is to work toward consistency, and closely review all financial measures, to ensure that a standard interpretation for basic financial measures is used.

Ensure competitive success by revisiting measurement

Let's say that one day you wake up to discover that your arch rival has made a major breakthrough in product distribution, and has reduced its lead time by half! Yikes — what a nightmare! Without a Balanced Scorecard, you can probably figure out that this happened, but not why. However, with a scorecard and real-time dashboard, you will be able to know specifically what the reason was for this increase, and be able to take quick action to keep your company competitive.

By having an active Balanced Scorecard, you will be able to detect changes in your competitors' behavior, understand these changes, and address them toward actions to both:

✔ React quickly to avoid loss in your business operations, and

✔ Ensure that the scorecard measures are still valid.

Considering all the changes going on in business, what was key yesterday is not necessarily key today, nor will it be tomorrow. Set up a your scorecards so that your KPIs and financial measures are reviewed periodically, to ensure they are still appropriate as your financial KPIs for your Balanced Scorecard.

Creating The Financial Scorecard

Balanced scorecards can give your business a tremendous advantage, if done right. However, if done wrong, they can create tremendous undo stress and anxiety, which will not add value nor help you to accomplish your goals. Which way will you choose to do them? Here's the way to do it right.

Select either a strategic, operational, or tactical level

It get where you want to go, you've got to start at the right point. In other words, you first have to decide where you are in the organization. For example, if you are strategic, you will be focusing on long-term planning and execution with financial measurements centered on high-level goals and objectives such as revenue and net income (or EBITDA, to some), cash flow, and working capital. If you are operational, you will focus more on delivery, quality and cost metrics, and how they affect your performance. For tactical levels, you would focus more on first pass yield, scrap levels, manning, and maybe some cost reduction and cash flow as well.

That's fine and dandy. But what does it all mean, especially to a non-financial type manager, which most of us are, anyway? Let's take one giant step back, and first make sure our financial measures are aligned with our organization's goals and objectives. To do this, we need to determine where we are in the organization.

Strategic

At this level, financial objectives are related to long-term goals such as improving stock price, enabling higher dividends, and generating high rates of return on investment. Financial measurements at this level will center around stock price fluctuation, market penetration, new technology leadership, with of course the standard revenue, gross and net profit, and several ratios related to performance, efficiency and profitability predictions.

Operational

At this level, financial objectives are related more to performance such as improving yield, reducing fixed and variable costs, improving margins, and increasing revenues for various products and services. Financial measurements at this level will center around delivery and budget vs. actual cost control, quantity of products sold, services rendered, and staff efficiency, as well as the same standard revenue, gross and net profit, and pertinent ratios as related to support strategy, but for operational profit and loss (P&L) based business units.

Tactical

At this level, financial objectives are much more specific, relating to performance of specific product lines or service offices, and looking to improve yield as well as first pass yield (each task done right and delivered on time the first time), reducing specific costs, increased shipments, and department budget vs. actual performance variation reduction. Financial measurements at this level will center around specific product or service line delivery, budget vs. actual cost control, shipments per day/week/month, and quality issues and how they are solved. Where continuous improvement is successfully implemented, there may be additional measures such as improvements, in terms of savings or reduced working capital (or increased cash flow, it is the same thing only the ratio is turned over) to the bottom line, and value flow improvements as well.

In table form, the above would look like Figure 9-1. Whichever level you selected, that level would form a framework for your financial measurement portion of your Balanced Scorecard.

Customizing your financial measures, and how to score them

Customizing financial measures is where the final financial measurements for your Balanced Scorecard are established. We bring together answers to the questions we asked in the first section with prospective KPIs from the sections section, and add our individual business situation, level, and positional responsibilities. The result is a set of critical, relevant financial measures with which you can track, manage and adjust your business actions, be they operations or administrative.

Looking at Figure 9-1 again, you see that you still need to look at your specific industry, market, and product base, and pick and choose which financial measures make the most sense for the particular level in which we work. A middle manager in the mobile phone industry would have a very different Balanced Scorecard, for example, than that of a law firm senior partner.

Level	Financial Objective	Financial Measurement	Example Target
Strategic	* LT Goals Achievement * Stock Price improvement * Higher Dividends * Improved Rates of Return on Investment	* Stock Price Trend * Market Penetration * New Technology Recognition * Revenue * Gross Profit * Net Profit * Strategic Performance Ratios * Strategic Efficiency Ratios * Business Profit improvement Predictions	* 10% better than previous year * 10% each year * 5 New Innovations each year * 15% growth over last year * 25% * 20% * Sales / Employee * Cost / Employee * Margin year/year
Operational	* Yield Improvement * Fixed / Variable Cost Reduction * Margin Improvement * Product / Service Line XX Increasing Revenues	* For each Product Line: = On-time delivery = Budget vs. Actual cost variation = Quantity (count) sold per day/ week/ month/ quarter = Customer services rendered successfully * Division/Functional Revenue per month/ quarter/ year * Gross Profit * Net Profit * Operational Performance Ratios * Operational Efficiency Ratios * Division P&L Performance * Product / Service Line Backlog – future business prediction	 * 100% * < 5% * # * 100% * Sales $$ * 25% * 20% * Sales / Employee * Cost / Employee * Margin year/year * 35% of total Revenue
Tactical	* Product / Service Line Yield Improvement * Product / Service Line First Pass Yield Improvement * Reducing specific costs * Increased shipments * Department/ Line Budget vs. Actual performance variation	* Product / Service Line performance * Product / Service Line delivery * Budget vs. Actual cost control * Shipments per day/ week/ month * quality issues – number, type, resolution * Savings per month/ quarter	15% over last year 95%+ Variation <5% 15-20% over last year 50% $250K/ month

Figure 9-1:
Tactical
objectives.

Figure 9-2 provides some insights into different financial measures as they might correlate to different industries and different applications.

Industry	Financial Objective	Financial Measurement	Industry Specific Example
Retail clothing	Sales Volume Cost Control	$$ Sold each day $$ Spent each day	Ave price per article Budget Compliance
Cell Phones	Reduce Churn Increase Customers	Customer Turnover Sales per customer	Customer Turnover Phones per customer
Jewelry	Revenue	Average Value per sale	Ave sale per item
Auto Parts Manufacturing			
Auto Dealerships			
Engineering			
Construction			
Law			
Financial Planning			
Function			
Human Resources			
Engineering			
Manufacturing			
Purchasing			
Sales			
Finance			

Figure 9-2:
Financial measures correlated to sample different industries.

Be sure to allow flexibility as you decide on what to measure. Some people review and revise their scorecards on a weekly basis, as they see changes in technology, consumer buying behavior, functional expectations, and other market and customer dynamics. You need to be consistent, of course, but be prepared to re-evaluate your metrics and change them if you need to. And believe us, in this fast-changing, global world of business, you will. Often.

Examining examples

One way to really see how financial measures can work for you, regardless of your industry or the products or services you produce and deliver, is to see examples of where different organizations have implemented Balanced Scorecards successfully, and understand how they did it. It might not surprise you much to learn that that's exactly what we're going to do next.

NOW Foods

NOW Foods is a manufacturer of vitamins, minerals, dietary supplements, and natural and health-related food products. In order to enable transparency of their KPIs from bottom to top, they established Balanced Scorecards at all three levels that linked their objectives to specific activities. Prior to this, monthly reports were the only way to find out what happened, and often they were not complete or consistent. Their Balanced Scorecard dashboard is at Figure 9-3. In order to see dynamic changes in demand and margin, they selected those financial measures pertinent to food product production and control, such as sales, profit and volume by geography, customer type and size. The dashboard, which we will discuss in greater detail with more examples in Chapter 10, also allows for daily status and tracking, such as volume shipped in this case. This dashboard has been deployed down to each cost center manager, with real-time data availability on yield, any quality issues, and shifts in delivery demand.

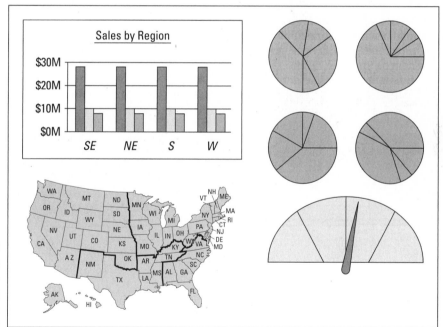

Figure 9-3:
Manufac-
turing
dashboard.

Vinfen

Vinfen is a not-for-profit human and health services organization, with 200 sites and a staff of over 2,000 within the greater Massachusetts area. As you can imagine, managing such a complex structure is very difficult, and given the added complexity of a changing in-patient need profile, and having to juggle distributed resources, the challenge to keep up with what was going on was more than they could handle. About five years ago, they embarked on a search for better methods to manage the operations, and they created a Balanced Scorecard. Their Balanced Scorecard dashboard is at figure 9-4. Here too, we see a balance with financial measures focusing on those important financial aspects of a not-for-profit business such as reducing overtime, and budget performance. Notice the direct connection to the financial goals of the organization as well.

Area	Sponsor	Objectives	Measurement	Target
Financial Perspective				
F2: Increase direct-care cost efficiency.	**Bruce**	1. Reduce overtime (OT)	1. % of direct care payroll, FTE of OT hours. (Report from Karen Stephan)	1. OT hours less than 6.5% of payroll
F4: Achieve financial sustainability.	**Bruce**	1. Meet budgeted growth targets	1. Revenue growth v. budget targets	1. Budget targets for growth
Learning & Growth Perspective				
L3: Recruit and retain a highly skilled workforce	**Tim**	1. Retain best qualified staff	1. Turnover Rate	1. Will not exceed 24% (annualized rate)
			2. Promotion Rate	2. Will not fall below 4%
L4: Ensure organizational learning based on data, outcomes, and experience	**Tim**	1. Increase organizational learning	1. Track all external trainings and conferences for divisions and departments. (Reports from VP's and Dept.Heads)	1. Baseline
			2. Number of hits to the Internet (report from Gary Herchek)	2. Baseline
Internal Perspective				
P2: Improve business practices and efficiencies	**Bruce**	1. Maintain the physical quality and appearance of Vinfen's group homes	1. Average response time to complete a work request. (Report from John Lind)	1. Improvement from FY05
		1. Manage the acuity level of clients through increased clinical consults and assessments	1. Number of clinical consults. (Reports from VP's)	1. Baseline
Customer Perspective				
C1: Deliver services consistent in service and value	**Gary**	1. Increase management retention	1. Management retention/ management vacancies for Site Managers and up	1. Baseline
C2: Increase public awareness and visibility	**Gary**	1. Increase positive media	1. Positive media placements. (Reports from Christopher Smalley)	1. Baseline

Figure 9-4: Vinfen Not-for-Profit health care provider Balanced Scorecard dashboard.

Defense Financial Accounting Services

The Defense Financial Accounting Services (DFAS) of the Department of Defense has established Balanced Scorecards and dashboards for the last 10 years, with remarkable results. Figures 9-5, 9-6 and 9-7 show a clear linkage from strategy to goals to specific scorecard measures, and explain why the organization has been so successful in establishing a direct link between its goals and the specific actions of each of the four legs which support the achievement of these goals. We can see that, once again, the financial measures are selected pertinent to the critical financial performance parameters of the organization, such as cost to client/customer, workforce/staffing ratios, and competitive sourcing implementation and expansion.

Goal / Objective	Customer	Financial		Internal Business Processes			Growth & Learning			
	Improve Client/Customer Satisfaction	Reduce Cost to Client/Customer	Expand the Use of Competitive Sourcing	Improve and Leverage Quality	Encourage Innovation	Deliver System Solutions	Enhance Employee Competence	Increase Employee Satisfaction	Enhance Ability to Recruit and Retain DFAS Talent	Develop a Climate for Action
Fully satisfy customer requirements and aggressively resolve customer problems to deliver best value services	✓	✓		✓	✓	✓				✓
Use performance metrics to drive best business practices and achieve high quality results	✓	✓		✓	✓				✓	✓
Optimize the mix of our military, civilian, and contractor workforce	✓	✓	✓	✓	✓					✓
Establish consultative relationships with leaders	✓				✓		✓	✓	✓	✓
Deliver business intelligence to drive better decisions	✓			✓	✓	✓				
Ensure everyone is working torward the same vision and can connect what they are doing to make the vision a reality	✓	✓	✓	✓	✓	✓	✓	✓	✓	✓
Embrace continuous learning for our workforce to ensure critical, high quality skill sets				✓	✓		✓	✓	✓	✓
Develop the next generation of DFAS leadership				✓			✓	✓	✓	✓

Figure 9-5: DFAS strategic matrix.

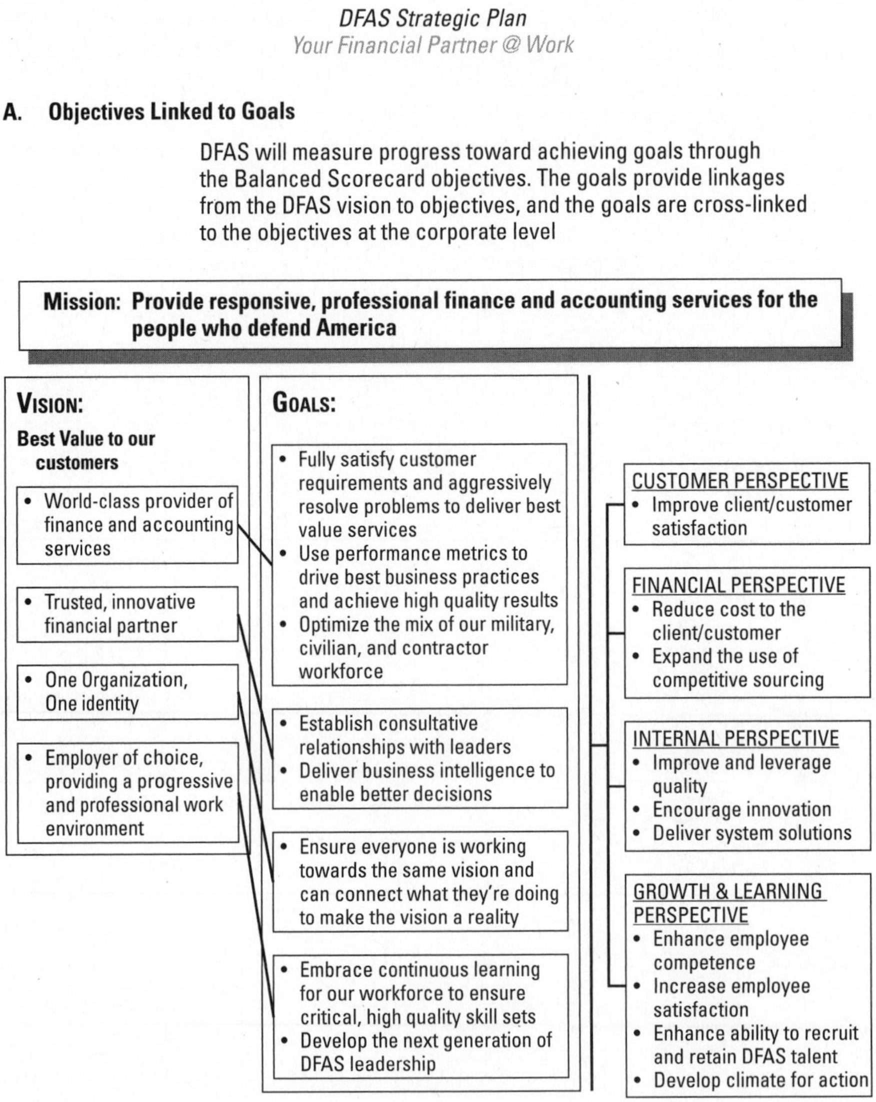

DFAS Strategic Plan
Your Financial Partner @ Work

A. Objectives Linked to Goals

DFAS will measure progress toward achieving goals through the Balanced Scorecard objectives. The goals provide linkages from the DFAS vision to objectives, and the goals are cross-linked to the objectives at the corporate level

Mission: Provide responsive, professional finance and accounting services for the people who defend America

VISION:

Best Value to our customers

- World-class provider of finance and accounting services
- Trusted, innovative financial partner
- One Organization, One identity
- Employer of choice, providing a progressive and professional work environment

GOALS:

- Fully satisfy customer requirements and aggressively resolve problems to deliver best value services
- Use performance metrics to drive best business practices and achieve high quality results
- Optimize the mix of our military, civilian, and contractor workforce

- Establish consultative relationships with leaders
- Deliver business intelligence to enable better decisions

- Ensure everyone is working towards the same vision and can connect what they're doing to make the vision a reality

- Embrace continuous learning for our workforce to ensure critical, high quality skill sets
- Develop the next generation of DFAS leadership

CUSTOMER PERSPECTIVE
- Improve client/customer satisfaction

FINANCIAL PERSPECTIVE
- Reduce cost to the client/customer
- Expand the use of competitive sourcing

INTERNAL PERSPECTIVE
- Improve and leverage quality
- Encourage innovation
- Deliver system solutions

GROWTH & LEARNING PERSPECTIVE
- Enhance employee competence
- Increase employee satisfaction
- Enhance ability to recruit and retain DFAS talent
- Develop climate for action

Figure 9-6: DFAS Link to vision, goals, and measures.

A word or two (or three) about information management

When company leaders decide to implement Balanced Scorecards, many of them believe that it is all about having the right data management system. As a consequence, many make the mistake of purchasing a Balanced Scorecard dashboard software program that has more bells and whistles and attributes than you can imagine, with the thought that, "If I have the right information management system in place, I should be able to manage my performance easily and effectively." Right?

Wrong.

DFAS Strategic Plan
Your Financial Partner @ Work

B.   **DFAS FY 2002 Corporate Balanced Scorecard Perspectives, Objectives & Measures**

PERSPECTIVE	OBJECTIVE	MEASURE
Customer	Improve Client/Customer Satisfaction	1. Client/Customer Satisfaction
		2. Commitments Met – Performance Contracts
		3. Commitments Met – Client Executive Contacts
		4. Specific Billing Rates
Financial	Reduce Coast to Client/Customer	5. Total Costs
	Expand the Use of Competitive Sourcing	6. Competitive Sourcing Performance
		7. Total Workforce Ratio
Internal Business Processes	Improve and Leverage Quality	8. Quality Index
		9. Rework Identified
		10. Rework Eliminated
		11. Best Business Practices Adopted
	Encourage Innovation	12. New Products or Services Delivered
	Deliver System Solutions	13. Commitments Met – System Milestones
Growth & Learning	Enhance Employee Competence	14. Employees in Developmental Assignments
	Increase Employee Satisfaction	15. Employee Satisfaction
	Enhance Ability to Recruit and Retain DFAS Talent	16. Core Competency Profile
	Develop a Climate for Action	17. Climate for Action

Figure 9-7: DFAS Link to Balanced Scorecard dashboard measures.

The problem is that the thinking here is backwards. The risk is that the software program won't meet the manager's needs exactly. But, the software was sold as a do-all, be-all, end-all management tool, so what ends up happening is that the measures are adjusted to fit the tool instead of the tool being adjusted to fit the measures.

To avoid this potential dissonance, managers need to define their measurements, and then look to see which software enables them to manage their measures most effectively. The software needs to:

✔ Enable easy flexibility and adjustment to measures as market and customer conditions change

✔ Link objectives and measures across the four legs of the Balanced Scorecard.

✔ Enable a wide access capability, with customizable dashboard capability for managers at the strategic, operational and tactical levels within the organization, and if possible, be offered in multiple languages as well, yet integrated at the executive levels.

Interpreting Financial Measures for Balanced Scorecards

Having an excellent Balanced Scorecard, with effective financial measures, is a big step forward, but is only half the story. The other half is, of course, being able to interpret what your scorecard is telling you, as it provides real-time critical data on your business. There is a saying that having information without an ability to understand it or to make use of it is often worse and possibly more dangerous than not having the information in the first place.

The basis for information provided by Balanced Scorecards and dashboards is that it is designed to provide up to date status and data on how well a company is accomplishing its goals and objectives. It's now time to consider how to use this information to help us see when changes are necessary, manage our business, and to make decisions to improve or adjust our progress.

Understanding scorecard financial measures, and what they tell you

Typically, financials can be pretty dry and complex things to work with, even for those lucky (?) people who deal with them every day. Yet, there are things that financial measures can reveal which can help on several levels with respect to your Balanced Scorecard and how you manage with it. In our experience, there are only a handful of key measures you need to be familiar with.

Realize that many financial measures are not as exact as one might think. Take sales, for example. Sales is most often recognized (recorded) at the time a service or product is delivered. In retail, when you buy something, you give money for merchandise, which results in sales equaling cash income.

But, for many companies, when a product or service is delivered is not necessarily when the company gets the payment. It may wait weeks or even months to get paid. Costs are also not necessarily recognized when they are accrued, but instead are often spread over a year or two, a process called amortization, so that there is less incremental impact on the business. For example, if you buy a truck for US$45,000, it could be devastating to your small business financial performance for the month in which it was purchased. To mitigate this negative impact, the truck cost is amortized so that each month only a portion of the total cost is declared.

The standard financial measures, such as revenue or sales, cost of goods sold, gross profit, net profit, Earnings Before Interest, Taxes, Depreciation and Amortization (EBITDA), and expenses, along with current assets and liabilities, form the basis for judging the health of an organization. These are mostly results-type measures, however, in that they represent the effect of many other actions taken in productivity or administration. While we certainly are interested in these figures, we cannot manage with them. It would be like trying to wag a dog using its tail. The dog wags the tail, not the other way around. So, we need more business process based measures, that tell us what is going on, not just what happened.

The key for you as a middle or upper manager is to learn your organization's rules of the road, and to manage your department or function within them successfully. To do this, you will need in-process metrics, available real-time, and capable of providing useful, critical information on a frequent — perhaps daily — basis. Examples include:

- ✔ Product value (delivered/time)
- ✔ Machine up time (machine operating time value/total time)
- ✔ Purchase price variance on a weekly basis (Purchase price/goal price)
- ✔ Daily work-in-process inventory value levels and trends
- ✔ Weekly customer issue handling costs
- ✔ Product sales by model, customer, geography, industry
- ✔ Budget compliance on a weekly basis, with clear reasons for actions, and trend analysis, to enable analysis of potential chronic repeating issues or first pass yield failure.

Industry-specific financial measures can also be of use, depending on the types and frequency of the decisions necessary to maintain a competitive advantage. Laptop manufacturers, for example, must know daily how their products compare to the competition in the eyes of their customers, and where to seek an advantage. Other examples include cell phone minutes charged (more is better), special services selected (more is better), and bundled service contracts (more is better), to name a few.

Pointing toward additional information and insight

Financial measures can also highlight when we do not have enough data or critical information to make sound decisions. Knowing how much work in process (WIP) you are maintaining on a daily basis is part of the story, but unless you also know consumption and delivery performance, you will not be able to impact it.

The same can be said for many of the most common scorecard financial measures. So, you need to be sure to tailor your financial measures to not only give you process performance information on a continual basis, but also to indicate where you can integrate performance measures for further financial intelligence gathering. And if they can brew your morning coffee and take out the trash, so much the better. The key is to always consider the cause and effect relationship of financial measures. For example:

✔ Per service value, coupled with frequency, becomes more useful in determining rates of performance, and adjusting as appropriate to need, pricing and delivery factors.

✔ Per component value, coupled with quantity per day, enables better decisions regarding speed, availability and costs.

✔ Per consulting service hour, coupled with value multiple for the client, helps plan and allocate resources.

✔ Days sales outstanding (ending AR/average revenue per day) calculated weekly, vs. monthly, coupled with collection status and progress, can enable strategy adjustments in billing, collecting old debt, and adjusting for capital.

There are many other examples that can illustrate how financial measures can help us manage our business, in many industries, and even according to national culture. For example, Japanese subcontractors must be constantly responsive to major industrial manufacturers, and succeed through collaboration in financial and other measures. As Earth Tech, a engineering and construction subsidiary of Tyco realized in the late '90s, in Mexico, daily environmental impact is more important to some communities than best price, and so will use such criteria to contract with water and wastewater treatment companies.

Investing in training

The same is very true for decision making and other analysis skills. Hewlett Packard — the 2005 award winner for best business performance management practices — has invested broadly and with some depth in their Balanced Scorecard initiative, and especially in the skills training and development around financial measures.

Their Performance Measurement and Management System (PMMS) provides transparency as well as centralized resourcing for status, data and progress anywhere around the globe through a web-based interface, and they spend many hours training leadership in its use.

Structures for decision making from scorecard financial measure

When we talk with managers about making decisions from financial measures, we find that very often there are no clear, concise systems or structures in place to provide guidance. If it were just about what to buy, or how much to spend on a trip, that would be easy. But today's budgets are increasingly complex, and managing operations has taken a whole new meaning in the multitude of contributing factors that influence our daily performance. Not to mention the unplanned stuff as well!

The fact is, nothing substitutes for good training in management decision making, where a system is employed whenever a decision is necessary based on financial measure performance. More and more companies are finding that, in today's fast-paced economy, managers must be able to collect and interpret financial information quickly. They create Balanced Scorecards for precisely this reason.

Remember, there is a difference between skills development training and experience. Experience is not a substitute for skills development. Just being familiar and experienced does not an expert make. For example, if you have been driving for say, 25 years, you should theoretically be eligible to race with a Formula 1 team, based on the years of experience you have behind the wheel, right? Not exactly. There are special skills required, like handling a car at very high speeds, negotiating curves around other cars, and maneuvering for lead, that are usually not learned nor practiced in most normal driving conditions. At least not in *our* normal driving conditions. Your own mileage may vary.

Risk analysis

When a leader has to decide between options, a special technique is used called a SWOT analysis, or Strengths, Weaknesses, Opportunities and Threats analysis. As each aspect of the SWOT is considered, sometime a weighting is assigned, in terms of high (9), medium (6), or low (3) risk to the company. The analysis is usually done by a leadership team, with members familiar with the different functional areas potentially impacted by the decision.

Specifically, each option is assessed in terms of these four areas, specifically:

- What strengths will the option capitalize on?
- What weakness can be overcome by this option?
- What opportunities become possible with this option?
- What threats to success and the company are likely with this option?

Once these four aspects area are considered and weighed, decisions can be made according to risk mitigation desires, and trade offs in terms of weakness offset by strengths, and threats offset by opportunities.

FMEA

The Failure Modes Effects Analysis (FMEA) is another risk mitigation decision tool that assess risks of different options in terms of three different considerations:

- What is the severity of a failure? High (8–10) would mean catastrophic to the company and the business. Medium (4–7) would be severe, but not fatal to the organization. Low (1–3) would impact minimally or not at all.
- How probable is the failure likely to occur? High would mean very probable to inevitable, medium would mean somewhat likely, and low would indicate an unlikely probability of occurrence.
- How detectable would the failure be if it should occur? High would mean its occurrence would be invisible to the organization. Medium would suggest some possibility to see it, but not much, and low would indicate there are detection systems or methods in place to alert immediate failure occurrence.

Each option is analyzed for possible failures, and each failure is assessed via these three considerations, with a score assigned in each, and multiplied together to give an overall risk value, or Risk Priority Number (RPN). Then, the option with the lowest RPN is the option with least risk.

Review structures are often used to ensure completeness, when time is available. When a decision is made, a review of that decision is conducted one level higher up in the organization, by a team of three or more, who would use a checklist or critical index of key considerations to ensure the decision took all appropriate aspects into account. This also enables a broader perspective for consideration, where the decision maker may not have investigated indirect aspects as well as needed, which may impact the company's longer term planning or other factors outside of his/her direct influence.

Different types of organization structures also can contribute greatly to operational success, especially where customer satisfaction is a big factor. Switching to more program and product or service focus from traditional functional structures enables a clear line-of-sight to the customer for every participating department, who together share responsibility for delivery, quality and performance. Added side benefits are greatly reduced rework loops, better hand-offs, and quicker response to problems or issues that arise from time to time. Figure 9-8 highlights this concept.

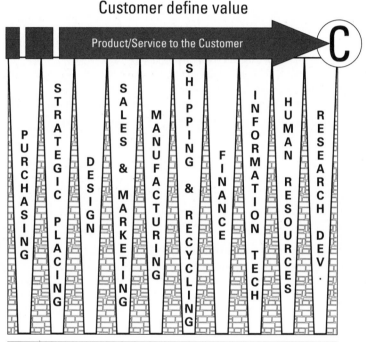

Customer define value

Product/Service to the Customer

C

PURCHASING · STRATEGIC PLACING · DESIGN · SALES & MARKETING · MANUFACTURING · SHIPPING & RECYCLING · FINANCE · INFORMATION TECH · HUMAN RESOURCES · RESEARCH DEV.

The key is to focus everyone away from their silos, on their specific role in supporting how well we deliver to the customer, and how to improve this above all else.

Figure 9-8: Financial measures can create transparency to customer created value.

Understanding the Essence of Accuracy

What happens when data is not what it seems, what we want, or what we need? Part of the problem is that if the data going in is not dependable, the data coming out will not be dependable either. But that is not the whole story. With errors in data, you may interpret such conclusions incorrectly. In the following section, we show you that, even if the data might be credible, the challenges in treating input as valid is actually a no-brainer, but often gets complicated in the day-to-day rush.

Oh no, the numbers are wrong!

The pitfall resulting from this exclamation is one of the most dangerous mistakes a company can make. We have done the math, analyzed the dashboard, and the results are in. The performance is *bad*. Put another way, the numbers represent less than stellar performance.

The most common mistake, and the most deadly, is denying the data. A lot of companies actually decide that the financial measures, as indicated on the dashboard, and as linked and integrated to the four legs of the Balanced Scorecard, must be wrong. They reason that, with the recent introduction of the Balanced Scorecard and dashboard, and the newness of the approach to the company, it must be the figures that are wrong, since the approach must be right.

This tendency is brought about by something called cognitive dissonance, or CG. CG happens when we encounter something that does not fit our 'rules of the road' or our cognitive map, which is a map in our minds of our hopes, dreams, ideas, impressions, rules of normalcy, and other things related to how we feel about things. When we come across a situation that does not align with our cognitive map, we experience CG. Since two truths cannot exist in the same time and space, one has to give. In this case, given that it must be possible to meet the numbers, politically as well as personally, then the numbers must be wrong. Very dangerous. Denial of accurate results has destroyed many companies, and rendered many more into bankruptcy or worse. However, there are other ways to slice a carp.

Some company leaders don't deny the data outright. Instead, they qualify the data, to render it safe, making the tenuous assumption that it might be true after all. For example, we need to meet the numbers, but the sales department projects that sales of a particular model will go down unexpectedly. So, typically the leaders might point to the data, and indicate that it is probably true for a specific set of circumstances, or a separate department or group, but because there are differences in departments, it does not apply to his or her particular department. This is equally dangerous, since it also results from taking drastic action, in order not to lose a significant portion of the company.

The key is to ask where are you focused, talk with your peers, your boss, and even other department heads, before you select your financial measures, so that what you measure aligns with what you want to ultimately achieve.

The right numbers, the wrong analysis

The pitfall here is the potential to draw correlations regarding performance that have no true link, but appear to be linked anyway. For example, we see an improvement in margin numbers, supported by an improvement in on-time delivery. The conclusion is that we are delivering on time, which results in reduced expediting costs. But we may find that the volume has reduced, making it easier to deliver on time and avoid expediting.

A small electrical component company was tracking its volume production, noting increases in specific current and capacitance based items, and began to analyze these items and their use in electronic stereo sound systems. Based on the volume increase, they revised their strategic focus, and laid groundwork for additional capacity to support such stereo sound systems in other ways, such as with additional components. They also established and staffed a new marketing strategy to approach such stereo sound system producers, in order to improve their market share. However, when they did approach these producers, they were told that their products were actually being phased out of their products, due to limits in capability. Surprised by this, they tried to analyze who might be buying such components, only to discover that hobby radio enthusiasts had found their particular products useful in controlling bandwidth and enabling parallel processing in short-wave communications equipment. Had they looked first at the consumer of their components, they would have saved hundreds of thousands of dollars in marketing to the wrong customer base and restructuring, and been able to capitalize on the increased customer base they did not know existed at all.

To avoid this pitfall, the key is to integrate your financial measures, such as margin and delivery with yield, takt (volume provided over available time), along with growth measures (shift rates to new products, for example) and internal measures as well (operational changes due to supplier or environmental variation) in the dashboard.

This will require a comprehensive review of your financial dashboard, to ensure its measures integrate and align with the other dashboard measures as well, so that the right analysis can be conducted, providing the correct decision choices for competitive advantage.

Tracking the numbers by automatic pilot

It's not uncommon for managers to create a dashboard that tracks "standard financial measures" in a way that reflects more of a reporting scheme than something that actually contributes to decisions. The problem here is that, while you set up your financial measures in order to monitor your company's behavior, you need to be sure to regularly check the measures as well, and not just depend on the 'automatic response' system to report irregularities.

The reason for this is that, while airplanes can use an automatic pilot system to monitor, detect, and signal an alarm when irregularities occur, they are flying level, with most environmental and mechanical factors known. Companies, on the other hand, ride their market waves with no warning to changes in trends, customer buying variation, new or competitor product introductions, supplier influence to your performance, and dozens of other factors that will have an effect on how you are doing today, and how you will do tomorrow. Many companies are brought down thinking they had great risk reduction programs in place, only to discover their market stolen out from under them.

The key to avoiding this pitfall is to provide for excellent risk reduction, based on Failure Mode Effects Analysis, or FMEA. Risks are assessed on the basis of three elements; severity of something occurring, probability of that occurrence, and detect-ability of the possibility of occurrence, or of the occurrence itself. As discussed in Chapter 10, this tool provides excellence risk mitigation, management and control for a company, and can guard against the automatic pilot tendency of financial dashboards.

To avoid these pitfalls, we need to review our rewards and recognition systems as they relate to achieving certain financial performance, and ensure we are not promoting any of the above behaviors. Remember: You get the performance that you reward! Especially vulnerable are compensation-related incentives.

However, equally strong in motivation are those factors that fuel such inappropriate behaviors through recognition or internal competition. We have seen where internal competition resulted in instituting cross-charging fees, delivering late, and questionable quality performance to sister companies, in order to gain an internal competitive advantage. The amazing thing is that management continues to advocate internal competition, in spite of the growing mountain of evidence of catastrophic damage caused to company, not to mention the fact that it does not add value anyway, nor would the customer be willing to pay for it anyway.

The bottom line is this: be aware that there may be a propensity to cheat, and that the measures recorded and reported may need an additional review, to ensure they are accurate and timely, so that you can indeed make the best decisions you can for your company.

Chapter 10

Building the Financial Leg Dashboard

A financial dashboard is just a Balanced Scorecard you use that tells you about your specific financial circumstance at a particular moment in time, just like your bank account statement. This dashboard contains the latest information — updated periodically — with enough detail to help you make decisions. By providing the latest information to you, financial dashboards enable you to choose appropriate actions to both avoid mistakes or errors in judgment and to make informed decisions for better results.

In this chapter, we discuss how financial dashboards extend the Balanced Scorecard, enable decisions, assist in assessing and decoding difficult business choices for competitive advantage. We also explore a variety of different examples.

The Basics of Financial Dashboards

The Balanced Scorecard provides you a vehicle by which you can make the best decisions, and track your progress toward achieving your business goals and objectives. It is an integrated road map (no, sorry, not a roadmap to the South of France), guiding you and enabling you to lead your organization, using a balanced approach focusing beyond financial performance and results.

Managing by scorecard alone, is, however, a very difficult and daunting task, as it truly encompasses multiple measures with multiple overlapping initiatives and activities, all managed at different levels and in different departments throughout the company. So, now what? How can all this complexity be turned simple?

One way executives and leaders have conquered these mountains of measures is by developing tools to help them quickly collect key timely intelligence data, and interpret, understand, and respond with execution actions and adjustments. These tools are call *dashboards*, and those that help you understand real-time performance of your financial measures are called *financial dashboards*. Often, executives combine dashboard elements of all four of the Balanced Scorecard legs into a single tool, with a limited set of key indicators by which they set, steer, and adjust the course of their organization. In this section, we will cover the basics of financial dashboards, who owns them, and how they can help you in your leadership role as managers of your company.

Determining ownership and responsibility of the financials

So, who is responsible for the financials of an organization? Typically, when you ask this question, you are told that is the job of the finance officers, directors and staff. Occasionally, you are told, "Who knows?" (Not the best answer for those who hope to keep their jobs, by the way!) Truth be told, there is something to be said for ensuring that a company's financials are accurate, timely and relevant. Often, this level of responsibility is seen as being the "owner and operator" of the financial data.

However, accuracy and timeliness, while important, do not a decision maker make. Ownership and responsibility will always rest with the managers and leaders that use this information in their daily task to lead and decide what actions are taken, what direction you go, and how you get there. This extends to all levels of management, and applies wherever decisions are made and actions are implemented.

The financial leg of your scorecard is different than the other three legs (customer, internal processes, learning and growth) because financial measures and indicators link directly to evaluated performance by the market, stockholders and owners. Having regular, updated visibility to these indicators, therefore, is vital for leaders to see not just how the company is doing, but also to link the four legs and their initiatives to these measures. This is because, as you might have guessed, you don't want to wag the dog by making decisions from your financial measures alone, yet you need to know how your actions are indeed affecting these same measures. Financial dashboards can be extremely effective because they provide a real-time window into performance measures, enabling you to adjust actions and respond to changes, hopefully before they become major problems.

But, and this is a *big* but, you will need to make sure that the right people are involved in selecting and designing your dashboard structures. Having only finance types take on this task may skew information towards financials, and away from key decision drivers found across all four legs. Similarly, having only business leaders select and design your dashboard structures may direct data toward decisions without clear financial justification. The best approach is a team approach, involving both financial advisors and business leaders, to ensure that the information provided in the dashboard is pertinent, real time, and accurate.

An emphasis on real-time measurement and response

Several years ago, a large government contractor submitted numerous bids for several large defense weapon systems contracts. The contractor's program office would monitor progress of these bids with monthly status reports and reviews, which would typically last about one day, and would usually require every program manager to fly in and report on their program (at no small expense, we might add!). The win rate was relatively low — about 15 percent — with this type of bid, so the contractor wanted to know what they could do to double the win rate to 30 percent or better. When we looked into the review process, we immediately noticed that it did not allow real-time feedback and adjustments to the bid process. We were in fact told that this inflexibility was a strength of the bid process, since the company was following strict, disciplined procedures, which discouraged and even punished deviation. Once we mapped the bid process, we were able to demonstrate that over 93 percent of the process added no value, and often delayed, misdirected, and imbedded additional errors into the bid itself, resulting in last-minute, crash timetables to meet deadlines. It took months to get the company to untangle its process. They did, however, and within two years the company's win rate moved into the 25 to 27 percent levels, with very encouraging prospects for the future.

So what is the point of that little tale? The point is that the typical financial reporting and review structure involves monthly reports, where each department compares actual costs and expenditures to budget levels, and explains variations in terms of unexpected events, unforeseen circumstances, changes in priorities, projects, focus, or customer requirements. These are usually accompanied by plans and actions designed to rectify these situations or compensate to get back on track.

The danger with relying on these commonplace methods and structures is that they are always reactive at best, responding to failures and unforeseen circumstances *after* they already happen, not *before* they happen. In addition, most of the so-called corrective actions are determined without a rigorous root cause analysis, so they will ultimately address a symptom or resolve a piece of the problem, without getting to the true root causes, which means you will be solving this problem again. And again.

A Balanced Scorecard approach can dramatically improve this condition. The financial measurement aspect of such a scorecard approach focuses on real-time indicators to both give warning and to provide sufficient information for business leaders to see potential issues coming before they occur, often with enough time for a thorough root cause analysis and preventative measures to be installed. The key is proactive, pertinent real-time information, useful in monitoring and adjusting actions by departments and divisions toward successful goal achievement.

Taking appropriate action: Who, when, and how

Once you have established your dashboards, you need to be able to read them, understand what they are telling us, and take appropriate action. For financial measures, this means looking at trends, ratios, and key performance indicators (KPIs), tying them to actions within the company's operation, and adjusting your specific actions in real time, to ensure that you stay on track.

This means moving away from traditional management practices, where financial reviews would show a specific problem had occurred, and corrective actions would be put in place to mitigate and correct for the next month or quarter. These methods are reactive, focusing on what has already occurred rather than helping you avoid the problems in the first place. Instead adopting an approach involving Balanced Scorecards supported by financial measures — monitored, tracked, and analyzed using dashboards — alleviate the need to construct a review and corrective action system, by enabling real-time response and adjustment to deviating trends in performance.

Using financial dashboards helps managers take swift and appropriate action to prevent problems from occurring — or at least mitigate their effect on business performance. They help determine who should be assigned to address the pending problem, when it gets done, and how. In practice, this process becomes almost automatic, because the elements of the Balanced Scorecard are assigned to key members of leadership, even as all decisions are shared by the steering team. This assignment, coupled with measures of timeliness in response, allows a smooth transition toward accomplishing key actions as planned, without unnecessary directing, delegating, or assignment, since responsibility and authority is already designated.

Creating Financial Dashboards That Have Impact

Managers create financial dashboards to provide not only real-time, up-to-date information, but also help enable informed decisions regarding contingencies, alternatives, and risk-avoidance strategies. It is also important for the financial measures to help managers assess and decide critical aspects across all four legs of the Balanced Scorecard, since each is a critical part for the whole — action in one leg usually affects others as well.

There are really only a small number of key things to remember in creating your financial dashboard:

- ✔ Your financial dashboard should contain no more than five or six key measures of real-time characteristics, capable of being updated often and accurately without special actions (in other words, part of the normal process would be not just to provide and assess, but also to update this information regularly.)

- ✔ Your financial dashboard must relate to *your* financial needs, in terms of what you are measuring in your business, either at the section, or department, or division level, providing line performance data to a line manager to help him or her make the critical daily decisions.

- ✔ Given options, always opt for graphics, gauges, pictures, and illustrations in your financial dashboard, rather than tables, spreadsheets or raw data reports. Dials, much like on your car dashboard, provide an excellent visual way to see immediately understand what is going on, aiding interpretation and accelerating the decision-making process.

- ✔ Make sure your dashboard links to your strategy map, such that you can connect your financial measures directly to the scorecard. An example of such a linkage is at Figure 10-1 below.

- ✔ And, don't forget, your financial dashboard needs to tie operational, growth and internal process performance together.

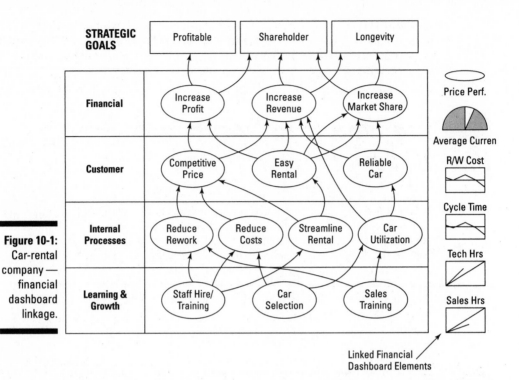

Figure 10-1: Car-rental company — financial dashboard linkage.

Linked Financial Dashboard Elements

Keep it simple, complete, and effective!

REMEMBER

The *raison d'etre* of the dashboard is to create a tool that is easy and quick to interpret, not difficult to explain or share with others, and that provides the best real-time updates. Here are some suggestions for keeping your financial dashboard simple, complete, and effective (and not stupid!):

To ensure your dashboard is simple:

- ✔ Keep your dashboard to one page, fit to your screen. Also, limit your sub-panels to no more than four or five. And, keep the data elements on each sub-panel to no more than five to six at most.

- ✔ Use a combination of daily, weekly, and monthly financial information, updated appropriately.

- ✔ Try to make the information readily useful. A good rule is to only take a maximum of three steps to get to clear, unambiguous data that can be interpreted, analyzed, and indicative of a clear root cause for effect.

To ensure your dashboard is complete:

- ✔ Once you have put your dashboard together, test your ability to explain it to a colleague in another area, taking no more than one to two minutes, and then ask for feedback. This will provide excellent information on what is clear or unclear, what is necessary or unnecessary, and how much detail you need. Be prepared to change your dashboard significantly.

✔ Check your dashboard to make sure you can link each measure across your scorecard, using your strategy map, as discussed earlier in this section.

✔ When it is finished, put it away for a few days, and then pull it out again, and look at it as if another manager developed it, and ask if it covers the necessary financial information and measurements.

To ensure your dashboard is effective:

✔ Test pilot your dashboard, before you publicize it, to make sure the data is relevant, accurate, and necessary to manage your group effectively.

✔ Show your dashboard to peers and colleagues, and ask specific questions regarding simplicity, completeness, and effectiveness, as well as overall design, and whether it is easy to explain to others. Ask for any suggestions, or additions in case you might have forgotten something.

✔ Build into your dashboard ways to evaluate the measures for effectiveness, and to change them immediately when necessary.

The key here is to create a visually attractive yet pertinent, informative window that frequently updates to help you determine how well your group or department or production line is doing, and provides what you need to know to make it run better and improve every day. That's not too much to ask for, right?

Types of dashboards

These days, you have all manner of dashboards, from hand drawn (for example, the primary visual displays common to production teams in lean manufacturing environments) to spreadsheet-based Microsoft Office designs (such as those in Excel or Lotus Notes), to those higher-level programs designed by professional organizations to enable managers to tailor their dashboards according to their specific needs. Let's take a look at each type, and see what the advantages and disadvantages are for each.

Manual dashboards

Hand-drawn and maintained manual dashboards are commonly used by teams and cells at the process levels of the organization, such as production (line or manufacturing cell teams), purchasing (commodity or buying teams), finance (receivables, payables or invoice teams), administration (travel or recruiting teams), or engineering (design or research teams). These dashboards are updated and reviewed daily, and are located where the teams work. They include key daily and weekly financial metrics indicative of performance to the Balanced Scorecard, such as output, rates of performance, and cost and defects rates as well.

Some advantages to manual dashboards are:

- ✔ That they are extremely current and usually accurate
- ✔ They are owned and operated by the teams themselves
- ✔ They provide any information regarding issues or concerns
- ✔ They enable customization to the specific group or department financial measurement needs, such as accounts receivable or assembly line performance.
- ✔ They usually link directly to higher-level key financial performance measures
- ✔ They provide real-time information to management, without need for translation, interpretation, or summary reporting.

Some disadvantages might be:

- ✔ It can be difficult to integrate multiple dashboards for trend analysis and other uses. This is usually handled by supervisors, who capture the data and share it with each other and other lines.
- ✔ Hand-updated dashboards are by nature not linked to financial data systems, so there may be a need to record such financial data electronically. Here again, supervisors who record the information from these dashboards share it, and also record it for financial analysis and reporting.
- ✔ There is very real potential for differences in visual display dashboards, making comparison to targets difficult. While creativity is encouraged within teams, standardization is important as well.

Spreadsheet-based financial dashboards

Spreadsheet-based financial dashboards provide certain systems and integration advantages over manual dashboards, by enabling teams and middle management common, easy-to-use tools to track and manage the financial measures of the Balanced Scorecard.

Some advantages to such spreadsheet-based dashboards include:

- ✔ Ease of use in format and data integration, since most people who manage are familiar with spreadsheets of some type or another
- ✔ Customized design, enabling implementation of exactly what you want in financial measures for your dashboard
- ✔ Some degree of brevity, due to high cost of customization, to include only what is required, enabling simplicity and efficiency

✔ Quick analysis of key measures, for trends and decision support

✔ Graphics which are usually enabled with spreadsheets, enhancing simplicity and visual measurement tools and techniques, such as graphical gauges or dials.

Disadvantages to this type of dashboard might include:

✔ Because they are usually custom made, they cost much in time, money, and trial-and-error testing before they become useful.

✔ They usually do not provide flexibility for rapid changes and revisions. When changes are necessary, they usually involve re-coding, re-testing and piloting before use.

✔ They cannot handle complex, highly integrated business systems such as those found in computer, software, and usually provide only limited integration to financial systems

✔ There are inherent difficulties in standardizing across continents, and with different companies in different industries, given spreadsheet differences.

Higher-level programs and software-based financial dashboards

Higher-level programs and software-based financial dashboards comprise the third key type of dashboard, and they provide enhanced programming capability as well as visual and numeric data tracking.

Some advantages to program-based dashboards include:

✔ Flexibility in design, enabling not only the ability to create your financial dashboard, but also to provide for real-time evaluation, revision and testing of your dashboard.

✔ Integration across business segments, and flexible integration with most major financial systems

✔ Ease of financial measures selection and assignment

✔ Best visual management systems of all three types of dashboards, and able to create Sect. 508 compliant (visually impaired) graphs, charts, and pictures

✔ Automatic assessment and adjustment opportunity, to enable the best use of this dashboard for any management level

✔ Ease of creating images compatible with different media, such as PDF, JPEG, PNG, SVG, Flash, EPS and others

Disadvantages to this type of dashboard might include:

✔ High cost to implement, requiring high priority of the company, and buy-in at all levels to be useful and provide maximum competitive advantage

✔ More complex to implement, requiring some training, development and systematic implementation.

✔ Unfamiliar formatting and programming requires special training and setup.

Some examples of dashboards that work!

Not all dashboards are created equal. Consider these examples of dashboards that work. They can provide you with some ideas for how you might select and format your own financial dashboards.

Figure 10-2, courtesy of Corda Technologies, depicts a four-panel financial dashboard from VisualCalc, showing performance against target, performance by segment, by teams, and background information (populations) for analysis. Note how easy it is to use, with the use of a meter or gauge to indicate level of performance, and varying bar heights and thicknesses for greater detail. The pie charts depict information per regions, and make it easy to see what the pieces are relative to the whole. This dashboard can show a manager — on a daily basis — performance, where problems are, and relativity of the problems to their customer population, for better prioritization.

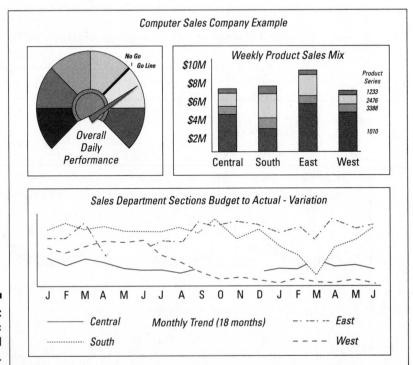

Figure 10-2:
VisualCalc
financial
dashboard.

Figure 10-3 was sketched from a very sophisticated software-program-based financial dashboard for a large oil refinery company — with locations in Texas — that manages its scorecards by state for maximum effect. Note that there are multiple indicators, all updated daily, regarding current status of each location, as well as other charts depicting different customers (A–G) and their contribution to profitability. Given certain changes in performance at key sites, the manager can mitigate risk by diverting levels for refinement, depending on OEE readings, all while avoiding serious equipment problems.

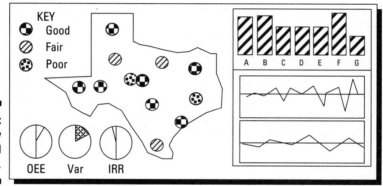

Figure 10-3:
Oil refinery
financial
dashboard.

Figure 10-4 is an example of a dashboard that a pizza delivery vendor uses. The data is updated after each delivery, in order to monitor profitability based on six indicators, all calculated and part of the excel program they developed, providing the manager exactly what he needs to adjust, in terms of risk, margin for error (level of wrong deliveries tolerable before financial impact, for example), and overall sales-to-cost rate of return for capital investments. Actions to adjust might include increasing deliveries, or switching delivery carriers, or initiating certain menu options that require special handling.

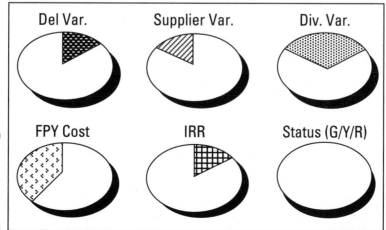

Figure 10-4:
Pizza
delivery
financial
dashboard.

Figure 10-5, courtesy of Corda Technologies, depicts a customer care center financial dashboard, at a corporate level. The dashboard uses a combination of bar charts and color coded indicators to help management immediately see where problems are, with different customer groups by region, and how current performance compares to historical performance. This particular dashboard can also enable flexibility in realigning customer care resources, no matter where they are in the world, in order to quickly recover from any difficulty in any region. By using this dashboard, and acting quickly to specific customer and financial data effects, significant negative impact can be avoided.

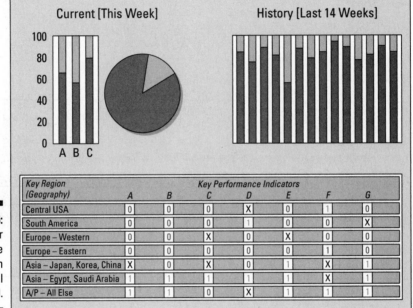

Figure 10-5: Customer care division financial dashboard.

Figure 10-6, is an excellent example of depicting multiple kinds of financial information to get the whole picture. In this example, you see the use of a tachometer, fuel gauge, and speedometer graphic to show multiple pieces of financial information, in order to get a better understanding of the entire financial and operational picture of the company. You can see that just looking at the dollar trends and levels per quarter might suggest good performance, but compared to ROA on the left, and calculating dollar trends as a ratio against ROA, there is an exponential spiral downward as early as a year earlier. Not only can such comparisons provide a more complete picture of the health of an organization, it can provide insights into what to do to recover should a trend become apparent.

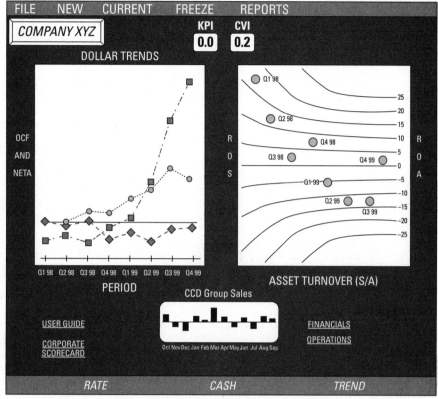

Figure 10-6:
Financial
dashboard
example
showing
multiple
information
formats.

Enabling response and adjustment agility and flexibility

To avert significant loss or damage to assets of the company (and, potentially to your job!), your financial dashboard needs to enable quick response,. Here are some ways to ensure you are able to respond quickly and with the right answers when things start to go really bad in a big way:

✔ For your electronic dashboard, think through what might be excellent early-warning signals, and design a way to detect movement in the wrong direction, such as trend tracking to show crossing bands of ever-increasing risk thresholds, accompanied by changes in intensity, and perhaps increases in voluble warning systems.

✔ Develop if-then contingency planning decision paths, and incorporate them into your dashboard, so that it will be standard operating procedure

(SOP) for your organization to follow the contingencies laid out, with options for detecting variation in expected response and added suggestions for variations in adjustments as well.

✔ Develop a series of decision maps covering impossible reasons for certain trends, to eliminate them from the logic and thus create a higher level of agility to get to the core issues and adjust for it.

✔ Enable point-and-click capability wherever possible, to allow users to drill down on a measure to see contributors to the calculation and their trends as well. This is particularly useful when multiple causes for getting off course present themselves, because it allows selective investigation and analysis of each factor and combined factors, to fully understand what happened, and what you can then do to adjust and get back on track.

Avoiding Pitfalls While Designing Dashboards

Here's a surprise: Financial dashboards need to be designed right to work right. When they are not designed right, errors are often made — resulting in data that is consistent and dependable, but not much help or use in managing a company because it is not what needs to be measured. Here are a few common problems:

Selecting the wrong measures

To avoid this pitfall, you need to select a balance of strategic, operational, and tactical financial measures for your dashboard:

✔ The strategic measures need to link to your overall strategy, yet also provide useful information, in terms of how well you are achieving your long-term goals and pursuing your strategic plan.

✔ The operational and tactical measures, sometimes called Key Performance Indicators or KPIs, are often the first financial measures selected, and while much easier to relate to actual delivery of products and services to your customers, they must work in concert with your strategic financial measures to give you the complete story. A good example of this is when you are comparing revenue to delivery performance, without taking special customer requirements into account. (This happened with a client who did not realize their customer needed delivery declared every Friday, regardless of actual delivery, for specific accounting reasons in their particular country. This caused some inconsistencies, which affected cash flow as well, and became a real issue for several months.) When these measures are not aligned, you can see where you might make operational adjustments which could compromise your strategic plan, or vice-versa.

Organizing goals and objectives poorly

Be careful here, because the tendency is to orient the goals specifically to that particular business or organizational entity, yet forget to ensure linkage to the overall strategy of the company. An example of this might be when shared services measures its collections performance, not realizing the strategic benefits of delaying long-term collections from some Asian and Far Eastern countries, where rates and other factors make short-term collections unfavorable, or investments in these areas are contingent upon special terms initially.

Having the wrong number of financial measures

If you have too many or too few, once again you will not get the correct picture from which to make your key strategic and operational decisions. A great rule is to have five to eight financial measures, combining strategy with operational perspective, and linked to some degree to the operational, growth and customer dashboards as well, so as to provide the best, most up to date and complete information.

Thinking in the short-term thinking

A frequent pitfall is when a company sets up its financial dashboard to focus on short-term performance only, and does not allow for long-term assessment. Some sure signs that you've got this problem are:

- Having financial measures that are strongly linked to compensation, bonus or privileges. This may result in focus on those aspects of performance that will only result in such compensation rewards, regardless of their long-term impact on the company. An example of this would be increasing revenue, without looking to the need to ensure successful delivery.

- Lack of solid linkage between financial and growth dashboards and scorecards, such that there is a balance, focusing on both short term and allowing for long term achievement of key measures. An example of this would be where certain products with higher margins are pursued, yet do not align with the long term goals and target markets of the company.

A tire manufacturer focused on larger tire products because of their profitability, even while customers were designing vehicles for greater efficiency, which is linked directly to smaller tire size and other design aspects. The result was a contradiction in measures, and ultimately a market opportunity for newer vehicles.

Even if strategic planning is incorporated into financial measures, you need to make sure that there is sufficient flexibility in your dashboard to enable adjustment, and allow visibility to key indicators linked to your financial measures even as they might change as planned. For example, when new products are planned that require changes or variations in operational financial measures, how will you enable such adjustment without missing a beat in performance? The key is to create flexibility in your collection and formatting system, so that when things change, variations are selectable easily, so that long term planning can always be incorporated into actual decisions.

Understanding Your Financial Dashboard

Practitioners who use financial dashboards to track real-time performance against their Balanced Scorecards have learned over the years that they need to understand what their dashboards can and cannot provide. They have refined ways to continuously improve these dashboards, which enabled them to achieve ever greater levels of understanding and response to their customer and business needs. Not too shabby, if you ask us.

The financial dashboard needs to eventually become part of your day-to-day work routine. A professional golfer relies on his drivers — in the way they handle and respond to his swing, how they feels when they impact the ball, and on his follow-through — to judge his resulting success in placing the ball near the cup. You should be relying on your financial dashboard in the same way, judging how well your group, department or organization performs based on significant real-time indicators you can see with your dashboard, and their expected impact on performance.

In this section, we explore what it means to understand your financial dashboard, how to make it work for you, and how you use it, appropriate to your business. We will also discuss what to do with the information provided from your dashboard, and talk briefly about follow through.

Make it part of your daily work

This is harder than you might think. Really. Making a financial dashboard part of what you use daily to manage and steer your business, division or department requires a fundamental change in the way you look at financial data. This is because:

✔ Non-financial managers view financial reports and information as generally unconnected to real life, fragmented, and therefore not easy to link in any kind of cause-and-effect relationship.

✔ The key financial ratios or comparisons are typically not even used in most financial reports, making it difficult to actually use the data in any meaningful way for line and department managers.

✔ Usual financial information is provided on a current versus past basis, and does not show trends, nor does it provide actual vs. budget data historical comparisons, again making it hard to know what to look for or interpret for corrective action.

✔ Most operational or department managers don't get foundational training in financial measures. Even worse, their perspective or knowledge is not often taken or considered as relevant in forming financial measures. Instead such measures are typically developed in finance groups or by the CFO, extending the gap between finance and people who manage systems that actually provide products and services to customers.

Given these historic obstacles and hindrances, it is a wonder anyone can get financial dashboards going at all! When you can integrate your financial measures into everyday business life, you can also begin to see how to use them, not just to monitor progress, but to really see where opportunities present themselves for a competitive advantage, or just to adjust specific activities or to reprioritize to maintain performance when things change or the unexpected happens. Here are some helpful ideas:

✔ Lean Daily Management System, courtesy of Dr. E.W. Lareau in his book *Office Kaizen*, talks about using a combination of short daily team meetings — about five minutes long — and visual management boards, to keep track of key metrics for a department or function that are updated daily by hand, and reflect the team's or group's important performance indicators. These indicators are then used by the team or group to adjust actions to correct, or to capitalize on any competitive advantage.

✔ If you work on a computer routinely, set up the dashboard to be the first thing you see in the morning. PowerSteering software, a program that tracks improvement projects for a company, provides for this capability, and enables executives, when they start their day, to see which projects are on track, off track, closed, achieved specific milestones, and can immediately know where the health of the continuous improvement program is at any moment in time.

✔ Proactively schedule a daily block on your calendar, maybe half an hour, within the first two or three hours of the day, to get together with your management team and discuss key financial measures, and work with them to understand what is happening

✔ Format your financial dashboard to one-page, and keep it simple. Also, organize it so that you show performance information from all four legs as linked to your financial measures, to overcome any perceived reality disconnect.

✔ Freely use graphics, such as the tachometers, speedometers, gauges, light indicators, and other examples shown in this chapter. Visuals are very powerful to show trends and key information. Stay away from complicated looking tables and exhaustive spreadsheets.

✔ You will need to discontinue current practices that do not help connect your financial measures to daily activities. This is important, since the first time there is any problem, there will be a tendency for you and your team will be to go back to what is familiar, even if not useful or even destructive to your purposes. Make it impossible to go back.

✔ Have patience, and make indoctrination of the financial measures something you will recognize and reward in your management and team members. Also, coach incorporation into daily reviews, conversations and planning meetings as a routinely included topic.

It is important to make it impossible to go back to the old way of working. Remember, the explorer Cortez, when landing at the New World, burned all the ships and navigation equipment, which helped his crew decide whether they wanted to stay or not. Once retreat is no longer an option, you and your team will also find it easier to discover other ways to incorporate financial measures into your daily routines, and to change your routines to accommodate the need for this information more frequently.

So what does it mean, and how will I know what to do next?

You may not be a financial wizard, but we'll bet you are clever and have figured out how to operate, perform, and deliver fairly well in your current job. you are managers because you got things done in the past, and will continue to do so in the future. Yet, if you can understand and take appropriate actions based on financial measures from a dashboard, you will be even more effective managers, and be able to avert some problems you otherwise probably might not even see until it was too late.

What we are talking about here is taking your financial dashboard and using it to tell you things about the health of your organization, how well you are doing, and if you are headed for disaster. Thankfully, interpreting financial measures from a Balanced Scorecard is not rocket science, and yet can prove invaluable regarding risk mitigation and speed to take advantage of opportunities.

There are ample software tools available today that actually enable managers to manipulate specific financial measures, once they have entered appropriate information into their models, such that they can see how specific actions can impact the three big financial measures for a company: return on assets (ROA, a reflection of the balance sheet), net profit (reflects profit and loss, related to the income statement), and operating cash flow (reflecting the cash flow statement). This is very useful, not just to understand the cause-and-effect relationships of actions and their impact on financial performance, but also as an effective model for management development.

So, what are these relationships, and how can they help you decide future actions? It is really about recognizing relationships and patterns in financial measures that indicate trends and suggest outcomes given current actions. Here are some basic relationships of financial measures to help you along:

- ✔ Looking at monthly rates of receivables (what you are owed) with revenues (what you sold) can help you see trends in cash flow, critical to whether you will have the capital you need at the right moment. If this is trending down, you may find you will be cash strapped, which makes it harder to invest, or fund improvement programs.

- ✔ Seeing market and industry changes in revenue or margins, or even in the key players and their position, for example, can provide key intelligence to be able to capitalize on opportunities for competitive or price advantage, at the right moment.

- ✔ Always look over the financial measures, and compare them to the current strategy. Any anomalies will send a red flag up the pole, and may provide for early warning regarding necessary changes in priority, especially if the strategy has changed or if priorities for the whole company have changed.

- ✔ Tracking trend operational measures, such as on-time delivery, cost against budget and rework levels can provide early warning of likely financial performance issues, if they are increasing, that can enable management to review and seek out unknown or unplanned changes in processes and take corrective actions.

- ✔ Continuous improvement programs need to be connected to financial measures and performance, at least indirectly through delivery, cost and quality, but the more direct link the better, since you want your resources, time and initiatives focused on supporting your Balanced Scorecard, and can see this best through your financial dashboard.

Follow through — it's what's for breakfast

This thought is probably one of the most important. Follow through involves staying the course, using the dashboard for more than a check-the-box activity, and leading the charge for incorporating financial dashboards in your work. Some ideas to ensure follow through include:

- ✔ Remember, you are a leader, as well as a manager, so your actions, and reactions are out there for everyone to see, every minute, every day. Make them count to your advantage, and consider how you respond to your subordinates' questions and concerns in your coaching them to their decisions.

- ✔ Lend focus every way you can, regarding financial measures. Define for your department what is important, and stick to it, don't change it every week.

- ✔ When you are starting out, many things will go wrong or just not work too well. At the worst of times, you will need to be persistent, stay the course, and be patient. At the same time, demand consistent use of financial dashboards, ask how well things are going across all four legs of the Balanced Scorecard, as they link to these financial measures.

- ✔ Ensure there are structures and systems in place based on your Balanced Scorecard, and the use of financial dashboards and measures. Recognize those who are using it, or even trying, and provide coaching by asking questions, let them come to their measures that they need, so that they own and operate them routinely.

- ✔ Highlight excellence in development, use and adjustment of financial dashboards, and encourage sharing of ideas among your teams, other managers, your executive team and others, and ask for ideas, thoughts, concepts. Also, don't be afraid to try something new, or incorporate someone else's dashboard, if it can work for you.

- ✔ Periodically review progress toward cultural incorporation of financial dashboards, and allow for intelligent, studied revision as appropriate to the needs of the group or department.

The bottom line is, financial dashboards are one of the most powerful tools for today's manager to use in making the right decisions, based on the Balanced Scorecard indicators of overall performance and opportunities for tomorrow. Use 'em, or lose 'em!

Part IV

Internal Business Processes – The Value-Creation Leg

The 5th Wave   By Rich Tennant

In this part . . .

*U*nderstanding how value is created within your business processes is critical to satisfying your customers. In this part, you discover the role you play and how to identify the critical few measures you need for your balanced scorecards and dashboards. You then see how to build your balanced scorecards for internal business processes, how to make process decisions that give you a competitive edge, and the pitfalls to avoid.

Chapter 11

Understanding Your Role in Internal Business Processes

*A*s a manager, you know you play a very important role in your internal business processes. Making sure that things are running smoothly is just another day at the office for you and your fellow leaders. Sometimes, though, with all the fires to fight and problems to handle (again, just another day in the office), it becomes a little difficult to focus your efforts, doesn't it? And focus is what the Balanced Scorecard is all about.

Well, there's good news! This chapter is all about helping you focus your efforts on your role when it comes to the internal process leg of your Balanced Scorecards.

First, we'll take a look at five key things you should know about your internal processes. Then, we'll explore your role in understanding and measuring how your processes create value for your customers and continuous improvement. Lastly, we'll dive into your role in creating and translating your strategies into your plans and tactics that will knock the socks off your competition. And if you haven't seen your competitors without their socks on lately, have we got a treat for you!

Five Things You Must Know about Internal Business Processes

When it comes to your internal processes, there are five things that we have identified time and time again — in businesses of all sizes in all sorts of different industries — that many managers know, but tend to not focus on. They are:

- ✔ Your processes are full of waste

- ✔ Many of your process measures don't link to customer defined measures of their needs and expectations

- ✔ Unless you've done a measurement system analysis, your measurement system is most likely broken, giving you misleading information upon which you are making important, but potentially flawed, decisions

- ✔ Process workers are often under-utilized and unappreciated by management

- ✔ There is often an over-reliance on technologies to try and solve process issues, leading to even more waste, disconnected process measures, broken measurement systems and under-utilization and lack of appreciation for process workers

Why are these five things important for you to focus on when doing your internal process scorecards? Because, if you don't pay attention to them, you will be frustrated and have serious issues when using your scorecards. And when we say "serious issues," that's just for starters. It's as simple as that!

Waste abounds in your processes

Did you know that in many companies, only about 10 to 20 percent of their processes actually add value? Would you believe that the remaining 80 to 90 percent are non-value added parts of the processes — they burn huge quantities of both time and money without making a contribution to the building or delivery of your products or services. This is waste!

Still not clear what we're talking about? Waste is things like inspection, auditing and monitoring, generating reports (unless that's what you get paid to deliver to your customers) — and yes, even management — are all considered waste. They do not transform your product or service in any way. There are actually seven commonly accepted forms of waste — what we call the Seven Deadly Wastes:

- ✔ **Overproduction:** making things that are not going to be used immediately — just in case you might need them some time in the future

- ✔ **Waiting:** idle time with people sitting or standing around with nothing to do, because they don't have what they need when they need it, or because of mistakes in scheduling

- ✔ **Transportation:** moving things around more than they need to be, often due to poor layout of the workplace and storage locations

- ✔ **Over-processing:** doing more things to your product or service than need to be done to satisfy the customer need

- ✔ **Inventory:** excess incoming materials, work in progress, and finished goods

- ✔ **Motion:** going on scavenger hunts to find the things that should be where the work is done, excessive bending, twisting or motions by workers

- ✔ **Defects:** not getting things done right the first time, causing rework and scrap and all the interruptions that they cause to normal workflow

A simple way to identify waste in a process is to ask this basic question: does whatever you are doing add value that the customer is willing to pay for? When we look at it from this point of view, you can see that your processes and systems are full of waste. But that doesn't mean you can go on a waste-cutting extravaganza and slash and cut your way through the organization. Many have tried that approach, with the best of intentions, to their own demise.

Talk about the best of intentions leading to the demise of a company's relationship with their customer, this story really makes the point! We had a client that, prior to our working with them, had a manager who went on an inventory cutting spree to cut costs and decrease waste. He slashed his way through the warehouses and cut over $26 million in inventories. What a tremendous benefit to the bottom line — or so they thought. He was hailed by his superiors as a hero — and he even got promoted as a result. But then, the problems really started. The company started having problems delivering products to its customers. Why? Because of stock outs — they couldn't deliver what their customers wanted, when they wanted it. Not only did this company have workers standing around — waiting for their materials to show up so that they could do their work — so too were workers at their customer's factories. This made the customer late in deliveries to *its* customers. You can see how the results of this well-intentioned manager's efficiency campaign flowed downstream. In the end, the end users — the ultimate customers who paid everyone's bills — were the ones left empty handed, not getting what they needed, when they needed it. It was a lose-lose situation all around. So be careful when you start to identify and eliminate the waste in your operations. Consider the full impact of your cuts before you make them.

Did you know that one of the most waste-filled areas — and the ones most often ignored — are the ones we call the transactional processes? These are the office processes that are found in the offices and cubicles where people are dealing with setting up and repairing computers and computer networks, handling paperwork, and the like. Very often, they are processes that are not core to your business and may have some potential for outsourcing to some company that does make money doing it and are a lot more efficient at it (and end up costing you and your company a lot less, too). When you go looking for waste, don't forget to look at these processes, for they can be a gold mine in waste reduction.

Many process measures don't link to the customer

Another thing you need to realize — or maybe you already do — is that many processes measures don't link to your customers. We often walk into a business and find measures that we wonder why they are being measured at all since they don't relate to things that directly impact the company's customers. In your Balanced Scorecards for internal processes, you should always try to link your measures to your customers, starting with your external customers and working your way back through your processes and your internal customers and suppliers, back to your external suppliers.

Now, we're not saying that all of the measures for your scorecard need to be directly linked to your customers. But, if they don't, you had better be asking questions about why they don't and if they are really necessary. After all, we spend a lot of time and effort measuring and tracking things with our scorecards. Let's make sure we're measuring the right things and not creating another form of waste — the waste of excessive and useless measurement!

When linking your customer needs to your process measures, always start with your customer's requirements and then work back through your processes to determine in what ways you and your process workers satisfy and measure how that need is met. These are then translated into process measures for your Balanced Scorecards and into the policies and standard operating procedure you use to make it happen.

Your measurement system is probably broken

Well, we'll put it very bluntly: most measurement systems we come across are broken, and they can't get up! Sure, they can measure things, but the answers they provide are located much closer to Fantasyland than reality. The reason is that no one has taken the time and effort to truly assess their measurement systems. Sure, you can get answers from any measurement, but what if the answers you get are the wrong ones? And when you make decisions based upon a broken measurement system, what kind of decisions do you think are made as a result? It's the old garbage in, garbage out scenario.

And decisions made from bad data and information will send you down the wrong path quicker than a drunken partygoer giving you directions to the bathroom.

Now, we're not going to get into the elements necessary to have a good measurement system. Heck, that would be a book in and of itself. We just want — more like need — you to be aware that the essence of Balanced Scorecards is measurement. So you'd better make sure that your measurement system is healthy and that it gives you good data and information so that you can make good decisions.

Here are just a few key areas that you will need to consider when looking at your measurement system:

- ✔ If your measurements are from subjective measures — people making judgment calls about how good your processes are — will different people make the same judgment call or will they come up with different answers?

- ✔ Will the same person, looking at the same thing over and over again, make the same judgment call?

- ✔ With your objective process measures — things measured by some measurement device like a scale, calipers, a micrometer and the like — will it really measure what you think it is?

- ✔ Is it accurate and in calibration — is there some error in the measurement device that you don't know about?

- ✔ Will different people using the same gage get the same readings time after time?

- ✔ If using multiple devices to measure the same process characteristic, will they consistently get the same measurement or will they be different?

If you don't know if your measurement system is working for you the way you need it to be, you should assume that the answer is a resounding no! Get online, get a book, or do whatever you need to do to better understand what is called measurement system analysis (MSA) or gage repeatability and reproducibility (gage r & r). Get your measurement system healthy before you start your Balanced Scorecards for internal processes.

Process workers are under-utilized and unappreciated

As a manager, one of your most important roles is to fully utilize and appreciate your people. And one of your key roles as a manager using the Balanced

Scorecard is to get your people involved and using their knowledge and abilities to the greatest extent possible. Actually, some companies — like Rolls Royce — identify the under-utilization of their workers as an eighth form of waste.

Your role is one of getting your employees involved in helping to develop the process measures, reporting and tracking their own processes, using the tactical level scorecards as a daily management system, and ensuring their involvement in improving their processes on a continual basis. Without their help, you will be very limited in your ability to fully leverage the power of the Balanced Scorecard approach, especially for internal processes.

You also play a key role in showing that your process workers are appreciated for what they do. Sure, we all know that nothing gets done without them, but how often do you let them know it? Do you find yourself looking more for people doing things wrong and punishing them for it, or do you look for people doing things right and telling them they've done a good job? When was the last time you said thank you and really meant it?

You see, in the end, your role as a manager who is using the Balanced Scorecard for internal processes is to be a cheerleader, teacher, mentor and coach for your people. Yes, it takes some time and a little bit of effort, but it is well worth it.

Technology isn't always the right answer

Technology is great! Some might even call it sexy. Not us, but some. Technology has an allure all of its own. Things done automatically, giving us capabilities that were undreamed of just a few years ago. And the pace of new technological development just seems to be getting faster and faster. And as a manager, your role is to sometimes identify new technologies and to implement them. All we can say is, *caveat emptor* — let the buyer beware!

Consider, for a moment, the example of the latest-and-greatest personal computer — with more memory than ever before, a faster processor, and the biggest hard drive this side of Bangalore. You buy the latest thing on the market and before you can get it out of its box, it is made obsolete by the next generation of computers that is, coincidentally, being released to the public next week. They're faster and more capable, and often less expensive than the previous generation but, here's the downside: they're also more complex and more difficult to use.

And then there's the whole learning curve thing. Software that you are comfortable with no longer works on your new system, so you're forced to buy the latest software offering, too. So, people have to go to classes or learn on their own and fumble their way through the new technological whatever that was going to increase your productivity and make life easier for everyone. On top of that, in our experience, few software packages are utilized at more than 25 percent of their full capabilities.

Do you see where all this is headed? That latest-and-greatest software package that is supposed to do all of your resource planning — and put gobs of cash back into the bank for you — may not be the big benefit that you think it will be. That new robot to save you all that money may end up costing you more than it's worth and be more of a headache than the old system it replaced.

When it comes to technology solutions and Balanced Scorecards for your internal processes, your job is to do the homework and make sound business decisions about which technologies to use. Explore your options fully and don't get sucked into the latest gadgets with all the bells and whistles attached before you have a chance to fully analyze their potential impacts on your organization — both good and bad. Often, solutions of the low- or no-tech type are just what the doctor ordered.

Creating Value

In a perfect world, your processes would be nothing but value adding: creating value for your customers at every step, with no waste, no problems, and no need for the firefights and chaos that so often are a part of a manager's daily life at work. Unfortunately, that isn't the real world, is it?

When it comes to value creation, your role is one of knowing what currently exists — what we call the current state — and then working on a continual basis to improve it by working with your people to improve things — what we call the future state. In this section, we'll take a look at your role when working on your current and future state of your value streams.

Looking at your value streams' current state

As a manager, one of your roles is to understand your value streams and where you and your employees fit into the big picture. And, you guessed it, this is another key area for you to understand when looking at your Balanced Scorecards for internal processes.

But first, it would be a good idea to define what a value stream is.

Simply put, a value stream is all of the steps required to bring a product or service from its raw state to the customer. It includes all of the information and data necessary to run and track the processes.

When looking at your value streams, you will identify things like work in progress (WIP), inventory levels, cycle times, customer demand rates for your processes (a thing called TAKT time), lead times, defect rates, value added and non-value added work content, along with important information. Once you've got your value stream current state mapped, you will have a very good picture of where your bottlenecks are located and where you have the most waste within the value streams and their processes.

You will also have a very good systems view of the entire picture: how your part of the value stream connects to other parts and functions within the stream. And in the end, it will help you to determine where you need to apply the resources and effort to improve the system, so that you can remove the waste and increase the value adding work and value creation within your processes.

For more information on Value Stream Mapping, we highly recommend the book, *Learning to See* by Mike Rother and John Shook.

When getting into your value streams, remember that it is your role as a manager to actually map them out and understand them. Do not fall into the trap of delegating the mapping of the value stream to others. If you do, you will lose the most important aspect of the value stream: gaining knowledge and a systems view, rather than a limited-process view.

Where you want to be when: The future state

Once you've identified the current state of your value streams, the next shoe to fall is that you have to get busy working on the future state. What are you going to do to remove the waste and improve the value stream so it maximizes value creation?

In moving to the future state, you have to let go of the reins and trust your workers to know what needs to be done to make the improvements. Yes, we're talking about your role as a cheerleader, teacher, mentor and coach for your people. If you want your employees to create a better future for your company, you've got to set the example for them by championing the improvements and the teams that are sweating bullets to get them in place. You are the one who must empower your people and give them the authority, autonomy, and resources they need so that they — and you — can be successful with their improvement projects.

You'd better believe that you play a critical role in the future state of your value streams. And you'd better be tracking your projects for the future state on your Balanced Scorecard for internal processes. It's all a part of your efforts with continuous process improvement, and an important job for every successful manager.

You Get What You Reward

What does rewards and recognition have to do with the internal process Balanced Scorecard? In short: everything! Oh, but that's a human resources or management thing, right? Remember: human resources and management *are* internal business processes. And nothing has more negative impacts on your ability to lead, manage and get your internal business processes working the way you need them to than your rewards and recognition processes.

Your rewards and recognition processes have to be well thought out and planned. You have to make sure that you aren't sending mixed messages, such as asking for new behaviors yet rewarding the old behaviors. And you have to understand that money isn't always the big incentive that you might think it is. Everyone's different and, while some may respond to cash, others might respond to a simple "thank you."

Sending mixed messages

Remember: people will hear what you say, then watch what you do. Any differences will quickly be noted and all those good words that came out of your mouth will be nothing more than cheap talk. And we don't want that, do we? Of course not. But it does happen.

Are you sending mixed messages, asking for one kind of behavior, then rewarding your employees for doing something different? Consider the following examples:

- Saying you want teamwork, but then fostering internal competition between individuals, teams, groups, functions, organizations: looking for win-lose scenarios, rather than win-win

- Saying that you believe in teamwork and cooperation, but management is at each others' throats with backstabbing and infighting amongst themselves

- Political agendas and pet projects and solutions that are not supported by the management team or data and information

- ✔ Agreeing to a set course of action, then saying negative things or disagreeing with it in private or while having water cooler discussions with others

- ✔ Not empowering your teams to make decisions about their work

- ✔ Saying you have empowered the team to make decisions, but then disempowering the team when they do make a decision by telling them to do this or that — and the this or that is usually a hidden agenda or pet project or solution

If you find any of these things happening with your people — or if you are doing them yourself — make sure you put a stop to it immediately! Your Balanced Scorecard for internal business processes will be much the better for your efforts. After all, everyone has to be on the same page, working together and pulling in the same direction for your scorecards to really work the way you want them to.

If it weren't so sad, we would have actually gotten a good laugh out of this one. Once, while mentoring a Six Sigma Black Belt in his training and project completion, the student told us — when asked how his team was doing — "Oh they are a very good team! They do everything I tell them to." When we asked the team members how *they* felt the project was going, they said, "It's no different than before — we are just told what to do and nobody cares what we think." It wasn't any surprise that team morale was very low and their performance was, shall we say, less than stellar. Needless to say, we coached the Six Sigma Black Belt on how to run and lead teams and we got the situation turned around in a hurry. Later on, the team members presented *their* solutions to the problems they had identified with *their* processes and the Six Sigma student got to teach them some new tools and ways of analyzing their data along the way.

Old rewards do not create new behaviors

Has this ever happened to you, at work or in your personal life? Someone says they want you to do something in a new and different way, but then you were still rewarded for acting in the same old way? And did you walk away thinking that there was just something a little bit wrong? Well, it happens all the time. It may even be happening in your own organization and your people may be thinking the same thing: there's something just a little bit wrong with the picture. And you better believe it, they are right!

Here's an example: We tell our salespeople that we want them to cooperate with one another — to work as a team — but we single out individual salespeople for recognition when they achieve their sales goals for the month. And then we're surprised when these same employees decide that it makes more sense to do whatever it takes to achieve their individual goals, even if it means cheating other members of their sales team out of potential clients or sales opportunities.

Rewarding old behavior and expecting new actions or different behavior just doesn't make sense. Yet, just like with all of the other pitfalls we've talked about, it happens all the time. Why? Well, we don't think it's a malicious or intended thing. Often, we find that the long-term results of the actions they take are not well thought out. They didn't take time to consider what kinds of behavior they were really rewarding.

So, the remedy for this one is really quite simple. If you are asking for new behaviors, then take a close look at what you are rewarding. If the old rewards don't make sense — and will instead continue to motivate people to act in old ways — then change them. Now.

Rewards that matter

We want rewards and recognition to motivate people, right? So the question then becomes: motivate them to do what? When you really get down to it and take a good hard look at many well-intentioned rewards and recognition systems, they actually de-motivate people. A poorly designed and executed rewards and recognition system can actually do more harm to an organization than good — destroying internal business processes and making score-cards miss target after target, and goal after goal.

Let's take a look at some of the things you need to think about with your rewards and recognition systems and processes so that you're not left scratching your head and wondering why your scorecards aren't getting you where you want to go:

- ✔ Remember that those whom you are going to reward should be part of the process to create meaningful rewards and recognition systems

- ✔ Money rarely changes behavior and increases performance — it rarely motivates people to do a consistently better job, but it does often de-motivate people to not care

- ✔ When using monetary rewards, tie them to the overall performance of the company, such as gain-sharing, so that everyone sinks or swims together and keeps them working together to win

- ✔ A simple "thank you" for a job well done often has as much or more motivational value than a big cash reward, putting someone's picture on the wall, or giving them the special parking spot for the employee of the month

- ✔ Showing you really care about your employees every day has more meaning to them than a special (but rarely given) reward

- ✔ Learn how to celebrate your successes and trumpet them for all to hear

- ✔ Be careful not to leave anyone out of the picture: we've often seen where someone got their feelings hurt when they were left out (like the people who took on someone else's normal job duties so that they could be on the team that ended up being recognized)

✔ Be clear about what will be rewarded, by whom and how

✔ Make sure that you reward day-to-day performance along with improvements

✔ Be very careful about rewards tied to suggestion programs: most suggestion programs are so broken, they are a running joke in many organizations, and ideas on how to improve one's work should be a natural part of their job anyway

✔ Don't keep your rewards and recognition static (never changing), rather, keep them a dynamic system that changes with time (the one thing that should never change is that you care about your people, how they feel, and that they are extremely important to you and the success of your organization)

✔ Make sure you have rewards and recognition for individuals, teams, organizations and the company as a whole

✔ When communicating your successes and recognizing people, make sure it is about them and not you (you should be like the proud parent beaming about the accomplishments of your children — it's all about them)

✔ Everyone appreciates a free lunch or dinner and they are a great way for you to not only reward teams and your organization, but they are also a great way to get some teambuilding into place

✔ Family fun days or open houses are a great way for your employees to show off their workplace and let the family know what they do — and to let their sense of pride in their work and the company shine

Finally, just remember that you need to always pay attention to your people and how they are rewarded and recognized. It should become second nature to you and your organization. It should be ongoing and real-time. And a simple thank you, with a smile and a handshake, doesn't cost you a thing, but may be priceless for your employees!

Building-In Continuous Improvement

Most things we do in business, and in life, are processes. Good processes deliver consistent, quality outputs in a timely, efficient and effective manner. The outputs are only a result of the activities in the process (what we do) and the inputs (the information, materials and services we use). Variation in the output — usually measured as cost, quality, or time — is the total variation of all of the elements of your processes' activities.

Therefore, continuous improvement concentrates on understanding the relationships between the process inputs, the activities performed within your processes, and the process outputs. By doing so, you can make the improvement necessary to deliver what your customers want, when they want it, and at the price they are willing to pay for it.

Variation is the enemy of continuous improvement and it is your role to lead the efforts to remove the variation: get rid of the defects, shorten the lead and cycle times, and reduce the overall costs of your goods and services sold to the customer. And while you're at it, you should use your internal process scorecards to measure these improvements. Remember: If you're not measuring, your only practicing. Let your competition practice and play at it, while you get serious about your continual improvement efforts!

Process improvement in a nutshell

Understanding what customers really care about is fundamental to continuous process improvement. Ultimately, you want your processes to perform at a consistent and measurable level that meets and exceeds the customer's needs and expectations. These customer expectations and requirements need to be translated into some kind of a measurable output.

When our processes fail to give customers what they expect in a consistent manner, we have those nasty things that we call defects or errors. Your improvement projects are supposed to resolve these nasty little problems. How? By reducing the variation, eliminating the defects, reducing the waste, and reducing the cycle and lead times within your processes. That's how. Your continuous improvement projects improve your process performance by getting to the root causes and getting rid of them — forever — rather than just applying some quick fixes that often only take care of the symptoms. At the end of the day, your projects must deliver real improvements for your customer and to the bottom line of your organization.

Determining, what, when, and where to measure

Performance measures are an important part of any continuous improvement effort. As a manager, you direct the efforts of your organization and have responsibility for knowing what, when, and where to initiate changes. These changes cannot be implemented without an in-depth knowledge and understanding of the appropriate information upon which your continuous improvements are based. To do so, they need to have an effective measurement system.

As part of an effective measurement system, we've already talked about the need for doing a measurement system analysis as one of the five things you must know, so let's take a dive into the what, when and where to measure.

When looking at your organization, there are many processes and functions that are required to deliver your products or services, with each one probably needing some kind of performance measure. In figuring out what to measure, you have to first consider their business impacts and select those areas that are most important to your organization and to your customers, both internal and external, in order to satisfy their requirements. You will also need to consider those processes with issues and problems that have been identified by management or the process workers. These then become those *critical* activities that you need to measure.

Critical activities at the tactical level are those that significantly impact your total process efficiencies, your effectiveness, product and service quality, timeliness, and productivity. At the operational and strategic levels, critical activities are those that impact your management priorities, organizational goals, and external customer goals.

In identifying what to measure, ask the following questions:

✔ Does it relate, directly or indirectly, to the ultimate goal of customer satisfaction? Every critical activity should. For example, on-time delivery is directly related to customer satisfaction. Use quality tools such as the Pareto chart, brainstorming, or examining data to help prioritize your critical activities and measures.

✔ Does everyone concerned agree that this activity needs to be watched closely and acted upon if its performance is not what you need it to be?

✔ Is it something that should be continuously improved? (Hint: if it hasn't been fixed lately, it is probably broken and in need of some improvement!)

✔ Does the benefit exceed the cost of taking the measurement?

If you answer "no" to any of these questions, take another look at the measurement and decide if it is really critical for you to measure it at all.

Figuring out when to measure depends upon the process and your needs for timely data and information. If you're going to make a mistake on how often to measure, it is generally better to err on the side of more often. You can easily back off and adjust if you find that you are measuring more often than you need, but we find that it can be difficult to ramp up to a more frequent measurement scheme.

Measurement often occurs at process inputs and outputs, or as a major step or activity within a process is completed. The measurement should be taken and tracked by those who do the work and not by some outside group or function, like inspectors or quality control. In this way, you get the most timely information and you can react much faster to problems than if you have to wait for someone to get around to taking the measure, reporting it, and then having some committee meeting to decide what to do. Employees empowered to measure and take action are truly a wonderful thing! Go give them a raise!

How to measure your performance

Learning to ask the right questions is an essential skill in the art and science of effective data collection. Accurate, precise data collected through an elaborately designed statistical sampling plan is useless if it does not clearly address a question that someone cares about. It is crucial to be able to state precisely what it is you want to know about the activity you are going to measure. Without this knowledge, there is no basis for making measurements.

To generate useful information, *how* you measure is extremely important. Here are some questions you need to ask about how you will measure your internal process performance:

- ✔ What question do we need to answer?
- ✔ How will we recognize and communicate data and information gained from the measures?
- ✔ What data-analysis tools do we envision using (Pareto charts, histograms, bar or line charts, control charts, etc.)?
- ✔ What types of data will our selected data analysis tools require?
- ✔ Where in the process can we get these data?
- ✔ Who in the process can give us the data?
- ✔ How can we collect the data with minimum effort and chance of error?
- ✔ What additional information do we need to capture for future analysis?

Acceptance and ownership means getting everyone involved

By now, you should be saying to yourself that you need to have your people involved in this. They've got real jobs to do, right? Not only can you not do it all by yourself, however, but when you get your folks involved, we can guarantee that the outcome of your continuous improvement projects will be far better and more likely to succeed. It's that simple.

According to a study on project success by VitalSmarts, 82 percent of employees surveyed said there are significant organization-wide initiatives underway in their workplace that they believe are likely to fail. And 78 percent said they were personally working on a project that was doomed to fail at the time of the study. In fact, over 90 percent of the men and women surveyed said they know early on when projects were likely to fall short, and 77 percent compared their failing projects to a slow-motion train wreck.

They also said that, basically, when it came to telling higher-ups about their misgivings, they didn't feel like anyone wanted to hear it. Eighty-one percent said that approaching a key decision-maker about it is almost impossible. There is a tendency for people to be quiet about important issues because they expect the conversation will go badly. It sure doesn't sound like there's much acceptance and involvement on their part, now does it?

Now, you're probably wondering how this can happen. What in the world is going on? In a word: fear. As the world famous guru of continual improvement, Dr. W. Edwards Deming, said in point 8 (of 14) in his influential book, *Out of the Crisis* (MIT Press): "Drive out fear, so that everyone may work effectively for the company."

Fear? You bet! If people are afraid to have those frank discussions about projects, what does that say about the environment in which they have to work? Do you know who controls that environment? Quick — go to the mirror and take a look. Surprise! It's you, the manager.

Here's another revelation for you. If employees work in an environment of fear — fear of reporting, of taking risks, of making a mistake, or even of saying what they honestly believe — how much ownership and acceptance do you think they will take for things like process improvements, team projects, the recording of data and the like? That's right — zero! Sure, you can form your teams and they will meet, but little will get done. They will participate, but they won't be involved and they most certainly won't accept any responsibility for the success or failure of the efforts of the team.

So, when you want your people to have high levels of acceptance and involvement in your continuous improvement initiatives and internal process scorecards, make sure that your work environment is one without fear, where the messengers are rewarded for their bravery, not shot. One where people are comfortable communicating with you, no matter what the news might be, good or bad. The kind of workplace where the old joke of "the beatings will continue until the morale improves" is just that — a joke. You can (and should) create an environment and organizational culture where your people can take ownership and are involved in its success.

Ready to do a quick check of your organizational environment? Here's a little exercise we often use as consultants to gauge our clients. You can use it, too. Take a leisurely stroll through your work areas and pay attention to how people act when you're walking through. Are they smiling and engaged — greeting you enthusiastically? Or are their heads down, hoping not to be noticed? Do they ask how your weekend was, or do they try their best to look busy for the boss? When people pass one another in the hallways, do they greet one another and have a bounce in their step, with their heads held high and their shoulders back? Or are they hunched over, walking slowly, looking like they have the weight of the world on their backs? When you pay attention to how your people are interacting, it doesn't take a rocket scientist to figure out what kind of organizational culture you have. If your people are walking around like a bunch of dazed zombies (like in *The Day of the Dead*), you'd better get to work on your organizational culture, and do it fast, because you have some serious problems that will devastate your continuous improvements and Balanced Scorecards.

Pitfalls to Continuous Improvement

Without a focus on the continuous improvement of your processes and people, you are leaving a lot of opportunity on the table and giving your competitors a major weapon to use against you. Continuous improvement is a necessary part of your internal business process scorecard.

Many organizations have some form of continuous improvement, whether it is total quality management (TQM), Six Sigma, Lean Manufacturing, Toyota Production System (TPS) or Theory of Constraints. Today, many have some combination of two or more of them, such as Lean Six Sigma. In fact, you would do well to learn as many different approaches to continuous improvement as you can because you will find, if you haven't already, that no one toolset or methodology is the end-all, be-all for improvement. Like any toolbox, you use what you need when you need it. Some tools are used often. Other tools are used not so often, but when you need them, it's kind of nice to have them around and know how to use them.

What we often see with continuous improvement efforts is a lack of focus on core processes, well defined procedures for who does what and when, and an over reliance on technology. In this section, we will explore the pitfalls that lead to these problems so that you and your organization won't have to suffer the pain and anguish that so many others experience. Learning from pain is, well, it's downright painful. So read on, avoid the pain, and enjoy the gain.

Implementing continuous improvement

Just a word about the pitfalls you'll find in implementing continuous improvement. All the pitfalls we've already mentioned apply to your improvement efforts, including:

- ✔ You need to integrate your strategies, plans and tactics for improvement.
- ✔ You have to take a systems view of your business and processes.
- ✔ You have to lead your people and manage your business.

In addition to what we've already talked about, there are some other pitfalls you'll want to keep in mind.

- ✔ Implementing continuous improvement is everyone's job: not just for those in quality control, or a special group of specially trained people (like six sigma black belts or what have you), or special teams that are come to help out.

- ✔ Process workers need to be trained and educated — and have experience — in using the basic improvement tools, like flowcharting, Pareto analysis, cause and effect diagrams, and control charting and SPC.

- ✔ Process workers need to be involved in creating the standard operating procedures for their processes so that they are not only understood, but will also be followed.

- ✔ Continuous improvement needs to be managed, but it should not be micro-managed: micro-management will kill team-based process improvements faster than you can say "our competition is killing us."

- ✔ New knowledge on methods and tools only comes from the outside, and only by invitation: don't be afraid to find the help you need from consultants, but don't make them the owners of continuous improvement.

- ✔ Management needs to be educated in the tools and methods, too: the quicky one or two day overview courses and seminars don't get you there — you have to know these tools as well (or better) than your people do.

- ✔ As mangers, you need to not only talk continuous improvement, you have to do the walk, too: you have thousands of opportunities everyday to show what you really mean, and believe us, your people are watching and all it takes is one misstep and they will know you are not serious about it.

We want to leave you with a little story before moving on. We call this nonfiction short story The Man from Saturn. No, we're not talking about some space alien who has come to visit us from the outer reaches of the solar system. We're talking about a fellow named Skip Lafauve, the first president of the Saturn division of General Motors. He was the guy that got the whole thing started. You see, Skip was an interesting guy. He really believed in making a quality car. And, maybe more importantly, he knew what had to be done to make it all happen. He understood that if he wanted to build quality cars and have a customer-focused organization, he had to do everything possible to make sure that his people had what they needed, when they needed it. If mistakes were made in the interest of quality, like shutting down the production line because someone honestly thought there might be a problem when there maybe wasn't, that was not only okay, it was the right thing to do.

He viewed his job as one of being a servant to his people. And he really loved his people, and let it show in so many different ways. And, wouldn't you know it, he would drop into classes on how to improve processes and measure process performance and sometimes teach the class. It was not uncommon for factory workers to learn how to construct and analyze control charts from the president of the company. So, when you go looking for examples and role models of what is needed out there when we talk about leading people and managing your business, pay close attention to The Man from Saturn: Skip Lafauve. Trust us, there are few, if any, that are better to model yourself after.

Identifying core processes and outsourcing

When it comes to identifying things that are considered wasteful — those things you do that don't add any value to your products or services — we often find that we are doing things that have nothing to do with our core processes, that is, the activities that produce the results we want. In the end, spending time on non-core processes is a waste of your time, money, and effort. Not only that, but we find that most companies are really quite lousy at doing them. Many have therefore found it to their benefit to outsource many of these non-core processes. All we can say is, be very careful when outsourcing!

We once had an interesting revelation while working at General Dynamics Convair Division in San Diego, California. The company's core processes were to build the aircraft body for the McDonnell Douglas MD-11 (a wide-body fuselage). That's what we got paid to do. As part of the manufacturing process, we needed a lot of perishable tools such as drill bits, sandpaper, tape, countersinks, and much more. We would order tons of the stuff on a regular basis. After all, we would drill well over one million holes in each fuse-lage assembly during the course of production. Now, that's a lot of holes! Of course, we had to have a place to store this stock of tools, and we needed systems and processes to manage it. We had to have people to stock it, track it, and distribute it to the people building the product. All of which cost a lot of money. When we looked at the overall system, we realized that managing the stock of perishable tools was not a core process for us — it was not an activity that directly led to finished aircraft bodies — and it was something that we could outsource to a local company whose business was to do all of those things and make money doing it. This was their core business. And you know what? They were a lot more efficient and better at doing it than we ever could hope to be because managing perishable tools was their core process, and they could make money doing it. In the end, we found that we could order our perishable tools and supplies and have them delivered to where they were needed within less than 24 hours on 98 percent of the things we needed. We had better fulfillment of our needs for a lot less money. We also found that we had opened up many thousand square feet of floor space for manufacturing when we got rid of the warehousing of the tools and supplies — space that we needed in the worst possible way. What happened to the people that no longer managed that perishable tooling and supply system? They went to work adding value to the product, working on our core processes! They started making money for the company, rather than being nothing more than an expense.

Ask ten managers or executives within an organization what their business's core processes are and you will probably get ten different answers. If you're going to use the internal business process scorecard (of course you are or you wouldn't be reading this book), you should have a good understanding and agreement on what your core processes are so you can effectively measure and track them.

✔ Don't be afraid to challenge what you do and ask if you really need to be doing it: Can someone else do it better, faster and cheaper than you can?

✔ Understand that there are risks associated with outsourcing, so be very careful and do your homework: Make sure of what you need and that those you partner with are capable of satisfying your needs.

✔ Don't make your decision to outsource based on price alone: The path to outsourcing ruin is filled with this type of decision, where contracts are put up for bid every year and awards are made on lowest price, alone.

✔ Don't be afraid to share information with those you partner with — they need just as much information as if they were your people — after all, they are in a way.

✔ Bring those you partner with into your teams: Have them become knowledgeable about where their products and services are used, how they are used, and that they become well known to your people — make them true team members and let them have a say in any decisions that affect the products and services they supply to you and how they are used.

✔ Make sure you measure and track your outsourced processes just as you do your own: You should have scorecards for your suppliers and anything that is outsourced.

Technology isn't always the answer

Did you ever notice that technology often creates more problems than it solves? Have you ever heard — or even thought yourself — why did we ever buy that fancy new gee whiz thingamabob? Have you ever wondered why new technologies fail to live up to the wonderful promises made by the guys and gals who sold them to you? Well, all we can say is, you're not alone and welcome to the club. And yet, so often we see that there is this almost obsessive need by companies to rely upon technologies to solve their problems and go into that downward spiral into the technology black hole, never to be seen or heard from again. Go ahead and do a web search on the topic if you doubt what we're saying. You'll find the stories all over the place.

So, you ask, why does this happen over and over again? Well, we're here to tell you. New technologies are cool! They can be fascinating — almost hypnotic — to watch. Have you ever watched a robot doing its thing? Pretty cool, isn't it? Software with tons of capability at your fingertips tracking this and that, spitting out tons of data and reports (notice, we didn't say information — someone actually has to look at it and analyze it to become information and so often that never happens). Conveyors moving tons of parts and assemblies all over the place, and hardly a human being in sight.

Not only do a lot of technology solutions not work as we intended them to, they also often create and hide a lot of waste. In fact, many of them just manage our waste a little more efficiently, but they do nothing to remove the waste itself. Things like automated inventory and warehousing come to mind. These systems will actually increase your costs of waste! And what happens when they break down? Your operations come to a screeching halt, or you go back to the good old fashioned way of doing things.

When looking to technology solutions to your problems, be very careful. Make sure they are not just optimizing ways of doing wasteful things. Remove the waste, instead. Also, make sure that your people are involved in the planning and introduction of the new technologies. You know, they may just surprise you and find a better, less costly way of doing it themselves. And always remember: New technologies usually have major price tags and, along with those major price tags, major risks associated with them. Make sure you fully understand the entire cost picture and the risks associated with your solution.

The Weakest Links in Internal Business Processes

You've heard it before: Your business is only as strong as its weakest link. We all know that once identified, we need to strengthen those weak links so that the chain becomes stronger, yet we see time and again that they are ignored and nothing gets improved, especially with internal business scorecards and the processes they track. Nothing is sadder to us than the myriad of process issues we've seen where everyone knew they had problems, yet nothing was done to correct them. And when the business is brought to its knees by the weak links, everyone asks how the heck it happened. Everyone knew it was a problem, right?

So, why didn't those weak links get fixed? Maybe the people in charge didn't think it was that big of a problem, or they were too busy fighting the day-to-day fires and other issues that invariably arise. Maybe they didn't have a good understanding of what the problem really was to begin with. Or maybe they were overwhelmed by the magnitude of the problem and just hoped it would go away all by itself. The list of "maybe's" is long and varied.

The problem with integrating strategies, plans, and tactics

Within many organizations, strategic planning is often looked upon as a necessary evil. Companies do it as a once-a-year (or even less frequent) exercise, and then the resulting strategic plan gets put on a shelf to collect dust, or thrown in a drawer to be forgotten. Then, at the end of the year, the plans get dusted off and everyone wonders why they didn't achieve any of the goals and objectives that they wrote down the year before.

The Balanced Scorecard is intended to help keep this from happening, but you have to avoid the many pitfalls that plague the process of tying your strategies to your plans and tactics for achieving them. This list of potential pitfalls will give you and your organization the information you need to make sure your strategies, plans, and tactics actually get done.

- ✔ No formal (and accepted) vision and mission

- ✔ Not communicating the vision and mission throughout the organization

- ✔ Not setting long-term (at least three to five year) and short-term goals

- ✔ Not establishing measurable goals for the various business functions and their objectives (profit and growth, market share, sales or production volumes)

- ✔ Not setting stretch goals: goals that are challenging but achievable

- ✔ Not having a system for measuring actual performance versus goals (that's why we do the Balanced Scorecard!)

- ✔ Not involving the right people in the planning process

- ✔ Top executives not taking a formal role and responsibility for the planning process: delegating the process to lower level executives, staff workers, or consulting firms

✔ Not making the strategic planning process a top priority for the organization

✔ Not providing resources for the planning process: not providing time, money, or people for the planning process

✔ Not having documented formal procedures and policies for planning

✔ Not getting all of the organizations, departments, etc. involved in the planning process

✔ Not doing SWOT analysis (Strengths, Weaknesses. Opportunities and Threats)

✔ Not comparing your analysis to your competition

✔ Not looking outside the box: not looking at new entrants into your markets, new technologies, methods, concepts

✔ Not looking at your own business objectively: being overly optimistic or having a sense that you're really not that bad

✔ Not including a deep dive into financial issues: cost of capital, investment strategies, taxes and all of that financial related stuff

✔ Not looking at your customers and strategies related to their needs and expectations for service, pricing, quality

✔ Not looking at your people and the human resources

✔ Not looking at information systems and technologies and their ease of use

✔ Not basing plans on risk versus return and feasibility

✔ Not basing plans and tactics on the strategic analysis and research

✔ Not assigning responsibilities and accountability for the execution of the plans and tactics

✔ Not allocating the necessary resources for making the plans and tactics happen

✔ Not having a formal system of review and tracking the strategies, plans and tactics — in other words, not using the Balanced Scorecard approach to managing the business

✔ Not having a regular review process — and by regular, we mean at least once a month and more frequently if necessary

✔ Not being flexible in your plans and tactics

✔ Not having a system for rewards and recognition for achieving and exceeding the goals and objectives (and make very sure that no one is left out — we like gain sharing where everyone has some skin in the game, and the executives have the most to lose if things don't get done!)

So, what can you do when you encounter one or more of these potential pitfalls in your organization? You can take action to fix them! Begin with the ones that will have the greatest leverage, that is, the biggest bang for the least amount of effort. Of course, don't forget to delegate responsibility for fixing pitfalls as widely as you can — you can't do this all by yourself after all. When everyone gets in the act, they are much more likely to become invested in the outcome — and in the ultimate success of your organization.

Systems thinking and internal business processes

No organization's processes work in isolation, yet we see time and again where they are managed by the company's leaders as if they do. Silos and barriers between functions and processes are built up and enforced as if they can operate on their own, with massive issues of bureaucracy that can kill the company and its ability to be flexible and deliver the elements of quality, speed and cost necessary to stay competitive.

When looking at your strategies, plans and tactics, you really have to take a systems view of your organization and its processes. And every system must have an aim — a reason for being. And by their very nature, systems must be well integrated or they will fail. We often see systems that do not integrate well with the organization in which they are supposed to smoothly function and add value. In many cases, the system drives the organization, rather than the organization driving the system — sort of like the tail wagging the dog. We particularly see this happen with material resource planning (MRP) and enterprise resource planning (ERP) software systems.

The following list of pitfalls will help keep you in the mindset of systems thinking with your internal business processes and keep your scorecards doing what they are intended to do — keep you ahead of the competition — and keep your Balanced Scorecard for internal business processes humming along smoothly.

- ✔ Forcing the organization to conform to system rather than having systems that conform and meet the needs of the organization (this is especially true with software solutions)

- ✔ Maintaining a functional (silo) view of the organization: focusing on the optimization of functions at the expense of the company as a whole: suboptimizing the whole for the sake of one part of the organization

- ✔ Focusing on turf battles rather than on collaboration

- Pursuing hidden agendas and pet projects or solutions

- Making decisions that affect others without including them in the decision making process

- Failure to build consensus on decisions when appropriate (caution: consensus is not always the best decision making approach — when the building is on fire, that's not the time to have a team meeting on the best way to exit the building!)

- Withholding information or viewing information as a source of power

- Making decisions from gut feel and intuition when hard data and facts are available or can be gotten

- Allowing people to be surprised by not communicating (often seen in meetings when tasks are due to be completed and the big surprise is it wasn't done and no one was told ahead of time)

- Not following through on commitments

- Looking for win-lose rather than win-win solutions

- A sense of competition between groups or other managers

- Not having a map of the system — only focusing on mapping your own processes

- Not understanding the nature and importance of your internal customer/supplier needs and relationships

- Over-reliance on the big home run or giant breakthrough solutions rather than on incremental improvements

- Micro-managing everything by requiring personal approval before moving forward

- Not educating and empowering direct report employees

- Not sharing corporate goals and objectives

- Taking a "that's not our problem" view to issues and concerns

We're sure that you can add some things of your own to this list, but this covers the main issues we often see when working with our clients. Taking a systems view isn't always easy, but then, most things that have tremendous payoffs usually aren't easy. So, belly up to the bar, take a systems view of your functions and the organization as a whole, and reap the benefits for you and your company. Believe us: if you can successfully resolve even half the things on the above list, you'll be far ahead of your competition!

It's a people thing

It sure is tough these days, knowing when to get involved and when to leave things well enough alone. As the famous leadership guru, Peter Drucker, once said: "Managers are more concerned with doing things right, while leaders are more concerned with doing the right things." We couldn't agree more. In fact, we would take Mr. Drucker's thought one step forward, by saying that you need to do the right things right.

For you to succeed with your internal business process scorecards, you need to be both a manager and a leader. You lead your folks, but you must manage your business processes. It is a delicate balance that the modern manager must find and maintain. Unfortunately, we see far too many managers and far too few leaders.

What this means to you is that the days of micro-managing your people, looking over their shoulder, tampering and meddling with them on a constant basis as they perform their work, are long gone, especially if you want to be a good leader. When it comes to your processes, translating your needs and expectations into those things that you can measure and track in your internal process scorecards along with all the other internal business processes and measures needed to run your business, you have to be both a leader and a manager. You have to lead your people, but manage your business.

So, as you've probably guessed, there are many pitfalls you need to avoid when getting your people involved with your internal business process scorecards. Here's a list of major pitfalls we have often encountered with our many clients.

- ✔ Not being situational in one's management and leadership style: fitting the style to the needs of the individual

- ✔ Not having a clearly defined, articulated and communicated vision and mission for the organization that your people can identify with

- ✔ Not communicating your strategies and tactics for achieving your goals and objectives

- ✔ Not setting clear expectations for your teams' performance and results

- ✔ Not letting your teams know why they are a team

- ✔ Not setting the groundwork for having team members committed to the team and its performance

- ✔ Not getting the right team members on the team — not having the cross-functional team members on the team when projects and issues cross organizational boundaries

✔ Not having a team charter that clearly defines the mission and objectives for the team, what they are to achieve, how it will be measured, what defines their success and the timeframe for results

✔ Not giving the team the empowerment they need to get things done — micromanaging the team, forcing them to work towards your pet solutions or hidden agendas

✔ Not providing effective team facilitation to get them through the tough times so that they can become a high performing team

✔ Not having a communication system in place for feedback to and from the teams

✔ Not valuing ideas from the team members: not allowing team members to be creative and to think out of the box or to seek innovative approaches to problems

✔ Not providing the teams with the resources of budget, time, materials, space and support that they need to get things done

✔ Allowing the scope of the team to creep and grow beyond its original intent without a clear and compelling need for it to do so

✔ Not having clearly defined rewards and recognition for the team

✔ Being too hands-off with your people: not being a coach, mentor and head cheerleader for them as they tackle problems and make recommendations

✔ Blaming the team when things go wrong: pointing the finger and trying to divert responsibility for it to the team (on this one, you'd better be looking in the mirror, not at the team or team members)

✔ Shooting the messenger: not wanting to hear the bad news and punishing the one who tells you by claiming they are not a team player

✔ Linked with shooting the messenger is maintaining an atmosphere of fear: fear of reporting, taking risks and making mistakes because the guilty ones will pay through reprimand, gossip, or worse

✔ Not having an effective employee suggestion program: by effective we mean making the suggestion go through so many hoops and hurdles to get approved that few ever are approved, and even if they are, it takes so long that the employee gets no sense of satisfaction from it anyway

There's one more thing that can be a real problem for anyone who has been assigned the job to manage a group of people: Not seeing your job to be a servant for your employees and truly caring about their needs in a loving way. If you want your employees to care about you, your company, and your customers, then you've got to first care about *them*. Leadership is a two-way street. Trust us, if you take care of them and really care about them, they will *always* take care of you.

Tying Internal Processes to Your Strategies, Plans, and Tactics

Just like with the other legs of the Balanced Scorecard, you have the center stage role in developing your internal business process leg scorecards. In this section, the first thing we'll do is describe something called catchball (and, no, it's not something you played in school when you were a kid). We'll then get into how to develop your process strategies, plans and tactics.

Playing catchball: The art and science of deployment

When formulating and deploying your strategies, plans, and tactics, it's extremely important that communication be two-way, and not one-way. This helps to ensure understanding and buy-in by everyone that is involved and affected by these new strategies, plans, and tactics. As it turns out, the catchball technique is very useful for achieving wide-scale deployment of your goals and objectives for your strategies, plans, and tactics.

Catchball is a give-and-take dialogue within the organization. It is a means to keep the dialogue going until everyone understands and agrees to the desired focus of the organization. Each level of the organization should, in turn, develop goals, objectives and action plans to support the overall goals. They will also need functional plans while monitoring and tracking their processes and product and service indicators to ensure quality consistently meets customer requirements and performance goals.

What ball game are you playing? The opposite of catchball is what we call dodge ball. This is where it seems like everyone is trying to escape the process, not work with other departments, executives and managers in the process, and do the minimal amount of effort to get things going. Make sure that when you play ball, you're playing catchball and not dodge ball, shall we?

Why do we say that catchball is both art and science? Because it is a process, and as such there is a method to it, just as with any science. But it is also an art because you will have to use your interpersonal skills of negotiation, compromise, and consensus throughout the process. You will even have to use some salesmanship skills as you try to get people on-board with your ideas that they are maybe, shall we say, a little bit resistant to and they may set up their barriers and defenses. And yes, you may even run into those who are trying to play the dodge ball game. So sharpen up your people skills when you get into the game of catchball.

Developing your process strategies, plans, and tactics

As you develop your strategies, plans, and tactics for your internal business process scorecards, you will find that your role is one of making it happen and getting it done. Along with the people skills and understanding the process of playing catchball, you also need to know what you have to accomplish during the catchball process. There are a variety of steps you should follow in this process:

1. **Establish the purpose of the process strategy, plan or tactic.**

2. **Define the goals of the strategy, plan or tactic.**

3. **Develop the scope and boundaries of the strategy, plan or tactic.**

4. **State your criteria for success.**

5. **Understand the barriers, constraints and risks and how they will be mitigated.**

6. **Determine who is to be involved in their development and execution.**

7. **Define who is to do what.**

8. **Determine how you will track performance and progress.**

9. **Establish how it will be measured.**

10. **Decide what methods are to be used.**

11. **Scope out any training or education that will need to take place.**

12. **Develop the schedule for getting it done.**

13. **Define the resources you will need to make it happen.**

Now, that wasn't so hard, was it? When you're done with this process, you should also be able to answer the following questions for each of your process strategies, plans and tactics.

✔ How much will your tactics contribute to achieving the annual operating plans and long-term strategic goals and by when?

✔ Who will be responsible for the various strategies, plans and tactics?

✔ How will those responsible for their execution be held accountable for getting them done, and how will you know when they are done?

✔ Who needs to be informed and how will you communicate them?

✔ When will you get them done?

✔ What are your contingency plans when things don't go as they are planned?

✔ Have you maintained enough flexibility to do the dance when things don't go as planned?

Yeah, there's a lot to get done, but you can do it! And never forget to have some fun along the way. All work and no fun makes for a very dull manager, indeed. And while you're at it, try to make it fun for your people, too. Get them out of the office every once in a while for some team building. Treat them to lunch at a favorite restaurant or meet up after work for some casual fun. Get to know your people on a personal level. Find out what makes their hearts sing and gets them excited. You may just find out that you have a lot more in common with them than where you work and what you do. And they just might find out that you're a real human being who really does care about them.

Chapter 12

Building the Internal Business Process Scorecard

Ask a bunch of different people what they value in life, and chances are you will get a bunch of different answers. Ask your customers what they value in your products or services, and you will probably also get a bunch of different answers. When you boil it all down, however, these answers will pretty much come down to the same basic issues that make a difference for the effectiveness of any business: quality, cost, and time.

When using the Balanced Scorecard to improve the effectiveness of your own business, it is your job to understand your processes and how they create value in the eyes of your customers. After all, it all starts with customers — no customers, no business. Unless your primary business is monkey business. Let's take a look at what might be some of the things that customers truly value, how they impact your processes, and how you can use scorecards to measure value creation.

In this chapter, we explore how to get in touch with the measures that are most important to your customers. We will also look at ways to focus on the issue of process variation, then build the Balanced Scorecard for internal processes and take a look at how to analyze it. Ready? Set. Go!

Finding the Right Measures for Internal Business Processes

There are as many measures for business processes as there are stars in the sky. Well, *almost* as many. The trouble is, we often make the mistake of focusing on things that really don't matter to the customer. Do you think, for example, that your customers really care about how many times your cashiers have been late to work this month? Or the percentage downtime of your janitor's vacuum cleaners? Does that mean we shouldn't measure them? No! But it does mean that we need to understand the difference between those measures that matter and those that don't.

Unfortunately, many companies focus on the measures that don't matter to customers, and only give lip service to the ones that *do* matter to them. The basic question that you have to answer is this: *What do your customers really value?* Once you answer that question, the next question you must answer is: *How do your processes fulfill what customers truly want and value?*

Identifying the critical few measures

First, let's take a quick look at some of the more common measures for internal business process scorecards. These are the kinds of things that have the greatest leverage on your organization's effectiveness, and many of them (for example, on-time delivery, customer response time, and warranty returns) are also measures that your customers really care about. Remember, we said that most measures involve elements of speed, quality, and cost, but there are a number of other useful measures we should look at, too.

Measures of speed:

- ✔ On-time delivery
- ✔ Lead time
- ✔ Process cycle time
- ✔ Machine or process downtime
- ✔ New product and process development time
- ✔ Time to market of products and services
- ✔ Customer response time
- ✔ Breakeven time

Measures of quality:

- Continual improvement
- Warranty returns
- Sales returns
- Field service representative calls and visits
- Defect rate: rework, repair and scrap (defects per unit, percent defective)
- Process capability
- Sigma level
- First pass yield
- Rolled throughput yield

Measures of cost:

- Costs of waste
- Cost per transaction
- Research and development cost
- Labor costs
- Costs or rework, repair and scrap
- Breakeven cost
- Appraisal costs (inspection, compliance)
- Environmental compliance costs
- Inventory and work in progress costs
- Cost of marketing and advertising

Other useful measures:

- Floor space utilization
- Inventory turnover rate
- Aged materials and finished stock
- Material stock-outs and shortages
- Forecasting and planning accuracy

As we said at the beginning of this section, these are just some of the more common measures for your internal business process scorecard. We are sure that you probably have several of your own that you can (and should!) add to the list, but these lists will give you a good start. What items are on your list? Why not tap one out on your computer right now?

Don't make the mistake of putting measures into your scorecard just because you can. Select only those measures that matter to your customers and to your business. This will take some thought and it also means that you will make changes over time. Stay on top of your scorecards and those critical few things that really matter!

The Input-Process-Output diagram: Your best friend

How do you select those critical few that really matter? Don't tell anyone, but here's our own personal secret: Take a look at your customer scorecard and tie together those things that you've identified as important to customers and to your internal business process scorecard. A simple tool will help you do just that — a tool that we call the Input-Process-Output diagram (see Figure 12-1).

	INPUT	PROCESS	OUTPUT
	PEOPLE		
	EQUIPMENT		NO WAIT TIME
Figure 12-1: Input-Process-Output diagram.	METHODS	**CALL CENTER SERVICE**	RESOLVED QUICKLY
	MATERIAL		FRIENDLY SERVICE
	POLICIES		FEEL VALUED
	PROCEDURES		

When using the Input-Process-Output diagram, always start with the Output requirements, first. This is the end closest to your customer and the requirements are the ones defined by your customers. These customer requirements are usually translated on the input side of the diagram as your specifications. As we've said several times before in this chapter, these will usually involve measures of quality, speed, or cost.

How about an example, focused on some element of quality — doing things right the first time? By focusing on quality, you can also improve (reduce) the elements of cost and speed. It kind of makes sense, doesn't it? If you improve your quality, you don't waste the time, money, and effort to do things over and over again to get them right. By focusing on quality improvement, you not only improve quality, but you also reduce the cost and time it takes to complete the process. The result? Happier customers and a healthier bottom line. Now you're getting the full power of the Balanced Scorecard working for you!

The IPO gives us a pretty high-level view of a process. It doesn't give us a lot of detail (like a process flow or values stream map would), but it does tie together the inputs required to achieve our desired outputs. Typically we have numerous processes joined together in a stream, each doing specific things and building one upon another in order to deliver the final products or services to the ultimate end user — the customer who pays the bills and keeps our lights on. We call these wonderful people our *external customers*. As we use the IPO to get in touch with our external customer requirements, we also need to identify the *internal customer* requirements: those things that each process requires from their inputs (or suppliers) in order to meet their internal process requirements.

And, while we're at it, we're also able to define those external supplier requirements for the things that we get from our outside vendors in order to do what we do. So, what we will end up with are the definition of our end user customer requirements, what we need to do in our processes to satisfy them, and the things that our suppliers must do to keep us happy, as well. It all flows from the end user back through our processes, tying our suppliers, processes and what they produce to our customers.

So the IPO answers the question: *What do your customers really value?* And this includes both the internal and external customers. The next question that needs to be answered is: *How do your processes fulfill what customers truly want and value?*

Waste, scrap, and other bad things

It's one thing to understand what your customers value, and it's another thing altogether to understand if your company's processes are designed to deliver what your customers value. When you get into processes for the production and delivery of your products or services, you will find out that most of what you do is what we call *waste*: things that take up time, money, and effort but that add absolutely no value to the resulting product or service. Some examples of waste include:

- ✔ Scrap and rework (things not done right the first time)
- ✔ Multiple approvals (you know, bureaucracy and red tape)
- ✔ Excessive reviews (again, more bureaucracy and red tape)
- ✔ Excess inventories (why not try just-in-time?)

Beware of waste in your business processes! These things — and many others — waste our precious resources and they add zero — zilch — nada — to the value of your products or services. And this presents us with the problem of finding out those things that we do that the customer is willing to pay for and getting rid of those things that are considered waste. For more on waste, visit Chapter 11.

Where's the variation?

No two things in life — or in business — are ever exactly alike, even though they may look the same on casual glance. Those little (and sometimes big) differences are what we call *variation*. In business processes, variation can kill your ability to deliver consistent products and services to your customers. And in looking at your Balanced Scorecards for your internal business processes, you want to look at those things that cause variation. Like a summer vacationer getting ready to swat a mosquito, you want to track them and eliminate them when and wherever they occur.

Okay, but how do you identify variation and where it exists? One of the best methods we know is to use two simple tools. The Cause and Effect Diagram, and a method called The Five Whys.

The Cause and Effect Diagram (see Figure 12-2) is a tool to be used by — you guessed it — teams. Can you do it by yourself? Well, you could, but going it by yourself may not give you the powerful results that you seek. Often, teams will start with the six basic legs as shown in the diagram:

- ✔ People
- ✔ Machine
- ✔ Material
- ✔ Method
- ✔ Measurement
- ✔ Environment

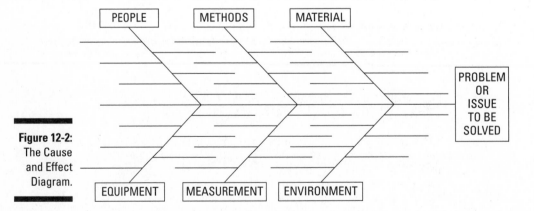

Figure 12-2:
The Cause
and Effect
Diagram.

What you're trying to do with this tool is to identify the issues and problems that cause the problem shown in the box to the right of the diagram. Get your team(s) to brainstorm ideas and put them onto the appropriate leg. Using the Five Whys technique, you'll ask the question "Why does this happen?"

Here's a simple example for you. Let's say you're having an ongoing and persistent problem with employees making mistakes that cause defects in your products. These defects in turn increase your costs and decrease your profit. And when every once in a while, a product with defects gets into the hands of your customers, well, you know — they aren't very happy about that. The old-fashioned way of dealing with this issue might be to punish the employee, give them a warning or maybe even firing them. However, by using the Five Whys, you might first ask "Why did the employee make a mistake?" Lo and behold, by asking that question first, you might discover that your standard operating procedures are ineffective or missing, or perhaps the employee was hired and placed into the job without proper training . Can you see where this is headed? Asking "why" enough times helps you to get beyond the superficial reasons and to the root causes for variation. And once you find those root causes, you can fix them so can't negatively impact your business or your employees again.

Remember, variation is the enemy, *not* your people.

Building Scorecards for Internal Business Processes

Okay, so now you've identified those critical few things that really matter to your business and your customers. You've taken a look at the sources of variation and the things that can (and will) go wrong in your processes. And believe us — there are things that will go wrong in any business. You've done all of the hard work, so let's have some fun and create some scorecards for the internal business process.

Strategic level scorecards

What are your plans for your business systems and processes for the next three, five, ten years? What do they need to look like and achieve to stay ahead of the game? Looking at your scorecards for the customer and financial legs, what is it about your long-term business processes that they will need to do to help you attain the goals you have in those scorecards? Strategic level scorecards give you the long view of your business — beyond the one-year view of the operational level scorecard.

So, when you're building you scorecards for internal business process, pull out your other scorecards and make sure you have them handy — you're going to need them! When you and your folks develop the goals, objectives and measures for the internal business processes leg of your scorecard, make sure that they tie together with your other scorecards (see an example of a strategic scorecard in Figure 12-3). You see, these scorecards do not work in isolation from the others. They are integrated and they work very closely together. If they aren't integrated, you're missing the real power of the Balanced Scorecard approach. Each leg has power, but — together — the sum of the whole is much greater than the separate parts.

Internal Business Process Leg Scorecard with Strategic Measures

	Three Year Strategic Goal
Increase Product Quality	75%
Reduce Cost of Processes	25%
Reduce Process Cycle Times	15%
Reduce Process Lead Times	10%

Figure 12-3: Example of a strategic scorecard.

Operational level scorecards

Looking at your operational level, what are the things you need to achieve, measure and monitor over the next year? What are the annual operational plans and goals and how will you make sure you're on track? The operational level scorecard tracks the things that you must do this year to achieve your strategic (long-term) goals and objectives.

Figure 12-4 shows you an example of an operational level internal business processes scorecard.

Tactical level scorecards

This is the scorecard that makes the rubber meet the road, as we business improvement consultants like to say. The tactical level scorecard is your day-to-day measurement and tracking scorecard (Figure 12-5 shows you an example). It is used on at least a daily basis, and perhaps even hour by hour and minute by minute. Everyone in your organization needs to be familiar with this scorecard and check it at least once a day to see how they are doing. This is a key management tool, used for gathering data and information and making sound business decisions by the right people in the right place. It is your job as a manager to make sure tactical level scorecards are being used effectively and that they always contain the most current data and information available. Ignore this, and you lose the power of this scorecard!

Figure 12-4:
Operational level scorecard.

Internal Business Process Leg Scorecard with Operational Measures	Three Year Strategic Goal	Annual Operational Goal
Increase Product Quality	75%	40%
Reduce Cost of Processes	25%	10%
Reduce Process Cycle Times	15%	8%
Reduce Process Lead Times	25%	10%

TRUE STORY

While working for one of our employers a few years back, we found a neat little trick that really helped us out. We called it the "Four Panel Chart," and we used it for our reviews with senior management. It was a great way to summarize what we were doing and where we were at in achieving our goals and objectives. At first, we tried to manage our business with them but, as part of our learning process, we soon realized that they were much better tools for communicating overall progress and status at the monthly reviews with our division management than for actually helping to run the business. As we put the charts into effect — and used them to brief upper management — the big bosses began to notice that we were hitting our targets consistently and we didn't have to produce recovery plans and initiatives to get our businesses back on track. Talk about feeling good when you go to meet with the top people in the company! Believe it or not, we actually started looking forward to those business review meetings! The moral to the story is that you can't manage your day-to-day business at the strategic and operational levels. That can only be done at the tactical level. Figure 12-6 gives you an idea of what a four panel chart looks like.

<u>**Internal Business Process Leg Scorecard with Tactical Measures, Performance and Trends**</u>

	Three Year Strategic Goal	Annual Operational Goal	First Quarter Tactical Goal	January Q1 Performance	Trend
Increase Product Quality	75%	40%	25%	12%	**YELLOW**
Product Line 1			15%	8%	GREEN
Product Line 2			**35%**	**4%**	**RED**
Reduce Cost of Processes	25%	10%	4%	2%	**YELLOW**
Product Line 1			**2%**	**–1%**	**RED**
Product Line 2			6%	3%	GREEN
Reduce Process Cycle Times	15%	8%	3%	2%	GREEN
Product Line 1		6%	2%	1%	GREEN
Product Line 2		10%	4%	3%	GREEN
Reduce Process Lead Times	25%	10%	5%	2%	GREEN
Product Line 1		40%	3%	1%	GREEN
Product Line 2		40%	7%	3%	GREEN

Figure 12-5:
Tactical level scorecard.

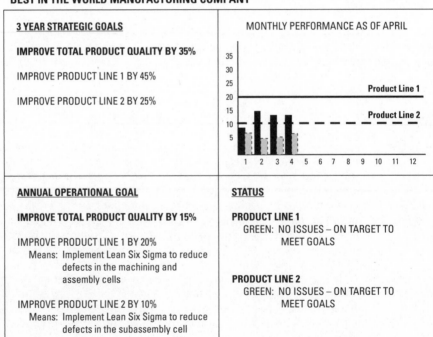

BEST IN THE WORLD MANUFACTURING COMPANY

<u>**3 YEAR STRATEGIC GOALS**</u>

IMPROVE TOTAL PRODUCT QUALITY BY 35%

IMPROVE PRODUCT LINE 1 BY 45%

IMPROVE PRODUCT LINE 2 BY 25%

MONTHLY PERFORMANCE AS OF APRIL

Product Line 1

Product Line 2

<u>**ANNUAL OPERATIONAL GOAL**</u>

IMPROVE TOTAL PRODUCT QUALITY BY 15%

IMPROVE PRODUCT LINE 1 BY 20%
  Means: Implement Lean Six Sigma to reduce
    defects in the machining and
    assembly cells

IMPROVE PRODUCT LINE 2 BY 10%
  Means: Implement Lean Six Sigma to reduce
    defects in the subassembly cell

<u>**STATUS**</u>

PRODUCT LINE 1
  GREEN: NO ISSUES – ON TARGET TO
    MEET GOALS

PRODUCT LINE 2
  GREEN: NO ISSUES – ON TARGET TO
    MEET GOALS

Figure 12-6:
Four-panel chart.

Making Process Decisions That Give Competitive Advantage

Making decisions and managing your business — that's what the Balanced Scorecard is all about. And managing your processes and making decisions about them should give you a competitive advantage whatever marketplace it is that your business does its thing. If they don't, you may not be around for the long haul. And that's not what any of us want, is it?

When making your decisions and using the Balanced Scorecard, you have to involve your people in the process. You and your employees need to have some basic tools in your toolkit, and you need to understand some of the most common mistakes that are made so that you don't make them — let your competition make them and learn the hard way. We don't want you to. That's why we wrote this book (and, we hope, why you bought it).

Involving the right people in process decisions

Who are the right people that need to be involved in making decisions? How do you know that they're the right people? In the "good old days," almost all important decisions were made by management. Well, let us tell you that those days weren't all that good and what we did back then often didn't really work out all that well, either. Many managers forgot that their workers not only had huge quantities of experience with their processes and the jobs they did, but — would you believe it — they had brains, too. The days of "we just need your bodies and leave your brains at the door" are long gone. And thank goodness for that!

If you're going to be effective using the Balanced Scorecard for you internal business processes, you're going to need to push decision making to the right levels and people within your organization. This often means front-line workers and their supervisors. You can't — and shouldn't — do it all by yourself. You need to involve the process workers in decision making, especially if you want to analyze and improve the processes and systems they use to do their work.

Of course, to make good decisions, your workers will need to have good data and information. Hey, here's an idea: Why not involve *them* in actually gathering that data and information — you know, let them "own" it? After all, they need to track their process performance and know how they are doing, don't they? They will need to see and use the Balanced Scorecards at the tactical level, see how they tie to the operational and strategic level scorecards. And they will have to be taught some simple tools that enable them to look at their work and also be empowered by you to make the decisions necessary to hit the targets that are set for your Balanced Scorecards. *Six Sigma For Dummies* is an excellent resource for your team-based data gathering and decision-making tools and methods. Check it out and help your people help *you*.

But one thing: Give your people the time they need to get this done. When we work with clients, one of the big problems we encounter time and time again is that they talk a good story about teamwork and employee empowerment, but trying to get the teams the time they need to gather and analyze data and information and to discuss problems and solutions is like pulling a wisdom tooth. And almost as painful, too. You have to give your people the time to do this critical part of their job. If you don't, you will have huge problems down the road in using and staying on top of your Balanced Scorecards for your internal business processes. Don't make the mistake! Give them the time they need. Trust us — you'll be glad you did.

Staying ahead of the competition: Tools that help

We've already talked about some of the tools that can help you stay ahead of the competition, such as the IPO Diagram. Here, we'll add a few more tools to your toolbox. Don't worry, we won't get too detailed. If you need to learn more about them, check out our Web site (www.psiassociates.com) and you will find detailed definitions, descriptions, and examples that will help get you going.

- ✔ **Quality Function Deployment:** A very structured approach to taking what the customer says they want and then translating that into measurable things that you do so you know you're hitting the mark (much more detailed and exhaustive than the IPO Diagram). This tool has also been used for deploying strategic goals and objectives down through the operational and tactical levels.

- ✔ **Design for Six Sigma:** Methods and tools for designing high performance processes and systems from the very beginning (in the design phase)

- ✔ **TRIZ (pronounced TREEZ):** A Russian acronym for inventive problem solving that is an established science, methodology, and tool set for stimulating and generating ideas and solutions for problem solving based upon knowledge gained from prior inventions and innovations, usually in industries and applications other than your own (example:

using a process for cutting diamonds that was first used to split sunflower seeds)

✓ **Maturity Models:** Tools and methods that present best practices and steps for what to do based upon where you find yourself (there are Capability Maturity Models, Product Maturity Models, Project Management Maturity Models and many others)

✓ **Six Sigma:** A comprehensive set of tools and methods for achieving continual improvement in systems and processes and improvements to the bottom line financial results

✓ **Value Stream Mapping:** A tool used to identify where waste exists and for designing more efficient systems and processes with the focus of minimizing or eliminating sources of waste and maximizing value creation

✓ **Lean Manufacturing (also known as the Toyota Production System):** A set of tools and methods for identifying and removing the Seven Deadly Wastes

✓ **Theory of Constraints:** A way to identify and remove bottlenecks and constraints to achieving optimal flow of products and services and aid in eliminating waste

Common mistakes made with internal business process scorecards

Here's a list of the more common mistakes made with the internal business process scorecards. We've already mentioned a few of them, so if we repeat ourselves here, that just means that they are really, really important! So, don't make them and you will come out way ahead of those that do — like your competition maybe?

✓ Losing focus and trying to track things that really don't matter

✓ Trying to do it all by yourself - not involving or empowering the right people at the right levels to gather data and make decisions about their processes

✓ Not giving people the time they need to gather and analyze data

✓ Not sharing or communicating information with process workers

✓ Declaring victory too early

✓ Not having the discipline to stick with your scorecard, regardless of what it says

- ✔ Not having systems and structures in place to support your Balanced Scorecards and dashboards in terms of response, review and decision support

- ✔ Resolving variation of steps without first deciding what steps can be removed or modified

- ✔ Not working on the important issues

- ✔ Cherry picking the easy things to tackle and avoiding the tough issues because they are hard to solve

- ✔ Having systems or processes that are "untouchable"

- ✔ Having preconceived solutions to problems or pet solutions driven by powerful managers

- ✔ Looking at systems and processes in silos — not getting cross-functional in your approaches and teams

Chapter 13

Building Dashboards for Internal Business Processes

*W*ould you believe that not everyone is tickled to death about Balanced Scorecards and dashboards? It's true. In fact, many who use dashboards are not thrilled with the results. But how can this be?

The reason often comes down to the same old thing: the results aren't what people expected. Who knows, maybe the expectation level was set too high. Or maybe the effort was more than it was thought to be. Maybe, interest was lost after awhile, like the new car that slowly — but surely — becomes a used car, and more trouble than it's worth. Or maybe, as happens in many cases, the design and use of the dashboards were flawed from the get-go.

Whatever the reasons, failures and false starts do occur with scorecards and dashboards. In this chapter you will get some good tips on how to avoid the dashboard graveyard. You'll learn the what's and why's of the internal process dashboard and how they help in getting to real-time data and information. You'll find out that dashboards are very effective for drilling down from high-level key process indicators so you can figure out where problems are coming from. Finally, you'll see how to create your dashboards for internal business processes and what they're telling you.

And if all that doesn't make for some thrilling dashboards, we don't know what will!

Understanding Internal Business Process Dashboards

Why do you want to use a dashboard? Well, it's quite simple, really. Just like you use a dashboard in your car to continuously monitor and display the performance of your car's functions and systems (in simple and easy-to-read and understand formats), you use a dashboard for your business to continuously monitor the performance of your business and its processes.

Can you imagine driving your car without a dashboard? Sure, you can get from point A to point B with no trouble, until you start to run out of gas, your engine starts to overheat, or your oil level gets low. Without your car's dashboard, you're totally clueless, just driving along as happy as a horse running through the tall hay. Unfortunately — unknown to you - you're headed for big trouble, and you won't have a clue until the engine overheats and you have major problems, some that are sometimes downright costly. Heck, you may even end up having to shoot the horse and get a new one, if you can afford it.

It's the same thing with your business dashboards. You use dashboards to tell you that critical need-to-know information not only so that you can monitor your business performance, but so that you can take the appropriate action when it's needed. In the end, dashboards make it easier to drive your business in the right direction and then keep running smoothly as you're hitting your strategic goals by staying on track with your operational and tactical goals and measures.

The what and why of internal process dashboards

The dashboards you use for your internal business processes and scorecards will use graphic displays that are tied to your various sources of data and their databases. You can either do them manually, or you can have them updated automatically. Either way, they require attention and regular updates to make them effective. Done properly, one click of the computer mouse will allow you to see the underlying data that is driving your dashboard gauge.

The one marriage that does seem to be made in heaven, so to speak, is the one made between Balanced Scorecards and dashboards. They just seem to go hand-in-hand with one another, like a couple of high school sweethearts. So, one of the obvious reasons to use dashboards is the decision you've made to use the Balanced Scorecard strategy.

Another reason to use dashboards is that once they are set up and running, they are — or should be — relatively quick and easy to use. It doesn't take a rocket scientist to read and understand them, providing you with valuable information at a quick glance. You can quickly figure out what's going on within your operations and processes because you can view your key process indicators at a single glance. Answers to how your business and processes are running are literally at your fingertips.

Dashboards give you drill-down capability. When one of your key process indicators isn't quite measuring up, you can quickly get down in the dirt, find the culprit that is causing you the pain, and take some corrective actions. And, unless you're a little bit masochistic and like pain, that's a wonderful thing, indeed.

The real key to having effective dashboards and not becoming one of those people who think they are just another prom date that's all dressed up with nowhere to go, is that you need to make them as simple as you can: (see Figure 13-1)

✔ Focus on the fewest number of key process measures that you can, while still getting the value that you need from them.

✔ Keep them to a single page, if at all possible.

✔ Select those really critical four or five things to put into your dashboards.

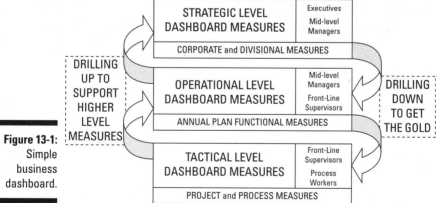

Figure 13-1: Simple business dashboard.

Another key is that you want to keep your dashboards without a lot of clutter. You don't want them looking like a college student's dorm room, with garbage all over the place, making it hard to find what you want when you want it. In the end, you want it to be nice and neat, with a place for everything, and everything in its place.

Variety is also good. Vary the types of charts you use. Don't fall in love with just one type of display, like only using bar charts, pie chart or line charts. Put some thought into the types of data you're looking at and how it will display data in the best possible way.

And finally, you want your dashboards to give you that sometimes elusive real-time (or as near real-time) information as possible. The real value of effective dashboards isn't just in providing you with the information you need It's their ability to give you that information quickly, so that you can take care of your problems before they explode in your face like a firecracker with a short fuse. In a nutshell, they prevent those unpleasant and often bloody surprises that make your job as a manager a lot more interesting than you want it to be.

Getting to real-time data and information

Timeliness of data, and the information you draw from it, is a beautiful thing. It gives you power. Power over your processes and over your competitors. Getting to it — well, that's the tough nut you have to crack. In cracking that nut, you have some things you need to do.

One of the first things you'll need to do is to go get some help from your information technology (IT) folks. Since you most likely will be using computers and display terminals to set up your dashboards, you'd better get the people who are the keepers of the keys to those things on-board, right up front.

Another reason is that they know what you already have with regard to your current sources and the types of data and information. They can get madder than a wet hen if you leave them out of the loop, and rightfully so. Go ahead and pay a visit to your IT people — we'll wait while you go get them.

Now, that wasn't so bad, was it? They're really nice people, aren't they?

You'll also want to get the business users into the game. These are folks like the business managers and supervisors that may report to you and who will be looking at the dashboards throughout the day to see how things are going so that they can keep you off their backs. These people will help you identify your dashboard requirements and the operational and tactical level data you'll need in order to satisfy the strategic needs of your dashboards. They will help you identify the pulse points for the data within their areas of responsibility.

You'll need some other folks to help you set up your dashboards so you can get to the real-time goodies — these folks are the people who work in the processes. Those guys and gals who do the office work and make the widgets. That's where most — if not all — of your real-time information will come from. It's where the work you'll need to measure is located. And who better to help identify what needs to be measured than those guys and gals who are doing the work? After all, they are the ones who are nose-down in the cactus with the processes and who know the details of the work that gets done each and everyday. Since you're busy flying at the 10,000-foot level, you'd better get the process workers involved when you want to get that up-close and personal view of your data for those times when things hit the fan.

 When getting to the earliest possible indicators of process performance for your dashboards and scorecards, your ability to do your data and information drill-down is essential. Well, then, let's find out what dashboard drill-down is all about.

Drilling down to get the gold

Drilling down isn't about getting your electric drill out and drilling holes in your computer when it malfunctions (though you may have been tempted to do so, at times). Getting to the meat of your business processes and projects, and those things that are causing you trouble and pain, is the purpose of data drill-down. And the key to data drill-down is linkage. Finding those things that aren't going according to plan, that are causing defects and errors within your processes or finding trends, and then being able to drill down to the root causes so that you can make some good decisions based upon that information. That is what dashboards are all about — that's where the gold is found. Without some good drill-down capability within your dashboards, you will never find the gold.

Now — quick — go to your computer and do a web search for dashboard software companies. It'll only take a minute or two.

Did you find that trying to identify all of the dashboard software providers out there is like trying to count the number of sand pebbles on the beach? There are zillions of them, aren't there? Unless you plan on growing your own dashboards from scratch, you will have to take a look at the providers and figure out which one best fits the bill for you. And, here again, you'd better get with your IT people and get them into the game. The earlier, the better. Yeah, the IT folks are going to become your newest and best buddies as you set up your dashboards.

The reason we bring up the issue of software and the IT types at this point is because most dashboard software will have drill-down capability. You will certainly want yours to have it. And the dashboard software you use will need to be compatible with your existing software and computer systems. So you need to give it some thought and planning before selecting a software package and provider.

Drilling down means being able to go from higher-level key process indicators and measures and finding the underlying data and information that lets you know what is causing certain trends or problems. Drill-down is like zooming in on your data and information with a microscope to pinpoint what you need to know. It let's you know the what, where, and why of your key process drivers. It enables your knowledge and understanding of your business processes. And it will ensure that you consistently hit your strategic goals and objectives

Understanding the drill down process is also important because you and your folks will have to be actively involved in setting it up and deploying it. You'll need to figure out what to put in them, how they will be linked, what they will be linked to, and how they will display the data and information that you want on your dashboard.

Creating Your Internal Business Process Dashboards

The process of creating your internal business process leg dashboards is just like the process of creating the other Balanced Scorecard leg dashboards. They take some good up-front planning and thought. And, just like the other dashboards, they need to have the right people involved and a good dose of critical thinking.

In this section, you'll find out who needs to be involved in creating your internal process dashboards and in what ways they should be involved. You'll then take a look at how your dashboards are created and ten common mistakes that are made with internal business dashboards.

Who should be involved with your dashboards and how

Not too many years ago, only top level executives and their direct report employees got involved in setting up and using dashboards. Today, dashboards are used throughout the organization, from the board room to the shop floor, and all sorts of employees at all levels are involved in setting up and maintaining them.

So, in answering the question of who should be involved with your dashboards and how, it comes down to pretty much *everyone*, in one way or another. Your people will be involved in helping you to create them, providing the data and information to maintain them, and using the information from them.

Maybe the best way to approach this is to go down the list of who should be involved and how. We'll start off with the strategic level dashboard, then hit the operational level, and then finish up with a look at the tactical level dashboard.

When developing the strategic level dashboards, you will be dealing with the highest level of measures. Things like overall company-wide key measures for performance and progress towards strategic objectives. In essence, they help to align the organization to its strategies. Strategic dashboards are typically highly summarized information, highly graphical, less frequently updated than the operational and tactical dashboards (weekly, bi-weekly or monthly), and include global, external, trend, and growth types of measures.

Strategic dashboards

To achieve your strategic alignment for your internal process dashboards, the senior executives, people with titles like Chief Executive Officer, Chief Information Officer, Chief this or that . . . well, you get the idea — will need to work with the people that report to them. Director or Managers are the people at the operational levels who will need to report upwards to the strategic level, ensuring that the operational initiatives are achieving the strategies set by senior management.

When the executives look at their dashboards and find issues and concerns that are highlighted, they will drill down to the operational level measures that are driving their strategic level measures. In this way, they can pinpoint the problem areas and take corrective actions.

Operational dashboards

In creating the operational level dashboards, Directors and Managers will need to work with the people who report to them. These people will be frontline supervisors and leads. Operational dashboards involve the annual operating plan measures and their drivers. These dashboards will typically report on key projects, initiatives and functional business operations that drive the strategic dashboard measures.

When the strategic level dashboards are drilled down to find the underlying data and information that drive them, executives will find the operational level dashboards and what they measure. The measures for the operational level dashboard will be at a more detailed level than the strategic level dashboard measures. They will be measuring things like project performance, ongoing business measures for the various organizational functions and those types of measures. When you drill down from the operational level dashboards, you will find tactical level projects, initiatives and process measures.

Tactical dashboards

Finally, at the tactical level, the supervisors and leads will get to the very lowest level of detail for their dashboards. In setting them up, they will work with their bosses at the operational level, and with their direct report employees — the process workers. These dashboards will be reporting on the detailed projects, initiatives and process performance measures that are established to achieve the operational annual plan goals and objectives.

In addition to the functional structure that was just detailed for setting up your dashboards, you'll need to get other staff functions involved, too. People from departments with names like Information Technologies, Finance, and Supply Chain Management, to name a few. And you most certainly want to include any vendors and consultants that you buy software from that will support your dashboard construction and implementation. You will need to involve anyone that will have input into the measures being tracked or that will aid in setting up the dashboards.

The key to the whole process of setting up your dashboards is that you need to take a collaborative approach. Consider who owns the various types of information you will need, where it resides, and how best to get at it. Then get the people you need involved early in the process.

Making sure you're hitting the right targets

Making sure you're hitting the right targets really comes down to following the thread among your strategic, operational and tactical scorecards and their dashboards. If you're not hitting your strategic goals and objectives and you can't drill down to find the culprits at the operational and tactical levels that are causing you to miss them, you've missed something very important.

By the same token, if you're having problems that are highlighted within your operational and tactical scorecards and dashboards and they are not showing up as issues in your strategic level dashboards and scorecards, you've probably missed a key strategy. If, in the final analysis, you find these kinds of issues with your dashboards, and you can honestly say they really don't matter one way or the other, then you have to question why you're measuring them in the first place.

The whole point to hitting the right targets is one of linkage. You have to make sure that everything at the operational and tactical levels ties to your strategies. If they don't link, you've got problems and you need to get them fixed, so get with your people and work the issues until they do link and that you can drill up and down through the dashboards

Ten common mistakes with business process dashboards

Here are ten of the common mistakes made when setting up and creating your dashboards for the internal business process leg:

- ✔ Not taking the time to plan for your dashboards and measuring the wrong key performance indicators
- ✔ Not including the right people in creating your dashboard
- ✔ Trying to grow your own dashboards when you don't have a clue what you're doing
- ✔ Going high tech when you don't need to — getting dashboard software with more bells and whistles than you need or will ever use
- ✔ Not integrating your dashboard with your IT systems, databases and sources of data and information
- ✔ Not providing effective drill-down capability within your dashboards
- ✔ Not using effective graphics and visualization techniques
- ✔ Cramming too much data and information into individual dashboards
- ✔ Trying to measure too many things and having too many dashboards
- ✔ Taking too long to get through the process of creating your dashboards — making it into a science project and trying to make them perfect on the first effort

What Your Internal Business Process Dashboard is Telling You

Okay. The party's over. It's time to put on your thinking cap and for you to apply your critical thinking skills. Now that you have your dashboards all set up and running for you, you have to ask questions and understand what they're telling you. This is where you'll be analyzing how well you're doing in your projects, initiatives and process performance.

In this section, we'll explore how to analyze your dashboards to figure out what they're telling you. You'll then get into what to do if your dashboards aren't getting you where you need to go, and then take a quick dive into the five most common mistakes made in dashboard analysis.

Analyzing your dashboards

The first question you should always ask when you start doing your analysis is this: Do you have the right measures identified for your dashboards at the strategic, operational, and tactical levels? You also need to ask if they are properly linked for effective drilling up and down through the dashboards.

Obviously, you'll want to do a drill-down on anything that shows up as a red (not performing as desired) on your dashboard. Quite simply, it just isn't measuring up and meeting your needs. You may even want to get ahead of the game by taking a look at things that show as yellow, or that are performing in a marginal way.

This is a good place to apply the Five Why's. By asking "why" several times, you get from symptoms of the problem down to the root causes. Perhaps you won't be surprised to find out that your issues will often have to deal with those familiar elements of quality, cost, and speed.

Remember, asking "why" five times isn't a magic number, and it's not fixed in stone (or concrete, or plaster, or anything else for that matter). It may take three or four "why's" to get to the root cause, or it may take six, seven, or more. The thing you must get to is the root cause of the problem or issue you're trying to uncover. Keep asking "why" until you get there.

You'll also want to look at your dashboards for trends — both good and bad. Take a look at your data in the line and bar charts and see what's going on with your data over time. You may also want to pull out your handy-dandy copy of *Six Sigma For Dummies* and do some analysis using some stats tools. Look for statistically significant changes in the data, take a look at your data in the form of control charts, and see what your confidence intervals are.

Yeah, we know, stats may not be the most thrilling thing in the world, but it's the only way you can really get behind the numbers and discover that need to know information that tells you what's going on and where you're headed.

Also, you'll want to look for emerging opportunities, and the things that are going really well for you. There is a lot of good information in the things that show as green (acceptable) on your dashboards and with which you have no worries about. Again, ask the five whys. You may find that the team is doing something that you want other teams to benchmark. You may find some processes, methods or approaches that no one else in the organization is using that would really help others within the organization.

There's an old saying in the military that goes something like this: The generals have their plans, but they are usually changed once the first round is fired in battle. In other words, you'll also want to do some contingency planning based upon what if scenario analysis. It's nice to have a plan for what you think will happen, but you'd better be prepared for those things that don't go according to plan. With a good set of contingency plans in your hip pocket, you will be prepared to do the dance when things don't go as expected.

And speaking of contingency planning, this is the story that drives the point home. When Chuck was working for a senior vice president at a company that for now shall remain nameless, he was asked a series of very hard, and — what at appeared to be at first glance — negative questions about his plan for a set of process improvements. Chuck was proudly presenting his scorecards and dashboards to the assembled group, and the senior vice president asked, "What if this doesn't go according to your plan?" and "What if this happens?" The VP called his approach Negative Objection Analysis. It didn't take long for Chuck to realize the wisdom of what the wise VP was doing. He was looking for the contingency plans — the what-if scenario analysis for the plan Chuck was presenting. Well, Chuck got the hint. He went back and did the planning and, don't you know it, shortly after implementation of the plan, one of those contingencies occurred and he was able to keep on going without skipping a beat. It was a very valuable lesson learned indeed.

What to do if you're not getting there

Don't expect to get it perfect the first time. There will most assuredly be things you need to tweak and problems with your dashboards that you'll need to solve. The real question is this: How will you deal with it? Sorry, "Give up" is never the right answer.

The right answer is that you need to regroup and go at it again. Get with the right people, get them together and tear it apart and put it back together again. Find out what the issues are, why you're having problems, and fix them. It may take a few tries — maybe more — to get it right. Not to worry. The effort will be well worth your while.

The key is to be persistent and never, ever give up.

Five common mistakes made in business process dashboard analysis

Here are five common mistakes made when analyzing your dashboards for the internal business process leg:

✔ Not taking the time to analyze your dashboards.

✔ Not including the right people in analyzing your dashboards.

✔ Not using analytical tools, such as the Six Sigma tool set, to do some statistical analysis of your data and information — making assumptions or going on gut feel instead of making decisions based upon data and facts.

✔ Using the wrong analytical tools to analyze your data.

When we do our consulting and Six Sigma project mentoring and coaching with Six Sigma Black Belts, this is one of the more common mistakes we find: the improper application of statistical tools to analyze data. This is a point where you want and need seasoned professionals, not recent graduates and novices. Sure, the novice can be a part of the team, but you'd better have an old data analysis war-horse on the team to keep things running smoothly and to get you the right answers from the right tools.

✔ Not doing "what-if" scenario analysis with your data and information: asking "what would happen if this scenario were to occur."

Part V
Knowledge, Education, and Growth — The Learning Leg

The 5th Wave   By Rich Tennant

In this part . . .

A company must look beyond financial performance for growth and development, implementing the knowledge, education and growth leg of the balanced scorecard. This fourth leg, the learning leg of the balanced scorecard, is presented in this part, starting with understanding the manager's roles and responsibilities, then discussing how to create an appropriate scorecard and dashboard and how they work together, and concluding with key information regarding pitfalls to avoid when implementing the growth and development leg of your scorecard.

Chapter 14

Understanding Your Role in Learning and Growth

In This Chapter

▶ Recognizing the power in your employees' knowledge, skills, and ability

▶ Evaluating the knowledge, skills, and abilities in your company

▶ Achieving growth at the strategic, operational, and tactical levels

*F*rom enhancing employee productivity to ensuring the long-term growth of an organization, the importance of training and development has never been clearer in the business world. The pace you must maintain to just keep up with ever-changing customer demands, coupled with recent technology breakthroughs, has produced the most exciting business environment since the industrial revolution. Innovations are making it to market in record time. Customer-focused value is the mantra of every company yearning to make it to the top, and to get there, you must acquire and develop new skills and capabilities to meet and lead market-performance demands for the future.

This chapter focuses on the role you as a manager play in growth and development for your company. In this chapter, you discover how to identify where you want your organization to go; how to design the systems, staff structures, and acquire the technology necessary to get there; and how to sustain a leadership role. You must focus on your current financial performance, but your organization wont' survive if you don't also have an eye out for the future and for competitive opportunities hiding around the next corner. For managers and supervisors, it is in the growth and development arena where an organization determines its destiny.

Getting Schooled on Knowledge, Education, and Growth

Defining your company's knowledge and skill requirements is a slippery slope, at best, because as your organization acquires knowledge, you almost immediately send up flares across your industry. The same is true for acquiring skills and abilities. In today's fast-paced business world, when new and innovative products enter the marketplace or companies develop new technology or acquire new knowledge, it isn't long before the products/knowledge move from unique to common, from niche to commodity.

Managers today need a deliberate, well-planned system to support their interests in new products and services; to satisfy and even delight customers with next-generation capabilities and new ways of doing things; and to push the ever-competitive envelope. You can focus on specific areas of interest to put your company on the right path, but you need to understand these areas at a fundamental level. The following sections explore five things you must know about knowledge, education, and growth for your company.

Putting your finger on the elements of productivity

Today, leading companies see their employees' productivity tied directly to their bottom lines and their long-term strategies. As a manager, your criteria for productivity elevates to the balanced-scorecard approach; where you must look beyond just productivity to other contributing factors such as teamwork, leadership, innovation, problem detection (along with problem analyzing and solving), and performance improvement. The following list presents some examples of how managers are measuring these contributing factors in today's business environment:

- ✔ **Teamwork:** Management and companies are drawing upon the military as an excellent resource to evaluate and develop teamwork. Such things as working with and relating well with others, developing trust and loyalty, allowing others to shine, providing support proactively, and helping team members learn from each other are some of the traits being measured and developed today.

- ✔ **Leadership:** Different than the "answer man" of old, leader traits today revolve around natural leadership, regardless of rank or status, and include how well leaders are followed and respected, as well as their abilities to focus, energize and motivate the team, and how they are seen to be able to get things done.

✔ **Innovation:** Creativity is certainly something we have not looked for in the past, as far as employees go. Today, though, creativity and innovation are seen, especially in knowledge-based companies (such as software, gaming, communications, and the medical fields), as critical to developing a continual competitive edge in their industry. 3M is known to allocate 15 percent of its researchers' workdays to creativity and innovation time, and Disney coined the word *imagineering* when talking about its cast members sharing new ideas and using their imaginations in every aspect of their jobs.

✔ **Problem detection:** Talk to the customer of any employee. Talking to the customer makes it easy to determine how happy or satisfied a customer is and what could make him or her happier. Try to link their needs to the capabilities of your products or services, if you can. Talk with customers, both internally and externally, to find out how you may be able to improve customer satisfaction. You may also find you can improve process flow, and reduce complexity as well within your business processes.

✔ **Process understanding:** The time it takes you to deliver products and services may be more important than how you actually deliver them to some customers. This time, called *cycle time,* is an indication of your competitive flexibility and certainly bears scrutiny. You want to measure cycle times to look for opportunities to build in better response and adjustment systems.

✔ **Analyzing and discovering:** Looking at where your employees spend their time may be the most important — and most ignored — area of opportunity to measure and improve productivity. Value-added flow analyses are great ways to see what happens to the products and services your employees provide. You want to see where you actually add value versus where you just move, count, inspect, log, stock, copy, and inventory products/services. This applies to every aspect of your business, wherever work is performed, delivering products, paper, reports, purchase orders, forms, white papers and various services. The productivity question here is how you can get more productive and less wasteful, which involves a look at your whole value stream. (For more information on this invaluable method, check out Part IV.)

✔ **Analyzing and solving:** Yield or volume is a major factor and can be measured daily or even hourly (as a rate for high-volume production). The key in a Balanced Scorecard approach is to measure yield or volume immediately; look for lost-time or lost-yield opportunities and for potential quick improvements.

✔ **Analyzing and improving:** After you determine the deliverables for a group on a regular basis — be it widgets, reports, purchase orders, invoices, or legal briefs — you can develop a standard rate (so many deliverables per day) to measure daily output. You can use the rate to determine how well a group or cell is doing and if you need any analysis to improve.

✔ **Performance improvement:** Certainly, you don't want your employees chasing information, reports, parts, and people to get their jobs done. To improve your employees' performance, look at various inputs to their processes to see if they're getting what they need — how and when they need it — or if you need to send some help.

You can use dozens of methods to measure productivity, including some we don't mention here. Just make sure that when measuring productivity, you follow this sequence:

1. **Decide what you want to see (in other words, what would define *productive* in your eyes?).**

2. **Develop a balanced-scorecard approach to measuring and improvement.**

Understanding how information flows

If you've been a manager for a while, you know that a company features an official communication chain and an unofficial chain (where the real information flow happens). You also know that the distinction varies, depending on the type of information being communicated. Formal notifications are likely to flow through formal channels. But informal information, irregular information (like weekly newsletters), or unapproved information still has a way of spreading throughout an organization — sometimes much faster than through the formal or public channels.

We also know that it is in the informal communication channels where opinions, ideas, prejudices, fears, concerns and beliefs are formed, in the hundreds of daily interactions and conversations happening all around an organization. Therefore, it is most probably in these channels and conversations where people are swayed to either support or oppose key initiatives such as the Balanced Scorecard.

As a manager, you can use the informal channels to get people on board with Balanced Scorecards and other changes you want to make in the company. One key way is to get everyone involved in setting up, measuring, and managing their scorecards — at least in their local areas of interest. Most changes succeed because people believe in and support them, not just because they're great ideas. You need to worry less about convincing people about scorecards and more about getting them involved on an individual and team level so they can see scorecards at work and internalize the concept for themselves.

So, where to look for these different information chains? Here are some information and communication paths — both formal and informal — to look for.

✔ Employee bulletin boards — whether established by the company or informal boards used to advertise items for sale or birthday announcements — are great for sending out information.

✔ Certain people in your organization may be known as great resources for information. Get to know these people and who they talk with. But be careful; these sources, although often entertaining, may not be reliable or accurate.

✔ Company newsletters, Web sites, and notices are very useful. The powers that be always sanction and approve these avenues, so they're usually reliable.

✔ Organizational chains are good for announcements and sharing key company information.

✔ Groups of people who share specialties or hobbies usually socialize in some way, and they often share a lot of information — such as ideas, innovations, or variations on current practices — that can help you and your company in many ways.

Examining leadership style and culture

When it comes to growth and development, you need to know your company's leadership style in order to incorporate the best program for training and growth and to have the best chance for success in implementing Balanced Scorecards in these areas. You need to understand the culture of your organization as well as the leadership style of your CEO, president, and even local managers. You also need to understand the relationship between leadership style and culture and how they influence a company's growth and development.

Your company's leadership style will set the environment for cultural influences to either flourish or struggle. For example:

✔ **When you use an autocratic, directive style** of leadership, you can be sure that your decisions are centrally controlled. In this culture, you expect everyone to do exactly what they're told. This style will stifle independent growth, innovation and development. When this style must be used, you need to narrowly bound its application and watch for long-term damage (such as increasing turnover, hesitancy, and frustration among your team).

✔ **When you use a democratic style** of leadership, you accomplish things in a highly collaborative way. You involve multiple groups and levels, and many channels of information flow and dialogue take place. This style creates more teamwork and develops the culture toward a better working environment. When you are using this style, be aware that there still needs to be some leadership, with key players focusing on the larger picture and developing overarching strategies for the company.

✔ **When you delegate decisions** as appropriate, you see much more involvement in the key aspects of managing as well as executing the business in a collaborative way. You involve people while also ensuring that you clearly define roles and responsibilities. This style develops your employees in teamwork, leadership and the other key aspects of a successful business culture. When you are using this style, work to develop your teams to delegate even further, sharing responsibility and authority, such that you are fully developing a knowledge and learning culture for the company.

Identifying and filling competency needs

Knowledge and experience *together* provide the competitive advantage to both recognize when change comes about and to learn new ways to embrace and use it to your organization's benefit. World-class companies see changes coming and embrace them immediately; they shift their focus and adjust for the changes in their strategies and actions. They do this by using a *critical link* between their competency needs (knowledge about the products and processes) and the best methods to fill those needs (experience in working these processes over time). The key is to establish this critical link or connection, and to build it into your Balanced Scorecard for growth and development for the future.

To establish this critical link/connection, you must first understand what knowledge and skills your company needs so it can perform to customer expectations. You then turn your attention to how your company intends to develop such capabilities within your existing workforce (in other words, how your employees can learn and your company can grow). Follow this general process when deciding on competency needs and how to fill those needs:

1. **Determine the competency requirements for new skills and abilities.**

2. **Pinpoint the best way to satisfy competency requirements through one of two ways:**

   • **Internal growth:** Design and implement the training necessary to develop the competencies in your existing workforce. With this method, you'll have a more dedicated, involved workforce.

   • **Skills acquisition:** Acquire the skills from external sources to fill your needs. External resources can have an immediate impact on performance.

Different places use different methods to fill competency needs. In North America, companies tend to train their own people or hire training companies to customize and conduct in-house programs. In Europe, companies tend to team up with universities and technical schools to collaborate on designing and conducting the required training and development. In Latin America, the tendency is to turn over the education, training, and even certification completely to local colleges and universities rather than invest in developing capabilities in-house. You should use the method that works best for your company, given the geographical, environmental, and cultural aspects where you are working. For global companies, this could of course vary throughout the company, and will therefore manifest itself in the resulting different approaches to your scorecard as well.

Aligning your employees organization

An important thing you need to know about growth and development is how well your organizational goals and strategies align with the aspirations, goals, and objectives of your workforce. Let us guess: You think that your employees will always look out for the best interests of your company, right?

Secrets, shiftiness, and sabotage

In a large North American automotive manufacturing company some years ago, a plant manager set up a competition between lines and shifts to try to boost performance. At the time, the plant couldn't keep up with demand, and employees were working overtime during the week and on weekends. The idea was simple: Whoever produced the most for their line and shift got a free pizza party at the end of the month, special recognition, and a paid day off.

The competition produced disastrous results. Handoff failures occurred between shifts; people developed secret ways to improve performance and didn't share them; and selective incidents of sabotage took place between shifts. Not only did production go down, but also dissention increased, fights broke out, and

personnel incidents increased. After two weeks, some supervisors went to the plant manager and pleaded with her to stop the competition. They explained that it was inhibiting collaboration rather than enhancing it and that they couldn't meet the month's production goals if the competition continued.

The plant manager was surprised, but after the discussion, she immediately discontinued the competition. In its place, she stated that if the entire plant met its goal for the month, everyone would enjoy a 24-hour pizza party; general recognition by corporate headquarters; and — especially if overtime was reduced — the possibility of a free day off. The subversive and destructive behaviors ceased immediately, and the lines and shifts began to work together to accomplish the goals of the plant.

Not so fast. Managers know, for the most part, what their companies want to accomplish in growth and development for the future, but where their employees fit into the picture often isn't so well-defined. In order to fully embrace your company's ideas for the future, your employees need to know that they're significant parts of the roadmap to get there. They need to believe that the goals of the company are aligned with their goals, aspirations, and needs. And as your company achieves its goals and objectives, you meet the personal goals and objectives of your workforce as well.

So why wouldn't these goals and needs be aligned? One reason may be due to a possible difference in perception regarding what's important to employees versus what managers *feel* is important to their employees. When differences exist, problems develop. You must recognize when a disparity in perceptions exists and work to better align the two belief systems, because real problems could occur otherwise.

Of course, the first step is to talk to your employees to get a sense of what their needs actually are. Be sure to also identify your organization's needs. To marry the two harmoniously, try these approaches:

✔ The key to avoiding such destructive behavior is to ensure that the needs of your employees are aligned with the needs of the organization, so that as company goals and objectives are achieved, so are employees' personal goals and objectives.

✔ Get employee feedback on how things are going on a regular basis, kind of like a reality check on the fulfillment of both sets of needs within the current work environment.

✔ It also helps to have an outside agency come in once in a while to do an external assessment of the organization, to see how well aligned your workforce is (or isn't, maybe) to your overall mission and operational direction. Many companies have discovered the root source of a key issue only after an outside firm pointed out some of the fundamental indicators, which are often not visible to the managing team (like where we can't see the forest because of the trees in our way...)

✔ Always use your scorecard and dashboards as guides to whatever decisions you make, and always check your decisions with your team prior to implementation. You can use several techniques to ensure a thorough needs assessment is done, such as a force-field analysis, brainstorming, or setting different perspectives for each team member to consider.

Have a Clear Direction for the Future

The most common answer we get from managers when we them to tell us about their company's vision and mission is usually something along the lines of "We are dedicated to achieving such-and-such lofty goal," or "We are committed to becoming the best in this or the greatest in that." Lofty goals they are, but most often without clear direction and focus. Indeed, such language is worth little when it comes to bringing an organization along. To be useful, a company's mission and vision must be articulated in terms of a clear direction for the organization to go, one which answers the what, why, when, who, and where questions easily and simply, so that everyone understands.

Clearly, then, when we are building the learning and growth leg of our organization's Balanced Scorecard, we need to consider not just the mission and vision, but also the direction necessary to achieve them. So what do we mean by "clear direction?" In this section, we will spend some time exploring this, and discussing how to avoid some of the more serious pitfalls previously encountered by companies that failed to clearly articulate a clear direction toward their mission.

Growing means changing: the concern of complacency

Guess what? The old rule, "If it isn't broken, don't fix it," no longer works. In today's fast-moving, ever-changing business environment, the new rule is "If it hasn't been fixed lately, it probably is broken!"

While this might sound just a bit trite, we really do need to take this to heart in looking at all aspects of our business, and especially when planning for growth and development. This is because new ideas and innovation will rarely originate near the center of an organization, but almost always occur at the fringes — in the outskirts, at the edge. It is only at the edge of a business — out on the front lines, or where the real action is — that we can see the real potential for new ideas, concepts and possible growth opportunities.

You can take advantage of this phenomenon in your business

- ✔ By ensuring that you have an effective business growth opportunity idea collection structure or system that permeates your entire organization.
- ✔ By ensuring that anyone anywhere can identify potential growth opportunities and have them considered by management within hours or even minutes.

Examples of how some very successful, big businesses are becoming more nimble and leveraging the brainpower of their workers' ideas are 3M's process of encouraging employees to generate new ideas every day, Toyota's standard expectation of 2-4 suggestions for improvement per employee each week — which generates millions of suggestions every year — and Chrysler's new product development team involvement method.

Getting clarity from learning and growth chaos

We know we need people with new capabilities, knowledge and abilities to enable desired growth in our competitive marketplace. So, to get this, we either train key people in new techniques and tools, we hire folks with these new skills, or we buy a company with the desired capabilities already embedded. In a combination of any or all of these scenarios, the tie back to our growth goals is difficult at best, since it is the practical application of knowledge, skills and abilities that provides the changes to processes and procedures, and reframes the new reality for your company. This connection can seem pretty loose at times — even chaotic — especially when we may be in the process of re-evaluating our growth strategies. If they change, so too must our approach to getting there.

So, how to avoid this tendency? The key is getting and maintaining clarity from this chaos, and driving it home throughout the organization. Another word for this is focus, but the meaning is the same. Let's see what this means for managers:

- First, you have to understand the current skills and capabilities within your department or function, and within your market and industry.

- Next, you have to understand your company's growth and development goals. Having a clear grasp of where you want to go — and what you will need to get there — forms the basis for developing your roadmap, and provides the clarity you need to focus your energies on doing the right things, in the right order. Planning is key, and determining the focus, sequence of actions, systems and structures needed, resources required and level of discipline are some of the key actions.

- Finally, you will need to communicate effectively with those who will be involved, those necessary to support and advocate these actions, and those outside support groups you will need to depend on as you implement the plan and track and adjust as thing progress.

 A critical point here, and one that ties well with your growth and development leg of the Balanced Scorecard, is to establish and maintain the key metrics that will tell you how well you are doing toward achieving growth and learning goals, for your group as well as for the overall organization. These key metrics include such things as:

For strategic interests

- Relevance and alignment of strategic initiatives, and decisions to pursue, hold or cancel — and why

- Alignment & achievement of strategy, and key strategic objectives

✔ Variation in strategy and direction, with reasons and analysis — especially in the formulation and review stages of business development

✔ Specific initiatives performance related to growth and development

✔ Board changes and revisions

For operational interests

✔ Employee survey results and improvement opportunities

✔ Key strategic knowledge, skills and training critical to growth goal achievement, including cross training and key competence levels

✔ Measurement against industry benchmarks regarding operational performance, stock performance

✔ Internal and external assessments against standards, such the Malcolm Baldrige National Quality Award or QS 9000.

✔ Volatility associated with changes in industry, and impact on performance

For tactical interests

✔ Use of the Balanced Scorecard, level of success, impact on performance

✔ Some standard human resource metrics, such as diversity, personal goal achievement, systems deployment, knowledge management and training hours per employee

The key is to measure relevant indicators to the business while selecting metrics that will tell you when things change — whether market, industry, personnel, or technology related — on which you can focus and react quickly and effectively. It is also very important to enable flexibility and some degree of adjustment here too, so that as market, customer and industry conditions change (as they often do), your metrics will be able to alert you to this fact, and you will be able to adjust. Again, this enables you to gain clarity in a moving, convoluted world that sometimes can be very challenging to understand and embrace.

Having a plan for growth and development

This is where most organizations get it wrong. Financial, customer, and process metrics are put into place, with strategies clearly laid out to achieve them. Then, almost as an after-thought, someone thinks about employee skills and knowledge development. Oops! In fact, employee skills development and knowledge growth are essential to every business because they enable the other three legs of the Balanced Scorecard to work. We can understand this when we realize that our workforce must be skilled to perform our business processes to the high standards of performance demanded by financial metrics, and to deliver the products and services that our customers want to buy.

To achieve success in this area, you must have a plan. This means more than just a training plan. You have to envision how you will be delighting customers, running your business and achieving financial success. You then must consider how your employees will obtain the necessary knowledge, skills, and abilities to achieve these accomplishments, and how they will acquire them within the planned timeframe. There are different aspects to planning growth and development:

✔ To develop your workforce means first assessing your process and business needs, assessing your current workforce, and putting training and development programs into place to close the gaps.

✔ To grow, you may need different employees with different skill sets and knowledge. So you will need to be able to acquire them, and quickly! At the same time, you will want to always consider using current employees, and providing them extra training if necessary. In this way, they acquire the added knowledge and skills needed to do the job in the new way, or do simply do the job better, faster, cheaper.

Above all, your plan must be flexible. Why? Because you may encounter changes in your assumptions about the market (such as a new type of metal, or a new process to inject plastic, or anything impacting your products or services), or changing financial conditions (changes in investment capital available, for example) which could impact your growth strategy. Always remember that the goal of the growth and development leg is to charter a path to new opportunities, and to do this, you have to plan well, execute well, and adjust when you need to. The following figure can help in tying your growth and development plan with some ideas for metrics, as they relate to the different considerations.

 You should never assume that other managers in your organization lend the same level of importance to each leg of the Balanced Scorecard that you do. In fact, as you develop your plans, you should be checking with key leaders to get their feedback on what you are doing, and where you are going with your scorecard. Why, you ask? Because, at the end of the day, it will be a shared success or failure regarding how effective the scorecard is, in not just reporting status, but providing key insights into helping to manage the business and determine decision criteria and direction.

Your colleagues, superiors and executives will feel differently about the importance and applicability of the growth and development leg to achieving organizational goals. Some may believe in a balanced approach across all four legs of the scorecard, to successful management of the business. Others may feel (quite strongly, by the way) that the financial aspect is the only one that really counts, and the others are just window dressing for the boss. Still others may feel that customer focus is everything, and they just have to satisfy whatever the customer wants at the time.

These differences in belief will impact behaviors, and in turn, actions taken to achieve results. Remember: Different strokes for different folks! For the growth and development aspect of the Balanced Scorecard to work properly, you must involve employees often and repeatedly in its planning, design and implementation. Any concerns, needs and observations must be addressed right away, both to gain credibility with these particular employees, and with the organization as a whole. Getting and responding to their feedback, as well as getting them involved, will increase their commitment and buy-in to the scorecards, as well as add value to the overall approach of the entire scorecard. This will also help to get commitment and buy-in, and even dedicated use of the necessary dashboards to indicate if and when the growth and development activities deviate from the plan, since they will own the plan, and actions needed to see its fruition.

Knowing and Understanding Liabilities

As managers and leaders, we have all heard of, seen, or been involved with the development of a SWOT (strengths, weaknesses, opportunities, threats) business risk analysis at some point in our careers. When we get to the growth and development leg of the Balanced Scorecard, we naturally gravitate to talking about our strengths and opportunities, as they quite naturally form the basis from which we see potential in setting and achieving our growth goals and objectives. Certainly, you need to know what you are good at, as well as where new product and service opportunities exist, in order to be able to grow and develop your organization in pursuit of a competitive advantage and greater market share.

What we often overlook, for a variety of mysterious reasons, are those considerations regarding possible liabilities and weaknesses, and even potential threats. In a case of acute myopia, many companies develop growth and development plans based only on the their strengths. We have seen detailed plans in this regard, sometimes extending five years or more, reflecting optimistic scenarios based on furthering key strengths and capabilities, with glowing expectations and promising high yields. Unfortunately, without taking the complete picture into account, two failure modes often occur:

 ✔ First, a company is caught unaware by factors that were not considered in the planning stages, perhaps reflecting some market limitation, or more likely, indicating a lack of a critical capability essential to the growth plan's success, but which was assumed as accessible or easy to achieve. The results of this can be anything from mild disarray or some delay in implementation, if it is caught in time, up to total devastation and bankruptcy, especially if these factors have patent implications (technology related, for example) or legal or governmental aspects not considered (needing higher levels of clearance, for example, is critical to working with some governmental agency or departments, such as defense).

✔ Second, without taking weaknesses or liabilities into consideration, a company does not give itself a fighting chance to develop the flexibility necessary for rapid response to ever-present changes, caused by customers, market trends, politics, economics, or a hundred other reasons that happen when we least expect it. Thus, a company will always be playing catch-up, with potential growth opportunities constantly eluding you and your leadership team, due to response time and limited flexibility and intelligence about your market and industry.

In this section, we will explore the potential pitfalls of considering only half of the total business risk equation, and see how we might be able to not only avoid these pitfalls, but even turn them to our advantage.

Turning liabilities into assets, weaknesses into strengths

As we mentioned in the beginning of this section (you do remember, right?), the pitfall many companies get into is when they consider only strengths and assets in planning for growth, but ignore potential weaknesses and threats. So, first, we need to make sure we also take our limitations, our liabilities and our weaknesses into account as we map out our strategies for the future.

One tried-and-true approach is to use the "2 up, 2 down" method that is used often in lessons-learned exercises. This approaches growth from a complete perspective by looking at business risk from all four sides: strengths, opportunities, weaknesses, and threats, or SWOT analysis. This method takes the perspective that everyone in the room must list at least two positive or strength-based aspects of how the organization can support the growth strategy and goals, and two negative or limiting aspects of what might impede such progress as well. This works great in planning or decision sessions, to flush out all perspectives and points of view, in the hopes that we can then better plan and consider our limitations and weaknesses.

So, once you have fully considered all aspects of the business risk, you might next ask: "How exactly do I capitalize on my liabilities and weaknesses?" Let's take a look at these, not from a 'what are my limits' perspective, but rather, 'where are my opportunities for competitive advantage?' instead. We do this through integrating customer and growth needs, as they both relate from a business development and expansion understanding. Here are several examples to illustrate this approach:

✔ You are in the retail dry cleaning business. While most of your competitors own their own equipment, you lease yours, because frankly you don't have the investment capital available to buy your equipment. While this initially looks like a weakness, it can actually be an advantage because you're better able to adopt newer technology or more modern equipment — with less risk of equipment failure as well.

✔ Your restaurant has great cooks, but has some limitations in space, which could restrict your clientele. You could turn this to your advantage by redesigning the seating area, going to the more modern 'group at the bar' design, or try other ways to redefine how people dine.

✔ You provide hardware to a manufacturer of automobile parts, but are somewhat limited in capacity. Rather than be slave to the limits of your production systems, you embrace lean concepts, coupled with other innovative ways to get parts to your customers, which gives you an edge for growth without investment risk.

As you can see, the idea is to reframe the market and/or redefine the consumer behavior or use of your product or service in a way that gives you an advantage. There are many examples of this:

✔ iPod, a part of Apple and a virtual unknown in the music industry, redefined music entertainment by rendering CDs no longer necessary, and creating the possibility to have many thousands of songs electronically available for play at the touch of a finger, in a very comfortable, easy-to-use platform. If you don't yet have an iPod, chances are you will in the not-too-distant future.

✔ Blackberry, also a prior unknown in the communications industry, redefined mobile data and communication management, combining phone with email and text-mail capability, available virtually around the world, in a device with full keyboard and data retrieval and interface features.

✔ Apple — with less than 3 percent of the total computer market — redefined consumer desktop publishing and reframed the PC marketplace for all time with its iconic Macintosh personal computer.

✔ Sinter Metals, a novice in scrap metal reuse, revolutionized the metal parts industry several decades ago, by introducing powder metallurgy, which reduced raw material and processing costs by at least 1/3 of conventional parts manufacturers, and today has been able to retain almost 100 percent of the powder metallurgy business worldwide.

There are literally hundreds of additional examples in the components (ITT), Defense (Northrop, Lockheed Martin), Hotel (Hilton), and many other industries where — recognizing their own limitations — managers were able to capitalize on apparent weaknesses by redefining and reframing the market.

Sounds easier said than done, right? Right. But the best way to do this is to work hard to understand the true nature of what your customers want, what they desire, and what they value, and think about providing that value in a unique way. This will give you a decided advantage while capitalizing on current limitations or weaknesses that, when they are successfully reframed, are no longer relevant to the market equation. Believe us — it works!

The dangers of shortcutting training for growth

It is hard for a company to see value in much of the training conducted today, just to achieve levels of competency necessary to attain or keep knowledge, skills and/or abilities in current key technology or business process positions. This is partially due to the difficulty in measuring value added through skills and knowledge enhancement or training, and partially due to overwhelming focus on standards of performance used to determine employee effectiveness, regardless of any special or additional skills practiced. In many companies, when budgets get tight, training is one of the first things to go.

But keeping up with current competencies isn't all there is to consider — you need to consider future competencies as well. But future competencies are often even more difficult to justify, as there generally is no current return. Most of this training can be viewed as an investment of sorts in the future rather than as adding value to current operations. And that's the rub: How would you then be able to justify conducting or investing in the critical training you need, to enable competencies in the technology of tomorrow for your products and services?

When it comes to it, there are several ways you can use to justify, plan, conduct and measure such training.

- ✔ Future potential, such as return on investment (ROI), as a basis for expected market share and resulting added revenue and margin can be used to calculate expected return on training to be conducted. This can then be monitored, as a part of the growth Balanced Scorecard as well.

- ✔ Redefining the context, or the relationship of the criticality of knowledge, skill and ability for the future process can also provide a basis for justification, which can be measured for determining forecast accuracy.

- ✔ Some of the same metrics that apply to lean, with respect to value added tasks, can apply to future training as well, such as cycle time, Return on training hours, first pass yield for competency, and integrating the timing of the training to coincide with the need for the additional competency or skills.

- ✔ Using a skills matrix, such as the one below, can help in defining what skills are key, and establishing a training timetable to meet the need as efficiently as possible.

Some managers fall into the trap of treating training for growth as an all-encompassing, comprehensive program. This is a mistake, and can cost millions. The thing to remember is to focus on the elements of knowledge, skill, and ability that are tied to the real, core competency you need to have with your growth products and services. This means that the other things you may want to train need to be assessed against this criteria, and if they are not linked to value and the core competencies you need to have, they need to be taken care of in other ways, to minimize the amount of resources they need, and even reduce or eliminate them from your scorecard. This is a very important point, so important that whole companies that had great growth plans failed because of the potential for distraction by mundane, non-value related tasks which were not related to the core competencies the company needed to design, develop and support to define their future.

Inventorying Knowledge, Skills, and Abilities

You need to know three things in order to get anything done:

- ✔ Where you are at the moment
- ✔ Where you want to be
- ✔ How to get there

In other words, you need to assess your knowledge, skills, and abilities (KSAs). They help you evaluate where you are now and how you can get to where you want to be. It's no different in business, but the rules may vary, because

- ✔ Where you are sometimes changes
- ✔ Where you want to be definitely changes
- ✔ How to get there is never the same way twice

But, even with the presence of this moving platform, you still need to know your KSAs well enough.

Knowing your skill and ability levels (and what you need to acquire) can be a tremendous advantage — not only to help you balance your scorecard for process performance and growth/development, but also to determine exactly how that growth and development needs to happen. Companies with this knowledge can develop an exceptional agility in responding to changes in the market or in customer behaviors. They also have a flexible resource base from which to staff and manage such adaptation.

Your company's wish list: Defining what you need

Companies that continually break through with new products and always seem to sell well in the marketplace have done their homework. They've developed ways to understand what their customers want — both now and in the near future — and have created flexibility in their workforce management systems that allows them to retrain quickly and effectively in order to answer changes in demand. In other words, they can effectively define what they need based on customer demand and value.

You need to deliberately design the flexibility you need to be able to respond to changes in customer needs. You should take several key steps to define what you need:

1. **Research your customers' needs and how they use your products.**

   The chapters of Part II on customers show you the way and help you develop your scorecards and dashboards around this information. Our advice in that part of the book also enables you to predict when things will change and shows you some early warning signs of changes in customer demand or need. Use the chart in Figure 14-1 as a guide.

2. **Put together a simple plan to determine the basic skills required for your current jobs and for any new competencies that may develop with new product and service requirements.**

   You need to talk with your employees about this plan. Ask them what they think they should know regarding how to maintain peak performance as their jobs change.

Product	Function	Fit, Form	Add'l Rqmts.	Technology
Toaster	Toast Bread just the way I like it	Size, Color, Shape, Useful, Fits with other appliances	Ease of cleaning maintenance	Power, Electrical heat, metal bending, mechanical, assembly
Can Opener	Open Can, Lid easily, cleanly	Size, Color, Height, how lid is removed	Ease of cleaning, reliability	Power, Plastic injection, motors, metals, assembly
Coffee Maker	Makes Great coffee	Size, Color, Style, Clearance, Ease of use	How easy to make coffee, auto water hookup, ease of maintenance	Power, Plastic injection, assembly, electrical heat, water systems, filtering

Figure 14-1: Customer need and use chart.

3. **Expand the plan to consider the skills you want your employees to have but that aren't specific to their jobs.**

   These skills may include good leadership, good communication, understanding of business, team membership, and good problem solving skills.

   Again, you should talk with your employees and their supervisors to get their inputs and ideas also.

4. **Share the results (your plan) with your human resources department to get input and guidance on how you should set up your structures to compare skills with your desired competencies and competency levels.**

   You can see a good example of a plan in Figure 14-2.

Technology	Components, Shaping	Assembly	Operation, Inspection
Power			X
Plastic Injection	X	X	
Motors	X	X	X
Metals	X		
Assembly		X	X

Figure 14-2:
Skills and competencies plan.

5. **Finalize a desired competency list, both specific and general to the skills and jobs you've identified.**

6. **Define the levels of competency you desire in each skill or job category.**

   Entry-level engineers will have different skills than 10-year veterans, so you must analyze on a case by case basis.

   Figure 14-3 shows what the finished product may look like.

Now you're ready to move to the next phase, conducting assessments, so you can understand your workforce — what they do well and where they may need some development.

Step away from the office! Getting to know your people

You need to get to know your people. You'd be amazed at the number of managers who have no idea what kind of people they have working for them.

They may know their employees' names, but that isn't the same as *knowing* who they are. The funny thing is, these same managers feel like they know their employees well enough to decide their career moves and give them advice regarding their futures.

This all-business approach is actually encouraged in North America, because if you have to lay off or reprimand employees, it's better not to get too close to them. However, in South and Central America, managers are encouraged to meet their employees' families and even get involved to some degree.

So, how well do you know your employees — even just professionally? If you don't know their professional competencies and capabilities, how can you determine where you want to develop them, expand their capabilities, and enable them to work in new products and services for the future? You really can't. It's clear that you need to have a way to assess your workers to determine their strengths and where they could use further development.

Competency Levels	Level	Motor Assembly	Operation, Inspection	Parts Buyer
Entry level	1	– Identify/inventory parts – Inspect parts for flaws – Understand instructions – Assemble w/o error – Use proper tools safely – Use safety equipment	– Understand motor assembly – Understand inspection tasks – Use proper tools safely – Use safety equipment – Can discriminate good from bad motor assembly – Understand corrective action – Works w/ Motor Assembly line	– Read and understand purchase orders – Can buy motor parts – Understands parts tracking, receipt and inspection – Understand part use in themotor
Certified	3	– Pass motor assembly test – No safety incidents – Min. 3 Mo. in this job.	– Pass motor inspection test – No safety incidents – Min. 3 Mo in this job.	– Pass Buyer test – No safety incidents – Min.1yr in this job.
Experienced	5	– Min. 1 year in this job. – Consistent safety record – Consistent excellence in motor assembly – Teaching new employees – Coord w/ Inspection	– Min. 1 year in this job. – Consistent safety record – Contributes to corrective action team, reducing failure – Teaching new inspectors – Coord w/ Motor Assembly	– Min 3 yrs in this job – Consistent safety record – Contributes to reduced purchase price of motor parts – Teaches new buyers – Coord w/ Receiving, Motor Inspectors
Master	7	– Min 3 years in this job – Recognized expert in motor assembly – Coord with motor vendor on assembly issues, improvement – Additional education in motor assembly and work – Certified motor inspector	– Min 3 yrs in this position – Recognized expert in motor inspection and problems with motors – Coord w/ design, vendors, and assembly on root cause and improvement projects – Support design teams to improve motor design	– Min 5 yrs in this position – Purchasing Agent Certified – Recognized expert in motor parts purchasing – Coor w/ design, vendors and assembly on improvements to motor, reducing costs – Participant on commodity team for motor components

Figure 14-3:
Different skills and competencies levels example.

The Italian automaker Fiat has done exceptional work in the area of employee assessment. The company's employee competency and development program first assesses each employee against target knowledge, skills, and abilities to determine any gaps (the work in this section) and then sets up development programs over the next two to three years to close the gaps (see the following section). Fiat boasts that it can correlate skill competency with performance with a high degree of reliability.

How do you get to know your people so you can prepare to close any gaps in knowledge, skills, and abilities? Follow these simple steps:

1. **With your assessment criteria and competency desires defined (see the previous section), develop an assessment model that asks employees to evaluate their capabilities with regard to the knowledge, skills, and abilities related to their jobs and to the company.**

   Figure14-4 gives an example of what an assessment model could look like. Note: You should develop the types of knowledge, skills, abilities with input from employees, supervisors, and managers so that no one feels surprised or threatened during the assessments.

2. **Have workers in the human resources department evaluate the assessment model and provide feedback and guidance.**

   You need to use the right language and send the right message in the assessment process. Convey your desire to help employees determine their strengths and opportunities for improvement.

3. **Begin the assessments.**

   Be sure to do the assessments in stages, with different parts of the company completing the form each month or quarter. Perhaps you can group different specialties such as finance, engineering, or manufacturing each month.

Take extra care to emphasize that the assessment process isn't a competition or a selection process for layoffs. You want employees to assess themselves first and then provide feedback to their supervisors so they can talk about and agree to any recommended changes. Also, you may want to stress that lower initial scores are better because they provide room for improvement. Giving this score advice should diffuse employee fears about looking unqualified or weak in specific areas and will further show that the assessment is a development program.

Mind the gaps: Determining knowledge and skill gaps and filling them

After you've conducted the assessments (see the previous section), you're ready to analyze the information and determine where you have strengths and where you can take advantage of opportunities for improvement. Here, too, you want to separate your current needs from potential future needs in terms of importance and priority. You should meet current needs first, but you should have a balance with respect to the knowledge and skills that you'll need on the horizon; you should begin to prepare for future development as well.

Determining gaps in knowledge, skills, and abilities actually isn't that hard; figuring out which gap to close first is much harder. In this section, you start to see how Balanced Scorecard integrates the different aspects of business into a focused, aligned approach to develop the right resources at the right time to meet your competitive needs. You need to know how well your processes are doing (by using the key activities outlined in the chapters of Part IV). With this information — combined with customer satisfaction understanding — you can begin to prioritize your knowledge and skills development to align with your customer value creation and delivery priorities.

Name: John Smith	Position: Motor Assembly Operator	Level: Entry Level	Time in position: Less than 2 mo.	
Skill/Competency	Detailed Task	Level [1, 3, 5, 7]	Expectation	GAP
Inventory Assembly	Identify each part	1	3	−2
	Inspect each part	1	3	−2
	Lay out Assembly	0	3	−3
Assemble Motor	Assemble Inner Coil	3	3	0
	Assemble Outer Coil	1	3	−2
	Assemble Electronic Switch	3	3	0
	Attach Power Line	1	3	−2
	Assemble Components	3	3	0
	Check for Power	1	3	2

Figure 14-4:
Skills and competency assessment form.

The following list presents the actions you need to take to identify your gaps in knowledge, skill, and ability and fill them to your needs:

1. **Compare the assessments you conducted (see the previous section) with the needs you've identified (see the section "Your company's wish list: Defining what you need").**

   The result should be a basic understanding of where your strengths lie and where you need to develop knowledge skills, and abilities to a higher level in order to meet specific needs. Figure 14-5 shows an example of such a result.

Name Skill/Competency	Task	Assessment	Need	GAP
Tom Johnson Welder	Operate Torch	3	5	–2
	Set up Operation	3	5	–2
	Prepare Materials	5	5	0
	Weld	5	5	0
	Clean Up Product	3	5	–2
	Inspect Product	5	5	0
	Clean Up Area	3	5	–2
	Use Safety Equipment	7	5	+2
Bill McKenzie Machinist	Operate Machine	3	5	–2
	Set up Operations	5	5	0
	Prepare Materials	5	5	0
	Program Machine	7	5	+2
	Clean Up Product	5	5	0
	Inspect Product	7	5	+2

Figure 14-5: Skills and competency need comparison.

2. **Examine the performance of your company by taking the measures from your internal business process scorecards and dashboards, and analyze this performance from a cause-and-effect standpoint with regard to competency in skills and work performance.**

   A good measure to use is *rework* (extra work done due to mistakes or errors specific to workmanship or skill-related deficiencies). Don't confuse errors or mistakes with material-quality issues or other external influences not specifically related to skills or abilities. From this analysis, you can determine where your workforce needs further development in order to improve company performance. Figure 14-6 shows an example of this type of performance analysis.

3. **Look to upcoming customer needs — by evaluating your customer scorecards and dashboard measures. In doing so, you can determine new and additional skills and abilities you'll need to bring in to your company so you can add value and improve performance.**

This is the last piece to help you prioritize which gaps to fill. This final step should show you what skills and abilities you need to develop in your workforce, and even when, so that you can plan an appropriate integration with your current skills assessment and development program.

Figure 14-6:
Competency
to perfor-
mance
analysis
example.

Performance Measure	Current	Goal	Skill / Competency	Need	GAP	Priority	Action
Rework	85%	25%	Welding	−2	2	2	Training next Qtr
On-time Delivery	90%	95%	Packaging	−4	1	1	Process Team Assigned
Errors in Delivery	5%	0%	Packaging/Shipping	−1	4	4	Insection in Shipping
Ramp up on new products	6 Mo.	4 Mo.	Assy Sys. Design Testing	−2	1	1	New Product Development project team assigned

You need to track and adjust the execution of the development programs for your workforce as your business environment changes. For this, you'll turn to your growth and development Balanced Scorecard; the dashboards will tell you how well your program is going and where you need to make adjustments as you change and improve the skills and abilities needed to create and sustain your competitive advantage.

Linking Your Strategies, Operations, and Tactics for Learning and Growth

In terms of your managerial duties, planning for strategic growth without defined specific operational actions and detailed, well-planned initiatives to achieve such growth is like planning on building an entire restaurant chain based on your one great stew recipe. Even if the recipe is world class, it doesn't help you navigate the many steps involved to get a restaurant to chain status — the how, when, where, and who to get it all done. Linking your planning steps and objectives ensures that

✔ You have a good plan.

✔ You can communicate your plan to everyone involved.

✔ You can make adjustments during execution to give your company the best possible chance for success.

Balancing at the strategic level for organizational knowledge and growth

Balancing your business at the strategic levels as a manager depends on weighting different factors for both growth and development and carefully aligning your initiatives with strategic goals. However, you must also ensure that you have leadership coalition overseeing and adjusting progress toward your objectives.

What happens if the boss doesn't care about something? Chances are, none of the workers will either, right? Whatever managers want, watch, or ask about becomes the talk of the day, and everyone has an interest. Given also that executives and senior leaders can best articulate the strategic direction, vision and intent of an organization, it makes sense for our Balanced Scorecard approach to align to their concepts and ideas as well, to help emphasize the scorecard's importance to the organization.

Executives should pay close attention to present performance while also focusing on the future. The future becomes the present tomorrow, so you always have to be looking to the future to sustain and grow. It is this fundamental fact that requires executive advocacy and support when implementing Balanced Scorecards for growth and development.

But advocacy isn't the only thing that companies need from their executives/managers; they also need their visions for long-term growth, how they plan to achieve the growth, and, most importantly, how they plan to assess, adjust, and ensure the success of the company's strategic growth and development process. You have to have a balance between the speed of your company's growth and development and how much change your company can pursue. You also must have an in-depth understanding of what you want to accomplish. For example, do you want 40 percent or 90 percent market share? One is a significant player, but the other dominates. Do you want financial reporting or financial information? One formats, but the other provides insights for clients into performance.

The following list presents some examples of where the type of industry and strategic desires play a significant part in strategic-planning decisions:

- ✔ Leaders of electronic component producers push for growth and new products several times a year.
- ✔ Construction leaders focus on building innovation into their construction processes and project completion cycle times.

✔ Leaders in the medical products and services field focus on a combination of new technology with patient care. They're also interested in new and breakthrough products at least once a year.

✔ Retail clothing leaders depend heavily on public taste in clothing — by geography, social class, community standing, profession, and even religion and family background. These tastes change almost with the seasons.

Having an operational focus for the future

The roles and responsibilities at the operational management level for growth and development are the most crucial of all three (above strategic and tactical). The operational level is where the rubber meets the road when it comes to planning and establishing the systems and structures needed to ensure your organization's growth for the future. Vision for the future is certainly key, but without support for the vision and sustained leadership toward accomplishing the vision, your efforts are hopeless. The middle managers should be there to provide the support and sustained leadership.

Here are some things for managers at the operational level to consider:

✔ **Collaboration among managers is key.** Managers have to work together and share their experiences in trying different ways to measure and manage growth and development. What worked, what didn't work, and what were some insights you gained?

✔ **Collaboration within functions is just as necessary.** Traditionally, functional managers on a leadership team make decisions within their respective functions. One way operational managers can make collaboration work is to have their teams make all key decisions regarding each area, with coaching being the main responsibility of the functional manager. In this format, decisions are made collaboratively. This forces all interests to come together, because a team has to prioritize what the business unit will do as a whole.

✔ **Managers need to link operational.** *Linking operational* means providing a bridge between strategic vision, concepts, and long-term goals and current/future initiatives and actions being worked on and planned. Managers provide this bridge by aligning initiatives, measuring them for medium-term performance trends (over 24 months, for instance), and adjusting initiatives and plans that focus on achieving long-term goals without appreciable risk to current performance.

✔ **Above all, managers must measure and adjust, measure and adjust.** The operational level must constantly review performance, plans and actions, and cross-functional team progress in key long-term initiatives. The operational level is where scorecards are kept balanced through the use of dashboards and leadership collaboration.

Acting tactically for growth, capability improvement, and retention

The front line — the tactical level, where plan meets reality — is where good planning bears out. Many companies lose it at the tactical level, because even if they plan well and link planning to specific actions, they don't successfully execute or sustain the efforts necessary to secure their growth and development goals and objectives for the long term. Executing and sustaining these efforts isn't easy to do. Balancing your efforts toward current performance with fulfilling developmental needs requires a shift in priorities and in the way you manage and support your team.

Traditionally, supervisors gave direction to their teams and then made sure their directions were carried out — observing the results and making adjustments along the way. Today, managers talk about a different approach, where supervisors hand over authority, process-performance responsibility, and even attendance and skill development to their teams; managers focus instead on coaching and removing obstacles that impede improvement. Managers are beginning to understand that their employees know what to do, how to do it, and what needs improvement. In addition, the work teams should be aware of how well they are doing, with respect to their immediate customers, and should be working with them to provide even better products and services in their department.

Linking tactical actions becomes something real for every employee at this point. The idea is to link growth initiatives to tangible benefits to the company and to track and adjust to maximize these benefits through various dashboards. Every employee should take an interest in knowing the overall ground rules, the strategy, and the operational focus. Each work team should come together to devise their dashboard that they'll use to track and manage their growth and development. The team will work on tasks such as the following:

- ✔ Tracking multiple skills capabilities by all team members and designing development programs for each team member to improve his or her weak areas.

- ✔ Completing section or group process-balancing requirements in order to better meet the needs of growth and development in their area.

- ✔ Organizing external training as appropriate.

- ✔ Devising measures that link performance to development (such as improved first pass yield, greater consistency after a technical course, or certification achievement in a professional area).

Chapter 15

Creating the Knowledge, Education, and Growth Scorecard

*T*he growth and development of any company is fueled by a desire to improve performance (with a better skilled, knowledgeable and educated workforce) combined with a vision for long-term success (with new and improved performance, coupled with new products and greater market share). The challenge is to determine how to meld these two for mutual advantage. The way to do this is through the Balanced Scorecard.

When all four legs or perspectives are balanced — with dashboards indicating any changes of significance — you can see the current performance providing the necessary financial, delivery and quality success. At the same time, you also see ahead to the future, enabling change as it becomes necessary and appropriate to the coming changes in your customers and markets.

In this chapter, we will look at how measures are selected, to be sure that you've got the best ones with which to build your scorecard. We will also talk about what these measures tell you, and how to capitalize on the indicators for your growth and development.

Finding The Right Measures For Knowledge, Education And Growth

As you might imagine, the measures for this leg of the Balanced Scorecard are different than the other three legs. Growth and development doesn't focus necessarily on financials, process performance, or customer desires. In this perspective, it is a whole new ballgame. Here you try to define your key competencies, both in people and processes, and determine what you need for your long term competitive advantage in the marketplace.

To tie your key growth goals to their related specific actions in any sort of orderly way, it is necessary to start with the overall strategic intent, branch to operational considerations, and then finish with key actions and initiatives designed to support the company's growth objectives.

Determine key growth goals for the future

It's not very hard to see where you want to go with your company, department, or group. Everyone has ideas about what they want to do, where they want to go, or where they want to take a company. The trick is to translate your vision and your ideas into goals and objectives that:

✔ Can be achieved in a reasonable time period

✔ Can motivate and create passion

✔ Can be realistically used to manage the planning and execution of the changes you have in mind

To begin, you'll need to review the basic steps that brought you to this point. Hopefully you have already become knowledgeable about your current state, either through mapping your value stream, or by using value flow analysis, or possibly as a result of accessing key steps in your processes at your level. If not, please refer to our discussion on this topic in Chapter 11. Next, you should have articulated your future state, or where you want to go. Finally, you will have envisioned the steps you will need to take to get there.

Are you with us so far? Good.

Now, think about what key growth goals and objectives you can put in place, to track and follow your progress toward your goals and objectives for growth and development. Then, as you plan and execute every task, action and initiative to be conducted. For example, if you want to expand your current market ownership, then your measure would be market share, with additional measures specific to the method you choose to achieve your objective, such as acquisition, capacity increase, or technology innovation. As you get further into the details key to achieving your objective, so will the measures and indicators you use to show you how you are doing, and what you need to do to adjust as you go.

Insufficient technology development, for example, can be countered by changing the resource mix, or adding academic influence. Internal capacity improvements that do not deliver can be assessed with detailed process analysis, Cpk and correlation indicators would tell you where in the process it is not working, and other continuous improvement tools can be brought to bear, to enable the appropriate adjustments.

Bottom line, once you have determined your key strategic growth goals and objectives, you can determine what key measures you want to use, and once aligned with the other measures of your scorecard, they can help you determine your course of action and adjustments to assure success.

Identifying operational goals, measurements for growth

The operational level is where planning is done, and — depending on how well this planning is done — it determines the relative ease of difficulty of achieving objectives at the tactical/action level. In other words, planning determines success. Otherwise, it is probably just luck. However, in great companies, "lucky" accidents are most often the direct result of people creating and working their plans.

Once your strategy and strategic goals and objectives have been formulated, the next step is to plan out the details of your strategy for each group, department, or division. This exercise includes the what, why, when, where, how, and with whom components of your overall strategic actions, and the Balanced Scorecard attributes, measures, and indicators that will show how well they are being accomplished. The challenges of planning at this level are threefold:

✔ Linking up to the strategic goals, direction, and scorecard measures is critical to ensure you are fully aligned at the operational level, with all actions, resources, priorities appropriately selected and supported. Failure in this regard can result in misallocated resources, selecting the wrong or unimportant projects for improvement, and may even confuse your workforce, all of which would be catastrophic to your business, almost guaranteeing failure to achieve objectives for growth and development.

✔ Linking down to the tactical actions selected and implemented, and their corresponding scorecards and dashboard measures and indicators is equally critical, so that people can immediately see they are directly involved with important improvement initiatives for the company.

Failure in this will produce projects and initiatives in a hundred different directions, consuming precious resources, and focused on multiple, individual objectives unrelated to overall company performance — virtually guaranteeing failure to achieve growth objectives.

✔ Linking across to other departments or groups is also very important to your scorecard for growth, leading to improved performance. Growth (increased revenue) and development (improved competencies and capabilities) feed the other three legs continually. Failure to do this will certainly result in sub-optimized improvements for specific areas, while causing significant damage to the overall performance of the company.

A good example of this comes from a former company's assembly division which was buying raw material and components from competitors, because they could avoid the surcharge that their sister company was charging them. An operational scorecard would have detected and revealed this issue immediately for the damage it was causing, and given this level of visibility, management would be hard pressed to continue the ridiculous surcharge practice.

Some considerations regarding operational scorecard measures:

✔ Seriously consider the linkage, both up to the strategic and down to the tactical and action levels, of your measures and your scorecards, to ensure alignment, successful fulfillment and achievement of your objectives.

✔ Select measures at this level that indicate how well your company-wide systems and structures are working to support your performance, and deliver products and services to your customers.

✔ Evaluate your measures for consistency and possible complacency. Many companies miss this very important consideration, and therefore see damage too late to correct, such as when data always looks the same, or doesn't vary much. Be critical of performance that looks too good, it probably is, especially early on.

✔ Be sure to measure for each detailed area within the denoted strategy. For example, if a strategy is higher yield, and the contributing factors are supplied materials, customer inputs, company and workforce capability and sustainability at key levels of performance. The operational measures must related to each factor directly, as they impact and influence performance within each factor at the tactical level.

Indicators at the action level

When you get trained, pass a test, or certify in a technical competency, that is at the action or tactical level. You are also tactical when performance improves due to a reduction in scrap or rework. The tactical, or action level, is really "where the action is." Products are conceived, designed, produced, assembled, delivered, maintained, and replaced at the tactical level. Services are rendered, reports are completed and delivered, and components are purchased, delivered and consumed at the tactical level as well.

Key growth and development indicators at this level show you the fruits of your labor. Up to this point, growth and development have been strategic and planned out. At the tactical level, the strategies and plans are carried out, tracked, monitored, and adjusted as appropriate. The key indicators at this level are specific to the kinds of actions related to growth and development. Some of the indicators we have seen used at the action level are:

For development interests (people concerns)

These are measures and indicators relating to employee attitudes about themselves, their jobs, their companies, and how this relates to their performance.

- ✔ Planned against actual trained employees, in specific fields, to passing and certifying on specific equipment or machinery
- ✔ Key performance improvements tracked and verified over several months after key training for select employees.
- ✔ Patents files and issued, per R&D engineer or scientist
- ✔ New technology achievements, recognition
- ✔ Retention and morale

For growth interests (company concerns)

These are measures and indicators related more to the organizational needs, to grow and develop within the company systems, structures, environment and corporate culture.

- ✔ Key initiatives achieving milestones to gain market share, such as initiating customer management systems, or Specific product deployment to select markets.
- ✔ Proven increased product use in expanded markets
- ✔ Overall patents submitted vs. issued, in specific areas or specialties
- ✔ Achievements in new technology project developments
- ✔ Specific skill or knowledge acquisition per strategic technology acquisition planned
- ✔ How available front-line information is to your front line leaders, regarding speed, accuracy, and reliability

Many companies will start at different places, with respect to what causes what. While this may suggest a chicken-and-egg situation, it all depends on what the company wants to do. For example, some companies focus only on profitability, so they start with financials, and try to work through the score-card legs in order to understand what balance has to be in place, and where. Many excellent companies are realizing they can't start with the financials, but that the financial results are a result of other factors, not the cause.

A good example of such a Balanced Scorecard approach is Sears. The company's management quickly realized that they needed to dig deep down, and explore true cause-and-effect relationships in the four legs of the scorecard, to ensure balance and a true strategic map. As a result of this analysis, they decided to start with the knowledge and growth leg, declaring that how employees felt about their job and their company set the pace for their performance, participation in process improvements and relationship to customers. They set up their strategic map in this way, and established measures accordingly. Figure 15-1 shows this relationship in a tabulated format, one of the many formats that are used for Balanced Scorecards today.

Scorecard Leg	Indicator	Measure	Units	Target
Knowledge and Growth	Employee feelings about work	Employee complaints Employee suggestions	Complaints Ideas suggested and implemented	0 10% more each year
	Employee feelings about qualifications	Employee turnover Training and Development	Turnover T&D numbers	<5% 25% per year
	Employee feelings about the future	Movement within Sears	Growth Successions	15% per year
Internal Business Process	Service oriented	Handling situations Movement of merchandise Ease of processes	First Pass Yield Inventory levels/ Turnover Cycle Time	>95% >5 per year 10% better each year
	Helpful to Customers			
	Value Merchandise			
Customer Focused	Customer ideas and recommendations	Number of ideas from customers suggested and implemented Customer surveys	Number, type % Implemented $ Saved/Improved	>300 per year >10% >$5M each division
	Customer impressions			
	Customer Retention	% Return customers	Percent, by demographics	>10% each year
	New Customers	% Increased customers	Percent, by demographics	>10% each year
Financials	Investment return Profit Sales Growth	ROA Operating Margin Gross Revenue Revenue Growth over last year	$$ Percent $$ Sales Percent	$XXXX YY% $$MMMM ZZ%

Figure 15-1: Tabulated format.

Constructing The Knowledge Management Growth Scorecard

The growth and knowledge perspective really focuses on two distinct areas: The growth of the company, and the development and education of the workforce. And, as we mentioned before, this leg of your scorecard needs to address not just your growth and development measures, but it also has to support the key indicators and success factors of the other three legs as well.

The actions and measures of your growth and development scorecard will talk to key elements of training and development that support both the current capability of the company, and fulfilling the future technology and customer requirements as well. In addition, these measures need to also address the strategic growth initiatives, which might be anything from new acquisitions to redefining the R&D and design process, to redefining market entry strategies, in current and possibly new markets.

The bottom line is, the construction of your growth and development scorecard starts with your strategy, developing measures that align to that strategy, and designing the scorecard to be flexible and provide good coverage across the strategic, operational and tactical levels. Let's look at each of these in turn.

Aligning key growth measurements, for strategies and their impact

The key to designing your plan is to first decide where you want to be, and then determine where to begin. While not so hard, this is very important for designing your roadmap or strategic plan.

Let's take an example. Suppose your company sells greeting cards, and you want more market share, increased sales, and higher profit margins on select products. (Okay, we know, who wouldn't want all that anyway?) What do you pick for growth strategies and tactics? Maybe you design a niche card style, unique and different. Or, you find a way to slash 30 percent of your manufacturing costs, and you go for volume increases. Or, you expand your business to include cards that can be transmitted using a variety of media, including cell phones, televisions, and more. Whatever you decide to do to achieve your strategic objectives, you will need to determine how you intend to measure your achievement, and what to do if you see changes you don't like, or if you want to make adjustments on the way. This is what we mean by aligning your measures with your growth strategies.

You can practice this. Think of your personal long term goals, where you want to be in, say, 20 years?

- ✔ On a beach
- ✔ At home, retired
- ✔ President of a corporation
- ✔ President of the world

Whatever it is, focus on it for a minute.

Now, how would one get there? Based on where you are, maybe you need further education, more experience, or to get into politics soon. Perhaps you might want to start saving, or investing, or start a business. The key is to determine what key strategic actions you need to take to achieve your goal. Then, you measure your progress in planning and executing these actions, and adjust as appropriate, to ensure success. Or, you reevaluate your strategic objectives, adjust, and recalibrate your actions accordingly. In this case, you might define a road to get the requisite college education, or take the steps needed to open that franchise, or affiliate ourselves with the right party, and get involved with local politics first.

For your business, it is no different. Figure out your strategic objectives first (or find out what they are, if they already exist), determine your roadmap to achieve them — given you know where you are today — and measure your progress to assure success. The key is to start with the strategy.

Determining the right measures for today and tomorrow

Most of you don't suffer from too few measures and too much time. Actually, if you are not careful, you might make a career out of measuring anything and everything. Some managers have done exactly that, and they sometimes fail as a result. The point to keep in mind is that the goal is not the measurement, but the performance you seek.

You can indeed design your measures for growth and development. A couple of key factors are worth considering as you determine your measures for this leg of the Balanced Scorecard.

- ✔ Measures for today's growth and development should focus on those things that affect short-term change, such as new skills and knowledge utilization, better equipment operation, and improvements in processes due to implementing learned lean tools and techniques.

✔ Measures for tomorrow's growth and development can focus on longer-term changes, such as new technology advances imbedded in new products, redefined advertising effects, integrated and improved product communications capabilities, or improved customer service system performance.

Again, remember that these measures cannot be implemented in a vacuum. The link between growth and development and the other legs is crucial to the overall success of your scorecard. This is primarily because growth and development are more the enablers of actions rather than actually delivering products or services. You will see this throughout the book, within each detailed discussion of the legs of the scorecard, and it makes sense, given Sears and others in their understanding of the cause and effect relationship between growth and overall performance for the future.

Always reassess and adjust, per market changes as well

So, everything is going great, your scorecard is in place — balanced well with the other legs — and it's tracked and managed through select dashboards deployed throughout the company. Then, something changes. Someone invents an iPod, or comes out with a new cell phone that, who knows, also becomes a laser pointer, wireless dog leash, and starts your car. All at once. The question is, are you ready for changes in your market, changes in your assumptions, and shifts in customer behavior that you did not consider?

There is an old saying in the Army, that is still very true today: All the best laid plans last about one minute into the battle, and then it comes down to contingencies and alternatives. How well you have planned for these alternatives will determine whether you and your company are still there a year from now. If you are not sure about this, take a look at whenever things shifted, and see who shifted with them, and who did not. Remember black-and-white television? How about the way you communicate? While letters, stamps, and envelopes — commonly referred to as "snail mail" — delivered by the post office have not yet gone the way of the dodo bird, email and mobile phone messaging has definitely put a big dent in their business. How about portable entertainment? Do you see any cassette tape players around anymore? Who does not have an MP3 player or an iPod by now?

The key is to design your scorecard and dashboards not just to detect changes in customer and market behavior, but to be flexible and adjustable as well, so that you can change your scorecard as the situation necessitates. Here are some suggestions:

✔ List all of your assumptions, and devise measures to test them, in the event that they change

✔ Characterize the important aspects of your strategy, your customers, and the important markets in which you currently participate. Then, devise measures and indicators that can tell you when they change

✔ Convene a growth and development steering team, which will review and make recommendations on possible changes to your scorecard from this perspective, as your actions and initiatives progress, and as other conditions change as well, to include staffing, support and funding

✔ Remember the new take on an old adage: instead of "if it isn't broken, don't fix it" consider instead "if it hasn't been fixed lately, it is probably broken!" In other words, look to keep things always in some state of change, continually improving and revising for better and more accurate measures.

✔ Share changes made to your growth and development scorecard and dashboards immediately with your peers and your teams, so that there are no surprises. At the same time, solicit any ideas from your peers and teams regarding your scorecards as well, to benefit from other's perspectives and vantage points.

✔ Keep track of your progress, and of any changes and their impact on the scorecard, and the measures as well.

Some examples of growth and development scorecards

The following examples are from different sources, and show how growth and development Balanced Scorecards can be and have been approached, both in industry and government agencies. There are many hundreds more, and many of the industry samples we wanted to include were confidential or sensitive. However, these particular examples show the key elements of the scorecard, and how to approach setting yours up as well, for growth and development.

Figure 15-2 shows an example of a Balanced Scorecard interrelationship diagram, one of the planning tools to better understand how each leg of the Balanced Scorecard relates and supports the others. Note the objectives/initiatives of the growth and development leg. The next figure, Figure 15-3, goes into depth on this leg, defining the key measures and targets for each one, and is an excellent example of the growth and development aspect of a Balanced Scorecard.

BALANCED SCORECARD
PERSPECTIVES AND OBJECTIVES

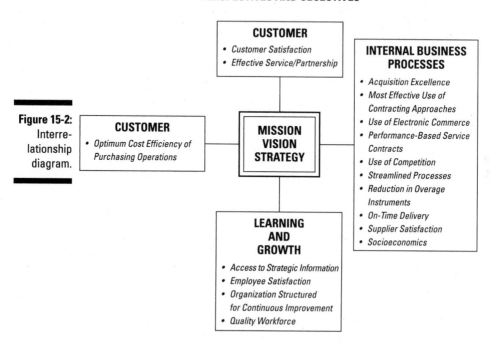

Figure 15-2:
Interrelationship diagram.

Figure 15-4 is an example of a strategy map, listing the objectives for the organization and the corresponding measures for each of the four legs of the Balanced Scorecard. As you can see, the objectives and measures for growth and development concentrate on those aspects related to skills, abilities and knowledge to be able to perform to the requirements of the other three legs. The strategy map is a key tool to ensure all objectives are integrated.

Figure 15-5 takes this relationship to the next level, where specific objectives are matrixed to specific goals and measures under each of the four legs of the Balanced Scorecard. you can see, with respect to growth and development, how specific objectives link to key goals by the checkmarks in the appropriate boxes. This sets up the detailed goal allocation and measurement for each strategy, as is depicted in Figure 15-6.

Learning and Growth Perspective		
DOE Fed Procurement Systems – 2003		
Objective	**Measure**	**Measure**

Access to Strategic Information:
    Data Source: Manager's self-assessment survey (data collection)
    Data Generation: Accomplished by using standardized survey instrucment. Individual survey responses are entered into Excel data reduction program which calculates results.
    Data Verification: Procurement directors are responsible for accuracy of data and retention of excel program reports in accordance with records management requirements. Reports will be made available for compliance and/or HQ reviews.
	The extent wo which reliable procurement management information systems are in place.	Strategic information System that is 100% accurate, timely and efficient.

Employee Satisfaction:
    Data Source: Employee Survey
    Data Generation: Accomplished by using standardized survey instrument.
    Data Verification: Procurement Directors as indicated above.
	Superior Executive Leadership: Employee's perception of the organization's professionalism, culture, values and empowerment.
	
	Quality Work Environment: Employee's degree of satisfaction with tools available to perform job, with mechanisms in place to ensure effective communication to accomplish job requirements, and with current benefits and job security.
		84%
		
		85%

Organization Structured for Continuous Improvement:
    Data Source: Managers' Self-assessment survey (Mission Goals Data Generation: Accomplished by using standardized survey instrument.
    Data Verification: Procurement Directors as indicated above
	Assessment of the level of continuous improvement including existence of an effective quality culture, extent of benchmarking and other improvement initiatives, and strategic planning actions.	81%

Quality Workforce:
    Data Source: Career Development
    Data Generation: Data is tabulated from the listed data systems.
    Data Verification: Procurement Directors are responsible for accurately reporting results and retention of records in accordance with records management requirements. Submitted results will be compared with data maintained by the Departmental Career Development Coordinators.
	Percent of all acquisition personnel meeting the qualification standards of the Acquisition Career Development (ACD) Program.
	
	Percent of certified acquisition personnel meeting the ACD Continuous Learning Requirements.
	
	Percent of all financial assistance personnel meeting the qualification standards of the Financial Assistance Career Development Program.
		90% (exception: Individuals receiving a written waiver from HQ)
		
		90%
		
		90%

Figure 15-3: Key measures for each relationship.

DFAS Strategic Plan
Your Financial Partner @ Work

B. DFAS FY 2002 Corporate Balanced Scorecard Perspectives, Objectives & Measures

PERSPECTIVE	OBJECTIVE	MEASURE
Customer	Improve Client/Customer Satisfaction	1. Client/Customer Satisfaction
		2. Commitments Met – Performance Contracts
		3. Commitments Met – Client Executive Contacts
		4. Specific Billing Rates
Financial	Reduce Coast to Client/Customer	5. Total Costs
	Expand the Use of Competitive Sourcing	6. Competitive Sourcing Performance
		7. Total Workforce Ratio
Internal Business Processes	Improve and Leverage Quality	8. Quality Index
		9. Rework Identified
		10. Rework Eliminated
		11. Best Business Practices Adopted
	Encourage Innovation	12. New Products or Services Delivered
	Deliver System Solutions	13. Commitments Met – System Milestones
Growth & Learning	Enhance Employee Competence	14. Employees in Developmental Assignments
	Increase Employee Satisfaction	15. Employee Satisfaction
	Enhance Ability to Recruit and Retain DFAS Talent	16. Core Competency Profile
	Develop a Climate for Action	17. Climate for Action

Figure 15-4:
Strategy
map.

Figure 15-6 is an excellent example of a growth and development Balanced Scorecard. The measures and actions are each linked to the objectives, and ultimately to the organizational strategies. It is this linkage that enables managers to use the scorecard to best assess alignment with key actions to the overall strategies, and to make adjustments as appropriate to ensure alignment as tasks and initiatives are executed.

Goal \ Objective	Customer	Financial		Internal Business Processes			Growth & Learning			
	Improve Client/Customer Satisfaction	Reduce Cost to Client/Customer	Expand the Use of Competitive Sourcing	Improve and Leverage Quality	Encourage Innovation	Deliver System Solutions	Enhance Employee Competence	Increase Employee Satisfaction	Enhance Ability to Recruit and Retain DFAS Talent	Develop a Climate for Action
Fully satisfy customer requirements and aggressively resolve customer problems to deliver best value services	✓	✓		✓	✓	✓				✓
Use performance metrics to drive best business practices and achieve high quality results	✓	✓		✓	✓				✓	✓
Optimize the mix of our military, civilian, and contractor workforce	✓	✓	✓	✓	✓					✓
Establish consultative relationships with leaders	✓			✓			✓	✓	✓	✓
Deliver business intelligence to drive better decisions	✓			✓	✓	✓				
Ensure everyone is working torward the same vision and can connect what they are doing to make the vision a reality	✓	✓	✓	✓	✓	✓	✓	✓	✓	✓
Embrace continuous learning for our workforce to ensure critical, high quality skill sets				✓	✓		✓	✓	✓	✓
Develop the next generation of DFAS leadership				✓			✓	✓	✓	✓

Figure 15-5:
Matrix of goals and measures.

Figure 15-7 is an example of a specific dashboard, related to the growth and development scorecard for L.L. Bean, regarding a particular product line. L.L. Bean, being in retail clothing, is real-time focused on its growth opportunities for new clothing designs, and aggressively pursues the use of dashboards and scorecards to be able to lead the industry in defining and changing styles for the future, and tying this to performance and financial return.

Figure 15-8, a potential application for a large software giant such as Microsoft, shows how it is vital for an organization to understand its strategy and the appropriate measures to ensure successful achievement of that strategy. The level depicted, while strategic, is a good example of recognizing that, due to different divisional strategies, there will be different measures appropriate to the strategy of each division. This is key, in that you should refrain from trying to always paint every department and group with the same color brush. Certainly, there may very well be some overlap, but be careful trying to fit the business to the measure, this usually leads to disappointment. Rather, define your particular business, group or department strategy or objectives, and design the measures to fit your needs.

THE LEARNING AND INNOVATION PERSPECTIVE

Strategy 1: Grow the Logistics Center as the provider of choice for aviation-related equipment through re-engineering, repair, and supply chain management of future and legacy systems.

STRATEGIC OBJECTIVE	MEASURE	TARGET
• Develop workforce strategies that will guide the Logistics Center to identify and train to competencies: acquire technical certifications; recruit, develop, retrain; develop leadership and plan for succession	• Strategic Workforce Action Plan • Managenat 380 degree assessment • Percentage of current competency inventories completed and training and development completed • Numberofcertifications • Percent of increase in indvidual • Development Pans (IDP)	• 100% implementation of Strategic Workforce Action Plan by end of FY05 • Leadership Development Program and Succession Planning Programs are implemented by end of FY04 • Competency inventory based on future state of the Logistics Center and training matrix by the end of FY03. • Certifications for selected series achieved by the end of FY04 • Increase IDPs by 10% per year
• Integrate an automated warehouse management system	• Implementation of automation	• Automation implementation by the end of FY03

Strategy 2: Enable our customer to address fast-paced needs by generating and marketing innovation solutions such as the Logistics Center "Results" vehicle.

STRATEGIC OBJECTIVE	MEASURE	TARGET
• Increase number of annual technology or tool renovations	• Number of innovations; scale of innovations	• Minimum of one major innovation per year and (2) minor innovations to achieve $50M in additional acquisition volume per year
• Improve format sales/CSR skills of sales and production teams	• Number of formal training courses completed annually per team member	• 2 relevant courses per team member per year

Strategy 3: Provide project management and consulting solutions to expedite NAS facility modernization.

STRATEGIC OBJECTIVE	MEASURE	TARGET
• Increase project management and consulting capability. (performance, schedule, cost)	• Number of certified project managers and engineer	• 85% of project management and consulting workforce certified by end of FY07

Figure 15-6: Growth and development Balanced Scorecard.

Strategy
Sales 15% increase
X Market expansion
6 New Products
Operational
30 % Fewer Sites
25% labor reduction
75% SCM Reduced
Skills up 25%
Tactical
New ERP Installed
30% More DE
25% Mgmt Reduced
45% Outsourced

**Product XX
Growth and Development
Q4, FY 2006**

Region A	18	6	33	-	98	17	Green
Region B	6	13	27	-	77	15	Red
Region C	12	9	45	-	93	21	Green
Region D	15	11	63	-	95	11	Green

Figure 15-7:
Dashboard.

Division	Groups	Strategies	Measures
Platform Products and Services Division	Client, Server & Tools, and Online Services Groups	Real-Time response, design and support worldwide	Response # and Type of Customers Customer Feedback
Business Division	Information Worker, MS Business Solutions and Unified Communication Groups	Provide solutions to any business situation worldwide	Client Business Performance RONA % Long Term Clients
Entertainment and Devices Division	Home & Entertainment and Mobile & Embedded Devices Groups	Lead the entertainment and devices market worldwide	Market share Innovation Client new applications

Figure 15-8:
Applying the scorecard.

Determining What Your Scorecard Is Telling You

When you have designed and implemented your Balanced Scorecard for growth and development, and the key indicators and measures are in place to help establish, track and adjust actions, you should next focus on determining what the scorecard is telling you. This has to do with interpreting these indicators and measures, and making decisions regarding the business on that basis, also taking into account the other three legs of your Balanced Scorecard.

So, we will introduce some ways to see where you are going for the long term, how you are doing, and how to avoid making mistakes or misinterpreting the information from the scorecard, so that the right decisions are made for the right reasons.

How to read your future

No, it's not a crystal ball, nor tea leaves, palm reading, or tarot cards. However, with the right scorecard and dashboards, it might look a little like magic when it comes to seeing what is going on, and the possible future opportunities.

What we are talking about is designing your scorecard in a way that the measures and overall balance can better indicate how well you are moving toward your long-term growth and employee-development goals. By setting up the right measures, and balancing through other drivers in all three of the other legs of the Balanced Scorecard, you can understand how different factors can influence growth and development success, and also influence the rate of success as well.

Here are a few things you can do to see and be able to interpret the key attributes and indicators for growth and development

- ✔ Trends are a good indication regarding progress or lack thereof toward achieving certain goals or objectives.

- ✔ Look to take a different perspective, focusing on enablers for growth, rather than pure performance improvement. For example, yield is production based, but yield related to increased sales or customers can indicate growth levels. Another example is where reduced costs are related to performance, yet costs related to employee levels, increased or added capacity, or per development product family can show a trend, either up or down, with respect to growth and development.

- ✔ Benchmark other industries, and look to see how their growth and development planning is measured. Be careful here, though, it is not so much the measure and the way and means used to measure, and its reliability and accuracy.

Many companies look to the operational level to measure how specific components of a strategy are doing across the organization. Their measures roll up tactical and action-based measures, and at the same time relate directly to overall strategic objectives. Remember to be specific here, and make your measures link both ways to ensure complete coverage and alignment.

Adjusting when it's not what you want

This is always a hard question. What if you have set up your scorecard correctly, balanced it appropriately to the four different perspectives, and you begin to realize that things are not going the way you wanted them to, given current plans and actions for growth and development? What do you do then?

In the mid-'90s, a large semiconductor company headquartered in Germany embarked on a new technology to revolutionize the television (TV) industry. Very little was known about this new technology at the time, so the company's R&D group was way out in front, cutting the path and redefining TV. Every indicator pointed to this new technology as the wave of the future, so the company proceeded to pull out all the stops, and go where no one had gone before. The technology? High Definition TV, or HDTV. The edge? .08 Mu size technology, smaller than anyone had ever achieved. And they were doing it! There was only one problem. Did you hear about this new technology sweeping the TV industry in the early '90s? Nope. And, while their marketing and sales groups predicted huge sales and orders for the future, based on their growth and development strategy, the public remained at a distance. Why was that? And why was there a significant difference between what was predicted and what actually happened?

No one understood it. Nor did anyone envision such a monumental impact on the TV industry. Consequently, there was no major impact, and in fact, the HDTV technology stayed relatively obscure until the early 2000s, where you finally started to see it emerge, as liquid crystal diode screens came of age, at about the same time. It turns out, it was the combination of both that enabled HDTV technology to really take off. Fortunately for this semiconductor designer and producer, the management team recognized early on that something was wrong, and that they were not getting the interest necessary to generate sales. Through a courageous shift in activities in packaging the microprocessors, coupled with an equally significant shift in screen technology through several partnerships, this company was able to redefine its roadmap, in order to take advantage of a parallel technological innovation, and couple it with their own discoveries in HDTV and wide-screen applications, to help define big screen LED based HDTV products. These products are selling like hotcakes today, and are predicted to do so well into the next decade.

The reason for telling you this story is to help illustrate that it is never too late to realize an adjustment is necessary, and to make the adjustment so that you keep or gain momentum in the marketplace for growth and development.

Some mistakes to avoid in interpretation

While you might be doing the right things when it comes to putting together your scorecard, and making it work, it's possible to run into problems when you finally get around to interpreting what your scorecard is telling you. Here are some mistakes to avoid.

Managing too close to the data

The biggest mistake companies make is to see one change in the overall scheme of things, and to make adjustments to compensate for it. Then, to see another change, and adjust again. This is called "meddling," and will almost always result in failure or, at best, marginal results.

The reason this happens is due primarily to the lack of patience at the top. When you think of growth and development, you have to think of it like a very large ship traversing an ocean. Small waves usually will not affect it, and if the captain corrected for every wave, he would not only be unnecessarily making corrections every few minutes, he might even miss the important turns when they are due, because of all the distractions.

The key is to try to avoid being distracted by the "small" waves, and to be totally focused on those things that are important to your overall growth and development strategy. Again, we can't emphasize enough that the actions and initiatives stem directly from this strategy.

Misinterpreting the trends

Another big mistake many companies make is to take the indications from scorecards and dashboards, and derive the wrong conclusions, and then take the wrong actions to correct. This especially happens when there are multiple objectives, and the possibility for confusion is high, such as when a company drives for higher sales and market share, and also cuts back on production, and talks about expanding product lines, while cutting back on engineering and new product development.

When this happens, managers will draw different conclusions, based on their background and work experience. Engineering managers might believe possible acquisitions are on the horizon, given no development budgets. Buyers will reduce purchases, to be in line with reduced production predictions, yet may anticipate new suppliers, in order to support sales.

The way to avoid this problem is to ensure your communications systems are as effective as possible, to get a consistent, clear, and repetitive message out to all regarding the strategies and goals of the company, and the part everyone plays in supporting them. You also want to check frequently, through talking with your employees all over the place, to make sure the message is indeed that which you intend.

Be mindful of the children's game called "telephone" (remember it?) where a message is handed off to one person in a circle, where it is whispered from person to person, until it makes it back to the original sender. Much to everyone's surprise, the final message rarely bears little resemblance to the original one. The fewer interpretations enabled, the less likely your message will be garbled or altered.

Misunderstanding due to lack of experience

This often happens when a manager is in a position where has to understand when certain shifts in measures take place, correctly interpret what they mean, and take appropriate action. But, sometimes the manager is not trained, or doesn't have the background or business acumen to fully understand what is going on, and will therefore miss the opportunity for action or adjustment.

This is very serious, and can impact a company's ability to achieve its long term growth and development goals. And, depending on how active and open your learning environment is, this may be difficult to see. Some of the indications to look for are:

- ✔ Key measures for growth and development shift, or indicate a trend, yet those directly responsible do not take appropriate actions, or don't even notice the changes.

- ✔ Decisions made by certain supervisors or managers that are clearly contrary to stated policy, strategy or long-term focus

- ✔ Actions taken by managers are inconsistent with the company's goals and objectives, and result in things getting worse rather than better

- ✔ Managers are hesitant to take any action, not knowing if it will help or hurt their department

- ✔ Conflicts arise in steering or management teams regarding actions to take in response to key measures for growth and development. Initially, conflicts can be good, but they also can indicate when there is a lack of understanding.

Again, this is serious, and must be recognized and corrected early. The way to correct this is to be open about having both strengths and weaknesses, or opportunities for improvement, and that we should all look forward to personal and professional development, that it is a good thing and will be recognized and rewarded. Also, you might do some personal one-on-one coaching with specific individuals, help them set up their development program, and review progress with them often, so they can see it is not threatening to admit the need to improve and grow, and to not always have all the answers.

Chapter 16

Creating The Knowledge, Education, and Growth Dashboard

*O*f the four different types of dashboards available to business managers, dashboards to help manage the company growth and development are the least commonly used. Yet, you can see where such dashboards can have great utility, such as for tracking strategic initiatives and their effect on capturing additional market share, increasing sales, or even increasing product and service demand.

Any time a company invests in growth or development initiatives, there needs to be a way to assess and adjust such initiatives based on performance against expectations, or at least based on progress made. The growth goals and objectives are usually far-reaching, yet with specific actions and initiatives that form tasks to be accomplished, some of which can be fairly short term — within the first 12 months — and can subsequently be measured and assessed for progress and adjusted as necessary to ensure the goals are achieved.

In this chapter, we explore how to design and create your dashboard for knowledge, education and growth, and the best ways to implement such a dashboard to capitalize on your long-term strategies for the future.

Requirements For Knowledge, Education, and Growth Dashboards

Your dashboard can do many things to help you track and manage your department or group. In order to design the best dashboard you can, however, it must align with the Balanced Scorecard and the goals and objectives of the company.

The essential elements for a successful dashboard involve translating the goals from your scorecard into pertinent daily measures and implementing them in the design of your dashboard. It is also important to do a "sanity" check, to ensure the measures respond to your needs, and to the needs of the company.

You will need to get this right, before you can actually design your dashboard. Keep in mind that your dashboard will have to be able to link to any other dashboards that you might need in the future.

Translating growth goals into meaningful daily measures

Growth goals, by definition, represent some desired future performance, capability, or business or market standing. Some examples include:

✔ Increase market share, from 10 percent (current share) to 15 percent (future share, usually higher), to be accomplished in a specific number of years, or by the end of a specific year.

✔ Recognized technology leader in a particular field, within a specific industry, also to be accomplished in a specific number of years, or by the end of a specific year.

✔ To be the number one or two recognized leader in a particular industry or industries, either in sales, profit, innovations, patents, sheer size in the market, new and/or retained customers, or technology.

✔ To be the number one or two recognized leader in a particular geographic or organizational region, in the same areas as mentioned above.

✔ Successful turnaround of a company, from poor performance to profitability, in a specific number of years, or by the end of a specific year. This is usually specified in ratios such as ROA/NA (return on assets/net assets), ROI (return on investment), and other performance indicators, usually financial.

Be careful taking these goals directly for measures of progress. Most of the time, growth goals are results-type goals and objectives, and so they do not reflect how a company achieves them.

In order to achieve these goals, you will need to have a plan which will clearly outline what specific initiatives and actions need to be accomplished. These initiatives might include acquiring several companies to increase market share in a certain industry, or developing a new variation of a main-line product at a lower price point to appeal to a different demographic.

All of these initiatives — and any others you might develop — can be measured, in terms of progress and performance. And, as you measure them, you can see their impact on progress toward achieving your overall growth goals. You can then make adjustments to specific actions as necessary, based on this information.

Table 16-1 is a table which suggests possible dashboard measures to help you achieve strategic growth and development goals and objectives.

Table 16-1	How Strategies and Growth Goals Link to Dashboard Measures	
Strategy	*Scorecard Growth Goal*	*Dashboard Measure*
Market leadership	From 35% to 55% market share	Monthly, quarterly market share, by business group, attempted vs. achieved, and trend last 10 periods
Technology leader	Association Recognition	Identify and implement association criteria, and measure progress against criteria each month
Leader for the Environment	ISO 14000 Certification and trainer in the industry	Certification achievement; contracts to train ISO 14000 each quarter/year
Number 1 or 2 in core product family	Greater than 35% market share	Monthly, quarterly market share, by business group, attempted vs. achieved, and trend last 10 periods.

Selecting key short- and long-term measures

For growth and development, there are both short- and long-term goals and objectives. These goals will be inter-linked in a way that accomplishing short-term goals will assure achievement of longer-term goals as well. Increased market share is achieved, for example, through a combination of specific entry into new markets with competitive pricing and technical innovation to create a better, more reliable product than the competitor's product.

So, how to select the short and long term dashboard measures that can work best for you? The key is to make sure that the combined achievement of short-term goals assures long-term goal accomplishment. This means listing your long-term goals first, and then identifying the short-term actions necessary to support and achieve them.

Keep in mind that short-term actions and objectives focus on specific tasks, related yet independent of each other. Also, remember that accomplishing one short-term goal does not guarantee that others will be achieved, so each goal must have a plan, with timing, milestones, key achievements, resources, and follow specific systems and processes in order to best assure their successful accomplishment.

Here are some additional considerations which can help in developing short- and long-term measures:

✔ After you have set up your short term goals and actions, go back and ask, if you were to accomplish all of them successfully, would you in fact have accomplished your long term goal or objective? If not, you probably forgot something, that is critical to complete success, that you will need to add in.

✔ When you have set up all of your short-term actions and goals, and verified their importance, check to see if there might be a sequence to them, that would work to your advantage in getting them done with the highest degree of success, and the lowest risk factor.

✔ When setting up your short-term goals, think about it from all four of the scorecard legs, to make sure you are looking at every angle related to growth, and its effect on the company's financial, internal business process and customer satisfaction performance as well.

✔ A good yardstick to use for "short term" is less than one year, with most shorter than six to nine months. Longer than one year can be considered "long term," with most long-term goals planned for three to five years.

✔ You should also consider and plan on some short term goals and actions overlapping others, as they collectively achieve your long-term goals.

Wait! It's time to do a sanity check!

Doing a sanity check may drive some people crazy, but, it is a necessary step — and one that many people miss. The thought is, you have picked your goals, linked them to your strategies, separated the short- and long-term goals, and you are now ready to measure progress against them. But this is where you need to check three key things:

> ✔ Go over your overall strategy and direction one more time, and compare your short term plans and actions, just to ensure they are linked.
>
> ✔ Check your assumptions in case you might have misjudged a risk or based a fact on bad information.
>
> ✔ Share your short- and long-term measures with your peers and your boss to get additional perspectives, and to see how your plan fits into your boss's plans, or if there are key assumptions he or she is making that you have yet to consider or work into your specific plans.

One excellent way to check the sanity of your plan is to exchange it with a colleague's plan, from a different department, and each of you analyze the other's plan from a critical perspective, asking questions as to who, what, when, where, how and — of course — why you would do each action to achieve each short-term goal or objective. In the end, make sure the sum of the actions accomplishes the long-term goals and objectives.

This is also a good place to do a check for what is reasonable and realistic. Far too often, lofty goals and objectives have been made with the best of intentions, only to fall into the abyss of not being able to get there, for any number of reasons. Maybe the resources aren't available, or the wrong assumptions were made. Whatever the reasons, you have to be on guard against setting goals and objectives that are too aggressive with no way to achieve them. Sure, you want to set stretch goals and not go for the easy way out, but make sure that there is a real chance for achievement and success!

Creating Dashboards That Increase Knowledge Management

The design of your growth dashboard has to reflect where you want to go with your company — the products and services you intend to offer and deliver in the future, along with how your organization will look and function. You can design your dashboard to help you not only achieve your vision for the future, but it can provide critical knowledge and information regarding how well your transformation is going toward achieving your growth and development goals and objectives.

Formulating the structure of your growth dashboard for action

Figure 16-1 represents a structured dashboard approach formulated by a medical services company to track key short-term measures as they worked to achieve their long-term growth and development goals. Each of the four charts shows a specific measure of growth, yet together they represent progress in implementing ideas, experiencing innovation and developing competencies necessary to future growth and development.

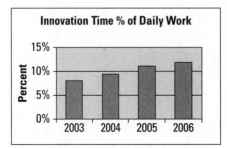

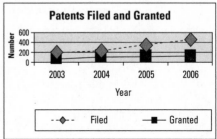

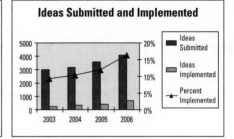

Figure 16-1: Structured dashboard approach.

This specific combination was designed to focus on development. To achieve their growth goal, such as increasing customers, they would set up charts measuring customer treatment increasing trends in total and by department, treatment, and maybe age and demographics as well, complaint resolution, and perhaps even specific trends in feedback.

Notice how the measures for this dashboard are closely related to customer satisfaction and performance as well as internal process tracking and performance.

To set up your dashboard, you first establish the different types of measures and information you will be tracking, and formulate a sequence of events. For example, in the above figure, the sequence starts with employee innovation time, and goes clockwise to patents (which are a result of innovation), then ideas submitted, and then finally to employee competency. Each of these measures are tracked daily, with the intent that, as they improve, the overall long term development goals will be achieved as well, which will also impact increased market share and potentially improve internal processes to higher performance levels.

This is easier than you might think. Just identify the overall objectives you are going for, by type, and set up your format to include the short-term goals and actions in an appropriate sequence to your decision needs. Your dashboard should show short-term performance, in ways that can help you understand not just what happens, but the reasons as well, to help you make better decisions and adjust ongoing actions to assure success.

Setting up feedback systems

When we talk about feedback systems, we are referring to ways that you can assess how well your dashboard is working for you. This is especially important for your growth and development dashboard, since you use it mostly to track progress in developing new products, markets or customer accounts, or the needed competencies and capacity for greater competitive position.

Some companies integrate their feedback process into their dashboards. This is the best way, as you can immediately see how reliable the information is. A good example of this can be found in clothing retailers such as J.C. Penney Company or Kohl's, which employ extensive dashboards to help them manage new product trends to help them with product selection and sales. The measures involve tracking volume and movement by model and product type, and show trends with different models, styles.

These measures are also able to relate certain characteristics or traits associated with clothing and their sales patterns, such as certain style traits, colors, patterns, or certain cuts. When styles would go in or out of fashion, the measures could be adjusted to enable some degree of visibility to shifts in product yield (reduction or increase in sales, for example), and could be regionally applied as well.

By building in reliability factors, the dashboard measures can be adjusted to account for variations and changes in the industry where they impact a company's competitive current status.

Using the dashboard to achieve greater potential

Your dashboard should do more than just tell you what's going on in your organization on a regular basis. Your dashboard should also enable you to make decisions regarding changes in company initiatives and actions across all four legs of your Balanced Scorecard that can improve growth and development progress toward long-term strategic goals and objectives.

Combining the proper formatting with feedback can create a formidable dashboard. One that can help you accurately track your key measures for growth and at the same time help you continuously improve the dashboard and your decisions as things change.

Always remember to review your assumptions about your market, products and services, customers, and especially the core competencies, knowledge, skills and abilities that are critical to developing and maintaining your competitive edge.

No one knows this more than those companies in the computer and communications industry, where change happens almost daily, and new product families and designs are introduced monthly. When you look at the growth and development dashboards of companies like Motorola, Compaq, Microsoft and Sony, you'll see similarities in technology measures that are not just product specific, but also relate characteristics and traits of these products as well. These measures change as consumer desires and expectations change.

In this way, these companies can see when certain traits go in or out of fashion, when new traits emerge, and how they can work them into the new models and service programs, in order to stay ahead of their competitors, at least for a little while.

The rapidity of such change has made Balanced Scorecards and their daily dashboards a standing part of life in these kinds of companies, and probably has saved them more than once in their ability to help shape decisions with appropriate information at the critical time needed to make the right changes in strategy, or to better time a new product launch, or better shape a new product design.

Analyzing Your Knowledge, Education And Growth Dashboard

As with the other elements of your scorecard and dashboards, you have to assess your dashboard regularly, in order to ensure continued alignment with your growth and knowledge goals, and to continue to support the other legs of your Balanced Scorecard as well, within a business environment that is experiencing change and growth at an exponential rate.

In addition, you want to be able to use progress measures in growth and development to tie to the performance of the other legs of your Balanced Scorecard, and to even try to make adjustments to the other legs as a basis of how successful you are at achieving your growth goals. This also applies should you need to make adjustments to your strategy in order to best satisfy the entire scorecard and each leg therein.

How to use the growth dashboard to make adjustments to scorecard balance

The power of the growth dashboard can help you make adjustments across all four legs of your Balanced Scorecard, when product or service deployment performance indicates potential market strengths or possible weaknesses. For example, let's say you make electrical components for the automotive industry, and you have several new, innovative connector systems for lighting and power control. Your growth and development dashboard can indicate measures related to trends in increasing yield, rates of design changes, and incorporation into different automotive products and models.

At the same time, these trends can indicate the entire maturity of a product's potential financial performance, given certain experience in product cycles, customer demand curves and other factors. In addition, depending on rates of increase in demand and supply, internal production and distribution process capability can be assessed and adjusted, and even customer behavior can be measured and tracked to detect changes and respond accordingly.

Another example presents itself in the medical services industry, where competition is heating up with respect to what facilities provide in health enhancing and maintenance services. This industry is growing by leaps and bounds, with the leaders only just barely ahead, enabled through real-time performance and development measures.

In fact, because of the level of growth in this market, hospitals and medical service organizations are redefining the way they provide services and in overall patient treatment, with emphasis moving from traditional systems to structures that focus on the total health of their customers and patients.

One large, Midwestern medical hospital services provider has actually designed their Balanced Scorecard around the growth and development trends, instead of the more traditional financial measurement and performance perspective. They fully integrate their growth dashboard measures and indicators into decisions related to internal business process performance as it relates to customer satisfaction, which eventually results in financial performance.

This particular hospital designed their dashboard to show all four legs on one screen, interlinking the four dashboard elements as related to their scorecard legs, so that their managers can see when any measurement moves in a particular direction, and can immediately see the effect on the other dashboards' measures as well, and make adjustments in services, take specific action, shift resources, or re-prioritize key initiatives in order to keep up with changes in demand or need.

The thing to remember and consider is to ask not only what growth measures can give you up to date information for real-time decisions, but also what these measures might be able to indicate with respect to your other scorecard legs, related to your market and product demand trend.

What your dashboard is telling you as you work toward achieving your future

What your dashboard tells you has a lot to do with what you are trying to do. This is pretty much common sense. Yet, what you want to do with your company will determine the steps you take, and the measurements of your Balanced Scorecard and your dashboards you will use to assess and adjust your progress. So, what is it all about anyway?

You use your growth and development dashboard to see if the decisions your company or group makes improves your growth position, and enables development toward improved competencies and capacities. How well things go depends on many things, but after all, it is very exciting to be able to grow and develop an organization.

As a manager and leader, you use dashboards to help you make important decisions, such as whether to pursue new technologies, reframe product families, and redefine customer approach and management strategies. There are some basic things to be on the lookout for, so that you take maximum advantage of the information, and make the best decisions you can. Here's how:

✔ Occasionally compare your dashboard data with outside information, not linked to your data collection or analysis process. Independent verification can ensure you are taking the right steps, and have not misinterpreted your growth data.

✔ Compare your steps and progress with those of your competition. Similar and different aspects of your strategy will bear out in this way, and can confirm the positive or negative impact of what you do and why.

✔ Refrain from making overly quick decisions or executing many changes as a reaction to variation in your measures. You need to realize that some variation will occur, so you want to focus on general trends, not specific points, when making decisions. You should allow for at least 10 to 15 points indicating a particular trend before you act on it.

✔ Require peer oversight in interpretation and resulting decisions, changes, or adjustments you want to make. Having someone else look at what you are thinking and what you want to do provides a good check system, just to ensure the right actions make sense given certain performance indicators in growth and development.

✔ Have some fun in interpreting your data and adjusting your programs and actions to enhance growth and employee development. As you work with your dashboard, you will learn which actions and variables can be manipulated to get the maximum benefit from your training and development programs, and other actions as well, to support strategic growth.

The importance — and the risks — of being truthful

Being truthful sometimes has its risks, especially in organizations where bad news is not well received or where admitting that you don't have the knowledge to perform a particular task or project will bring disfavor to the management team. The fear of reporting information that may not be well received will often force numbers and information to be fudged in ways that can permanently hurt a company and the people who work for it. This is why you must encourage and atmosphere of dealing with the truth.

Remove the fear, and if mistakes are made, find out what went wrong and take steps to learn from your mistakes. Shooting the messengers and hanging the guilty are the fastest way known to man (dogs and cats, too) to getting what you want to hear, not what is really going on and what you need to hear. After all, making mistakes is part of the learning and growth process. Just make sure you don't repeat them!

Another key factor that contributes to unrealistic assessments of what can be achieved is overconfidence on the part of the management team. A feeling that they are invincible and can do anything. Recent surveys have shown this to be a key factor in why some companies have failed miserably in achieving their strategies.

With growth and employee knowledge and skills development, it is more important than ever to realistically understand and interpret your dashboard and measures. The risks are greater here, not necessarily for the short term, but definitely for the longer term effects. Errors in interpretation can result in subsequent missteps in planning and executing key strategic initiatives, or even selecting the wrong actions, focusing your organization away from where it needs to go, or allocating resources in the wrong way or not at all.

Often, what happens as different strategies are attempted, is that the data can sometimes indicate that specific actions are incorrect, or you might be taking the wrong steps, or that steps are being taken in the wrong order. The key here is to honestly evaluate and adjust, and not worry about whether this might appear badly to your boss or others in the organization.

Of all of the legs of the Balanced Scorecard, growth and development are most dependant on looking to the future and determining what you need and when, and what to do to ensure your future initiatives can be successfully planned and executed. In other words, this is the least certain of the four legs, because it talks about the future, and developing capabilities you do not currently have.

World-class companies will assess the risks of this, and ensure that

✔ The data and alternatives are thoroughly examined and understood, including executing a good FMEA (Failure Mode Effects Analysis) to determine and prioritize their risks and impacts, to minimize distractions in decisions and possible actions resulting from incorrect risk assessments.

✔ Analysis methods are used which ensure objectivity in the collection and interpretation of the growth and development dashboard measures, to guard against perceptions and beliefs not based on fact.

✔ Often, an organization will have considered contingencies with respect to potential alternatives as shown in the data and measures of the growth and development dashboard. By having these alternatives taken into account, this helps managers overcome possible risks in going down the wrong path by having the different paths clearly defined. In this way, the decisions can be based on specific situational indicators, and the risks can be assessed more accurately against achieving critical strategic goals and objectives.

The decisions made using growth and development data can have far-reaching effects, and influence future initiatives, endeavors, and even key acquisitions or strategic development in new technologies. Because of this risk, it is imperative that managers double check decisions which affect the long-term growth initiatives, as well as key knowledge development and deployment actions.

While you know that the growth dashboard can give you a window into your future potential, it is also directly linked to your current performance in internal business processes and the resulting financial performance, and ultimately customer satisfaction. Yet, in the end, the growth and development dashboard provides the best way to see where you are going, and how to get there, in a way that still enables your competitive advantage — now and in the future.

Understanding the Pitfalls of Analysis

These days, it seems like everyone is referring to benchmarking for a variety of things, to include comparing to best practices, baselining (which is actually not benchmarking but rather defining current state or baseline), and results in decisions and changes in organization which most of the hurt more than help a company. Most managers think they understand what benchmarking is all about, but few actually get benefits from the concept, and most just get frustrated. There should be, one would think, a certain usefulness one can gain from looking at how others are able to perform key business processes better than anyone else, to see how they do it, and what you might be able to learn from them. Yet we see time and time again, where this is done badly, and where more damage is done to the group than was ever expected, all in the name of benchmarking.

So, we need to understand the pitfalls of analysis, and avoid them in our desire to capitalize on examples of key processes in our industry that clearly demonstrate excellence in performance and results. This section will explore some of the key reasons why most companies don't get it right, and provide some suggestions on how to get to the good stuff of benchmarking business processes and performance.

Performance results alone do not a benchmark make

Benchmarking consists of three key tasks, and they must be performed in order for the overall effect to be successful for an organization:

✔ First, you have to select which business processes you want to benchmark. For example, you might want to improve your month-end closure. Whatever you select, you then, as a second part of this first step, need to thoroughly understand your own business process in this area, to a fairly detailed level, in terms of who does what, when, and what specifically is handed off through the process, and to whom. You also need to know the level of first pass yield at each step in the business process, as well as the cumulative first pass yield. So, what does this mean? It means, at each step, how well (defect free) the task is performed, and the deliverable provided to the next step.

✔ Second, after you have internally mapped and measured the area you want to benchmark, you then go out and identify world-class examples of where this is being done, and gather further intelligence about these examples, perhaps set up a visit, ask for any information they would be willing to share, and do research as well. The key here is to gain sufficient process information about the benchmark best practice example to be able to compare process elements, internal to external, to see where you can change things internally, and which changes would impact or cause the appropriate improvement you are seeking.

✔ Once you have compared and extracted appropriate elements for incorporation into your business process, you will need to put together a transition plan, to implement the changes necessary within your internal business process to see the improvements and be able to measure a positive impact on the business as desired. Then, of course, you execute, monitor and adjust your transition plan activities to their successful completion.

The problem is, many companies see the results of world-class benchmark business processes, and invoke or dictate that their own business needs to achieve the same level of performance within a specific time period. However, they have no idea how the benchmarked example company achieves its performance levels, and just expects that, since they did it, it must be possible for us to do it too. So, we see the pitfall to avoid is when we only set parameters and performance metrics objectives, based on the industry best practices, without fully understanding the process level relationships that are fundamental to this performance. We have to make sure we can actually improve to best practice levels, and without actually analyzing the process steps, we cannot know whether our systems are even compatible or can even perform to the best practice levels, given possibilities for different systems and structures supporting the benchmark. So, you see why we have to break it down, to then know how to implement those compatible practices in the benchmark organization.

Comparing apples and elephants: best practices where?

As the title implies, another pitfall to watch out for is comparing two processes that are clearly unrelated or that represent markets or industries that are so vastly different that it would be clearly impractical to compare or measure one against the other. Let's look at some examples where this might apply:

✔ Being interested in improving customer service, a manufacturing company researched best practices and contacted the Minneapolis City Police Department, which had been cited with exceptional customer service awards for several years. It became obvious that, whatever customer service attributes were highly regarded at the police department were probably not going to relate to customer satisfaction of clients receiving high quality parts on time.

✔ There was a big push for software companies to improve the design and development process performance (mostly cycle time and reducing rework), in order to reduce costs. Several companies went out to seek benchmarks on design cycle time and cost reduction, and set their sights on Chrysler's design office in Michigan. As it turned out, unfortunately, the characteristics of software design and development did not lend sufficient alignment in core design elements to be able to be compared to any other design process. The process used to design Chrysler's new models was based on CAD and CATIA, which is solid 3-D modeling with some intelligence built-in regarding solid clearance, stress and other physical factors. For software, it is about testing software commands, loops, and detecting electronic impulses in system operability and fault isolation tests (SOTs and FITs).

✔ Financial management processes are sure to be common in all companies, so one would think. However, a bank recently tried to benchmark a stock broker's financial management processes, but without any success. The reason was that the way the broker was organized and operated, with the open policies, enabled multi-skilled financial management group, and U.S.-specific policies and procedures did not work when applied (or attempted to apply, thank goodness). The way which the bank closed the office and the safe each month, as well as other processes, confidential and for customer's eyes only, contrasted starkly with the openness of a broker, where all information is common knowledge, and that everyone works fairly close together.

These are just several of the hundreds of examples where we are trying to compare pepper shakers with mayonnaise. As you are looking for commonality, always be sure to check the validity of any comparisons, and if they do check out, we should support them as well.

Beware of cookbook approaches and case studies

Another way to benchmark best practices is to go to an official, recognized publication, and extract best practices based on highlighted articles, touting them as the holy grail of performance. The pitfall with this is that sometimes management teams will have a belief that they can take a business example from a quality or operations or engineering periodical, and make copies, pass them around the operations or engineering group with instructions to read and adopt within 60 to 90 days, and report back when completed and the new processes are working up to expectations. Again, this is taking the assumption that there is a standard or cookbook approach to implementing benchmarking practices, which results in inappropriate applications, caused by senior leaders who want to apply a peanut butter approach to improvement programs.

Put another way, each company is different, which means that they manufacture and deliver products, of course, but also that there are a lot of processes that could be done better, but have not been mapped or understood to the appropriate detailed level. As a result, when management doesn't have the maps or deliberate roadmap to improvement, they still mandate change on behalf of continuous improvement, even if they do not know what they are changing. So, we have to watch for this, and not allow rank and armor to redefine benchmarking just because they want it a certain way. There are ways to do this, but all in all, it is about working together through underlying assumptions, and getting to answers.

Part VI
The Part of Tens

The 5th Wave   By Rich Tennant

"I like getting complaint letters by e-mail.
It's easier to delete than to shred."

In this part . . .

Here are a few quick reference chapters bursting with insights gained from our combined experience implementing balanced scorecards in industries, from hotels and banks to electronics and automotive, from retail to wholesale, in both private industry and public service and government organizations. We cover tips for balanced scorecard success, scorecard mistakes to avoid, and tips for overcoming barriers.

Chapter 17

Ten Tips for Balanced Scorecard Success

*E*ven as you get your Balanced Scorecards going, and everyone starts to see the benefits, your job isn't over. You're going to need to continuously sell the Balanced Scorecard idea and help your co-workers pull together to get the most benefit from this powerful tool. If you stick with it, your Balanced Scorecards can help you succeed in adapting quickly to changes in performance, market demands, and new product or service introductions. Not bad, if we say so ourselves! In this chapter, you can find ten of our favorite tips to help you ensure Balanced Scorecard success.

Establish (and Remember) Where Your Company is Headed

Fundamental to the success of *any* endeavor (big or small) is to first know the direction in which you want to go. Balancing the scoring of a business is no different than arranging a vacation: You have to decide what you want to do, how you will finance it, how you will get there, and how much fun and exciting the process will be.

Like planning a vacation, a business also has to have an idea of what it wants to do, how it will finance and accomplish what it wants to do, and what it will look like in the end. From these key elements, the Balanced Scorecard is formed. In order to keep your company going in the right direction, you need to make sure you have the following:

- ✔ **Mission:** In the form of a statement, the mission is what gives the organization its purpose and its link to the customer.

- ✔ **Vision:** The vision sets the future state in mind, and it forms the growth direction. In other words, the vision answers the question, "Where do we want to go?"

- ✔ **Strategies:** The strategies are those overarching intentions and initiatives which will, when pursued, ensure accomplishment of the mission and enable the vision. Examples include commanding a specific market share in a specific industry or market sector, providing a competitive return on new product investments to stockholders, entering new and emerging markets successfully, growing margin on key products or in key regions, or expanding a customer base in a particular technology-based product family.

- ✔ **Guiding principles:** These are the principles by which we conduct ourselves (some examples might be agility, competitiveness, and putting our people first), how we treat each other and our customers and suppliers (examples here might be honesty, trust, respect and teamwork), and the guidelines and ethical rules that govern our business decisions.

Be sure that you have all four of these pillars in place to ensure your own Balanced Scorecard success.

Understand and Stay Current with What Your Customers Want

Knowing your customers and constantly being in tune with their needs and how to satisfy them is fundamental in order to make Balanced Scorecard strategy work. The leading company in any industry is one that is constantly updating customer knowledge, including how the customer is thinking about its products and services, and where customers could be better served tomorrow.

L.L. Bean cornered the retail market by getting right next to its customers and relentlessly pursuing ways to meet and exceed their needs. Southwest Airlines turned vital customer desires into a competitive advantage in the way they approached air travel services. Through the use of Balanced Scorecards and a customer dashboard, these and other companies aggressively went after the needs of their customers, and constantly measured and adjusted their performance to achieve their goals. (See Chapter 5 for more details on working with your customers.)

Define Your Scorecard and Dashboard Roles and Responsibilities

As you can imagine, simply installing scorecards will not a successful dashboard make! You have to have an understanding of who is responsible for doing what, when specific actions and adjustments are to be made, and by whom. You should always have agreement on who supports the Balanced Scorecard — and in what capacity — *before* you put one in place, not after.

For example, even as your finance team may track performance, the leadership team together owns the responsibility to achieve goals and expectations. It is crucial that the leadership team roles and responsibilities be clear, unambiguous, and complimentary regarding the establishment and monitoring of the Balanced Scorecard and key overall dashboard performance.

Charter Effective Steering Committees

The leadership steering a company's decisions about what to pursue and support toward continuous improvement and lean performance are profoundly linked to the Balanced Scorecard, the direction of the enterprise, and how performance is targeted and achieved. You need to ensure your leadership teams work together on key decisions and take an active role in coaching and leading critical initiatives affecting your scorecard. One way to do this is by establishing a steering committee comprised of a company's leaders, to take responsibility for these tasks and ensure that the Balanced Scorecards are instrumental in helping to achieve the goals of the organization.

There are a variety of different ways to establish a steering committee, depending on the size and complexity of your organization. The following are some suggestions:

✔ For simpler organizations, the leaders at the top should come together and form a steering committee, to integrate and share their actions and key decisions regarding business prospects, operational performance improvement, and any strategic direction changes. Priorities are set as a team, and leads are selected and assigned through this committee as well,. The Balanced Scorecard is brought into alignment and integrated with these priorities. .Key leaders can then take an active role to champion those critical initiatives — such as supply chain, retention improvements, or reducing working capital, because they are directly related to their appropriate scorecard legs.

✔ For more complex organizations, this type of structure is based on delegation, with leadership teams at the top as well as at the divisional and departmental (functional) levels. The framework is similar to that described above, except that there would need to be an executive steering committee responsible for strategy alignment and directional focus. For divisions and departments, additional steering committees are needed. These committees focus more on the actual initiatives and activities to support the overall goals and objectives, and set the scorecards in place as aligned with the strategic approach and complimenting and integrating with each other as well. Each division and department steering committee would take on the responsibilities for their particular organization or function, and would be of the simpler type as described above.

Establish and Maintain Accountability

You may have heard a saying from the southern part of the United States regarding participation versus commitment:

> In an American bacon-and-eggs breakfast, the chicken participates, but the pig is committed.

The same is true when scoring business. *Accountability* means holding yourself responsible and staying committed to achieving certain goals and expectations — "owning" the scores and adjusting for them to meet your goals. All leaders are accountable to each other and to the company for performance against the Balanced Scorecard and for carrying out necessary adjustments to maintain balance and achieve, and even exceed, expectations.

Be sure that you establish and maintain accountability in your organization throughout the Balanced Scorecard process.

Link Your Scorecards and Dashboards to Your Strategies, Goals, and Objectives

When you drive, you rely on your dashboard to see how fast you're going, how far you've gone, how much gas is left and how well your engine is performing. This information is critical to see whether you can get where you're going. Leading a business is a lot like this, in that you look to your scorecards and dashboards as indicators to tell you how far you've gone, where you're heading, and how you can get there.

Build links between your scorecards and dashboards as well as your objectives and strategies. These links enable your organization to respond quickly to changes in customer demand, capabilities, and markets. While this advice may seem like common sense, the key here is to have a solid, unambiguous connection, so that every action and every task can have a direct impact in some way to your overall mission.

There is a story from 3M some years back where everyone, even the janitor, could explain clearly how doing his job to keep 3M cleaner contributes directly to the company's ability to achieve its margins and remain competitive. The connection from actions to measures to monitoring to goal achievement is the secret many companies miss, but by linking every component of your company, you can ensure that you not only meet your strategic goals, but also outpace and outmaneuver your competitors.

Communicate Your Personalized Four-Legs Approach to Everyone

In sports, each team member needs to know his role as well as how the play comes together in order for the team as a whole to be successful. For example, the center fullback in soccer has to be able to absorb the stopper role to key in on the opponent's dangerous striker, to be able to anticipate the other team's movement of the ball. If the center fullback didn't do his job, his team pays the price.

In business, success likewise depends on how well everyone understands the overall mission and direction of the company as well as how each person's role is impacted. Each person, whether management or employee, needs to understand her part and how they can best support the four legs approach to make Balanced Scorecard a success. You can accomplish this by discussing it over and over, constantly reinforcing the basic principles, and ensuring that everyone is personally involved in the process.

Use Feedback and Feed-Forward Loops

Just like you would tell someone if something were wrong that required action on his part to correct, you should expect to be told as well. For the Balanced Scorecard to work well, you need to understand that feedback status and performance into the system as well as the feed-forward status and performance is important.

In other words, you need to hear feedback on how you're doing and where you need to make course corrections during the year. You also need to take prior information and knowledge and — coupled with other predictive factors — feed forward key information regarding trends in sales, costs, markets, consumer behavior, and the supply chain, to be able to adjust actions prior to experiencing significant losses to the business. In this way, you make adjustments from both factors.

As Dell developed in its early days as a computer hardware- and software-customizing company, it used data from both past performance as well as predictive programs to go after the next customer desire or idea. The Dell company capitalized on this approach to leap over its competition.

Plan and Execute Your Balanced Scorecards Relentlessly

Leading companies make their Balanced Scorecards (and their dashboards) part of their daily management and leadership practices. They ensure that both existing and newly appointed managers are trained in their Balanced Scorecards and the roles and responsibilities they have.

To make Balanced Scorecard work for your business, you not only have to create an effective plan, but you also have to follow through with that plan. The following are some guidelines for planning and implementing your Balanced Scorecards:

- ✔ Make sure that your plan integrates the evaluative elements with key performance indicators (KPIs) as well as regular reviews and follow-up to keep on track, and adjust when getting off-track.

- ✔ Execute the plan in line with other foundational initiatives by having each initiative and task laid out in a structured road-map — measurable and with clear roles and responsibilities.

- ✔ Make sure that the leader follows the road-map closely, with check and balances in place both to detect and correct side tracks.

   Leaders must work closely with their champions or sponsors to remove barriers and to enable real-time adjustment when priorities shift, as they sometimes do.

- ✔ Constantly evaluate your scorecards — planning, executing, and adjusting your scorecards and your performance as the market, industry, and customers' requirements change.

This approach can maintain balance between the four legs of the Balanced Scorecard and assure market leadership or a significant competitive advantage.

Synergize Your Scorecards for Competitive Advantage and New-Market Entrance

Your scorecards help you achieve a competitive advantage and key business performance. By constantly reassessing the overall goal and by stepping out of your area once in a while, you can use your scorecard to see the broader picture of which you're a part and see whether things could be done even better. You look for continuous improvement, not just locally to your own scorecard, but as part of a larger business focus, where you may be able to see greater opportunities. Sometimes we refer to this as: 'the whole is greater than the sum of its parts.' In other words, when everything works in a collaborative and coordinated effort, you will be able to see greater opportunities than would be typically visible just to accomplish your local goals and objectives. Maybe, for example, there is a way to revise your product development approach, because of the unique manufacturing processes you have designed, or because of the peculiar customer relationship you might have, such as greater sharing in technology, or closer links to the value stream.

In addition, your scorecards should help you seek out and define potential new markets and opportunities for your business, through a balance between customers and operations and between financial performance and new growth opportunities. For example, in the early '90s, Chrysler developed its integrated design organization to reduce time to market and enable faster design capability as well as a smooth transition to manufacturing. However, as it experienced these and other benefits, the Chrysler company saw customer opportunities through better and faster survey data, coupled with more up-to-date operations information, to create additional growth through its new Concorde family, which took off immediately and was a serious threat to Ford's Taurus and GM's Oldsmobile leadership.

As your scorecard becomes more and more a part of your business, you will see increases in flexibility, response time, and other traits, making you more competitive. You must be prepared to shed old, outdated processes that at one time may have seemed cutting edge, but could prove obsolete with new production techniques, better customer feedback, and technological advances enabling higher performance and achieving greater market share.

Chapter 18

Ten Biggest Scorecard Mistakes to Avoid

In This Chapter

▶ Keeping your focus on what's important

▶ Recognizing common pitfalls — and how to steer clear

. . . .

*T*he use of Balanced Scorecards can enable a company to achieve a clear competitive advantage through integration and synergy in an overall, four-leg view of its business opportunities and challenges. However, several mistakes can be made along the way. Your job is to avoid these mistakes whenever possible, and our job is to point them out. In this chapter, you can explore ten of the most damaging mistakes that you can make with Balanced Scorecards, and how to avoid making them.

Cherry Picking

Implementing Balanced Scorecards is an all-or-nothing kind of thing for a company. One quick way to destroy any possibility for success is to apply the scorecards only in special cases or circumstances, outside the normal function of the company. When you reserve the use of scorecards only for special cases, you lose a lot of their benefit. We saw this in one company where the financial performance aspects of a company were tracked well, but little attention was paid to the internal processes. This resulted in focusing on reducing costs (a good thing for sure), but without process understanding with respect to these costs, which ultimately resulted in workforce reductions and cutting in travel and expenses. As this company happened to be in the entertainment business, where everything is customer focus, impeccable performance in all processes, and a realization that service levels define cost levels (not the other way around, as in production, for example), this company was quickly forced to sell off about 45 percent, and close the rest within a matter of months.

By picking and choosing where you implement balanced scorecard, you risk different levels of visibility and reaction to failures or challenges when it comes to key aspects of the performance of the company. This can result in haphazardly allocating key resources, putting too much emphasis in one or two areas, and under-resourcing critical elements of the other legs of the Balanced Scorecard.

An organization's priorities and business focus must be in alignment across the company, to help decide what is important and to ensure limited resources are focused and applied accordingly. And, how do you do this? Simple: Use the scorecard in a consistent, uniform way. Balanced scorecards aren't just for breakfast anymore.

Following Case Studies Too Closely

You may see the success of other companies and want to know what made it that way, so you can apply that knowledge to your own business. But while you want to study successes (*and* failures, by the way), you also need to consider that your company is unique — it isn't GE, or Toyota, or Harley Davidson. Instead of getting hung up on case studies of successful companies, focus on your own business, and remember the rules for successful benchmarking:

- Identify the best practices you want to model.

- Map your own processes and practices to a detailed level, specific to these best-practice areas.

- Go and look at the company with best practices and capture the detailed-process characteristics.

- Compare process characteristics to determine portability and transferability of the process steps, actions, and resulting performance.

- Develop, plan, and execute a step-by-step activity that transitions your organization to the new best practice.

- Develop excellent tracking and adjustment processes to this transition plan, so that as things develop, you can fine-tune the approach and the systems or structures to support the change.

Delegating Responsibility without Authority

Have you ever been given responsibility for doing a job, but your boss didn't give you the authority you needed to carry it out? Not a very fun (or successful) position to be put in, was it? Unfortunately, this happens all the time, in all kinds of businesses. Putting people in a position where they're held responsible yet don't have the requisite authority to enable them to carry out crucial actions to support that responsibility results in frustration (at a minimum) and undermines the systems and support structures by which Balanced Scorecards are defined. Plus, you can get a big headache.

At its worst, when responsibility is delegated without authority, projects and indeed whole companies become disjointed, disconnected, and distrusting, because suspicions arise about hidden agendas — and people start getting paranoid about being set up for failure. The sad part is that none of this adds value to the products or services you work so hard to provide to your customers. In fact, it creates inefficiencies that increase costs and decrease quality.

When you delegate responsibility for performance of key aspects of the Balanced Scorecard, you must trust and enable your managers and leaders to be personally and professionally responsible for performance to the scorecard. Consider, as you assign tasks, what responsibility and authority *you* would need to successfully complete the task. Then, work with other leaders to make sure that the assigned individuals have the tools to succeed in carrying out critical activities. Of course, you must coach and mentor those assigned individuals as they follow the appropriate processes as well.

Ignoring the Soft Stuff

Putting your Balanced Scorecard into practice is more than just installing a series of measures, setting expectations, and monitoring results. A *lot* more. To capitalize on your company's strengths and synergies, you must integrate the four legs of your scorecard with your organization's leadership style — that is, the "soft stuff." This is especially the case in communication within the organization and the coordination of different functions and departments toward providing products and services to your customers.

We have seen numerous industry examples where mergers or acquisitions have failed miserably, and where companies have failed to capture market leadership, due to imbalances in leadership and employee motivation. When we take a closer look, we see this imbalance stems from the way individual performance is separately evaluated and rewarded, and how managers are promoted based on their individual achievement, with no regard for teamwork or shared responsibility for the overall performance of the company.

Don't let your company make the same mistake. You need to make sure you're integrating what you do with how you do it, by taking the "soft" skills into account in your quest for competitive superiority. Ready to get soft?

Here are a few things you can do keep an emphasis on leadership and motivation within the company:

- Set up and enforce steering team behavior, where key engineering, operations, staffing, supply chain, and financial decisions are made through a leadership team approach, in which every member of the management team participates — not mandated by one functional manager alone.

- Require employee involvement in every aspect — including financial — of any project that improves a process, and ensure a management team member is championing each project, providing coaching, and mentoring the project leader and team throughout.

- Expect employee work groups to develop their own visual display boards to manage their daily work; require each group to meet daily at this board for about five minutes, to discuss work, handoffs, and issues that have arisen or may arise.

- Require supervisors to also meet daily to discuss their work cells, daily work, issues, and any barriers needing leadership support and removal.

- Establish regular leadership reviews, perhaps weekly, for the management team to visit all the employee work group visual display boards to see what they're working on, what they're improving, and their current issues, so that staff members can better support the needs of the employee teams.

- Create rewards that focus on competition with external competitors, not internal organizations, with appropriate recognition for achieving greater market share as well as sharing best practices within the company.

- Establish multiple review processes for performance management, incorporating team-based metrics, leadership traits with concrete examples, and motivating a shared leader environment.

Above all, remember that you also need to actively participative as you bring the organization to the future state.

Focusing Too Much on the Tools

Many companies focus so much on the tools and techniques that they forget that a framework that enables and focuses these practices is just as important for success. Just applying the methodology without a concept, idea, or sense of direction, coupled with focus and a sense of discipline, results in blind practices with a hit-or-miss mentality. This way of thinking doesn't work in an increasingly competitive environment, where one slip-up puts you at the back of the pack playing catch-up.

This framework is more important than you may initially think. Without a sound strategic and overall business framework within which your business employs the Balanced Scorecard tools and techniques, you run a great risk of misalignment in department goals and objectives, which could result in optimizing scorecard performance in one aspect at the expense of another, causing loss and potential reduction in market share.

For a company, *Balanced Scorecard* means achieving balance in the way it approaches the challenge of providing products and services to its customers in a continuous learning and improving environment. The way to ensure balance is to develop such a framework for planning and executing your scorecard, ideally with the steering committee, and definitely with key leaders of the business. For more information on the development of such a framework, see Chapters 3 and 4.

Overanalyzing

While you may safely subscribe to the old adage that "what gets measured gets done," you also need to be careful not to measure everything to a point where you have so much information that you can't determine what to do. Paralysis by analysis is one sure way to help your business get nowhere fast.

In setting up and sustaining Balanced Scorecards, you focus on establishing critical measures around the four legs (customers, finance performance, process performance, and growth potential), so that you can assess the organization's overall health in performance and then adjust emphasis and priorities as appropriate to maintain the balance for sustained competitive advantage. After the scorecard is constructed and working, more information can clutter the data and make it difficult to see how you're doing.

Examples of how too much info can hurt the decision-making process abound in the cell-phone and electronic-entertainment industries, where companies were late in launching key innovations (and upstaged by their competitors) when they decided to gather more information instead of taking quick action.

The bottom line is this: Always ask yourself whether additional or more detailed information would be critical to taking certain actions aligned with performance of one of the four legs. If not, don't waste time collecting or analyzing the information — unless you're planning to look for a new job as your competitors leave you in the dust.

Not Dealing with Key Detractors

Thinking that if you establish the four legs of the Balanced Scorecard and communicate effectively, then everything will work out great all by itself and your business should see remarkable results in a few months is a dangerous tendency. Oh, and that cows will grow wings and start flying, and you will stub your toe on a buried treasure chest on the way to work tomorrow. But back to the real world. . .

You face plenty of barriers to Balanced Scorecard success, including those key detractors which can undermine everything you do with respect to Balanced Scorecards. While you shouldn't be deterred by negative feedback, you need to be cognizant of the following common key detractors that can derail scorecards:

✔ **Lack of critical information:** Such as, failing to measure key process indicators or failing to analyze data in a timely manner

✔ **Lack of a structure to support scoring to the necessary level:** This one works two ways, both up and down the organizational structure by; not delegating the responsibility and authority for scorecard to the lowest appropriate levels; and by not getting scorecard information properly fed upwards through the management levels of the organization.

✔ **Limitations on sharing best practices:** For example, when offices or plants are in direct competition with one another

As long as you reward and encourage internal competition, you can't be successful in utilizing Balanced Scorecards. Why not? Because employees aren't inclined to help each other achieve the best performance for your customers when they are rewarded for their own performance and ranked against other employees and departments doing the same work.

These and other types of detractors must be recognized and dealt with quickly, by establishing detection and intercept policies and procedures, and making the elimination of such detractors a high priority in deploying Balanced Scorecards for everyone involved.

Sending Mixed Messages

How well the company is doing and where it may want to invest next is clearly a business decision. However, the direction, vision, and focus must also be clear, unambiguous, and in sync with the actions the company is taking; otherwise, you're sending mixed messages. For example, a company stresses in its vision continuous improvement in processes, yet layoffs abound as the company struggles to meet quarterly sales and EBIT (earnings before interest and tax) targets.

When a company sends mixed messages about what is important, the Balanced Scorecards are directly impacted — how they're managed and used and whether they help or hinder the company's performance. A company's vision, direction, expectation, and measurements all have to be aligned and communicated in a clear way for the scorecard to be used effectively. To accomplish this, here are a few helpful hints:

- ✔ Centralize your communication messages, so that only one interpretation is published and discussed among your management team.

- ✔ Frequently discuss the messages you and your leaders need to convey, and ensure you have alignment and a coalition among leadership.

- ✔ Have your leaders check frequently with different employees and groups, to see whether the message is understood or whether issues have come up. Work to resolve issues in real time.

- ✔ Make use of communication professionals to get the different messages developed and communicated effectively. Working with these professionals to put together and execute a comprehensive communications plan with checks and balances can help your company ensure that mixed messages are avoided and when they do occur, to make sure they're detected and eliminated immediately.

Exaggerating the Returns

Anytime returns or results are exaggerated, you detract from the potential success and true contribution of the Balanced Scorecards to your business. Anytime you exaggerate performance, you do a disservice to the company and to yourself, by damaging the credibility of the data systems and the decision process you chose to accept. The impact of this loss could potentially close a company, depending on how deep the effect on performance, especially when the customer is aware of the exaggeration.

Exaggerating returns never works, and seldom gets the desired results from a performance and customer satisfaction perspective. Be straight with your results — good or bad — and you can sleep a lot better at night.

Ignoring the Customer

You may not think it is possible to ignore the customer. Yet, more often than not, we see organizations that feel they understand their customers so well that they don't really need to check every once in a while to see whether they're right. This tendency is especially prevalent when a company has a large sales presence, and feels that sales knows what the customer wants anyway.

With customer demands changing more than ever before, and technology and innovation constantly paving the way for new products and services, going back often and checking in with your customers is more important than ever. You need to ask your organization, and especially your managers, the following questions:

✔ Are you meeting your customers' needs well and completely?

✔ Are customers looking to partner with you and your company as they see new opportunities?

✔ Do customers see your company as highly responsive and quick to support change?

One of the foundational principles of Balanced Scorecards is the concept that everyone in your organization, from the CEO to the guard at the gate and everyone in between feels they are contributing to the success of the company by tying their performance and activities to one or more of the four legs of the scorecard. The customer's interests must also tie to all four legs, so that everyone sees his role as supporting the customer's needs — thus enhancing the company's health and continued success. (And maybe even getting you that promotion you've been hoping for.)

Chapter 19

Ten Tips for Overcoming Barriers

Successful companies have to work hard, over several years, to sew Balanced Scorecards into the DNA of everyday company life. Many obstacles and barriers have to be overcome, and a number of folks need to be convinced. Your organization can benefit from the lessons learned by the many organizations that have successfully *and* unsuccessfully developed and implemented Balanced Scorecards and dashboards. In this chapter, we review ten key tips for overcoming barriers when implementing Balanced Scorecards, based on these lessons learned.

Empower Your Employees

Employees are the process experts for their jobs, so they have the best insight as to how to do the jobs better, faster, and cheaper. However, many companies limit their employees' roles in planning and improving the work processes in which they perform. You can spot these companies if you look way behind organizations that empower employees to take an active role in such improvements.

We're taking a wild guess here that you want to be the surpasser and not the surpassee, so, follow these guidelines to empower your employees in the job-improvement process:

> ✔ **Get your employees' input on what could be done better.** Do this not through suggestion programs that just offer ideas, but through involvement. Have your work team select, prioritize, test, prove, and optimize the ideas.

✔ **Allow your employee work teams to share in the tracking and management of their performance.** This is already practiced in many leading companies, such as GE, Varian, Saturn, GKN, Sara Lee, and others, and is a foundational concept to lean enterprise theory. Rather than waiting for the 'boss' to decide what is going well, and what to do different, companies all over the world are embracing the idea that the work team itself can best decide what works, and how best to improve performance, given that the members are working in the process daily. This is fundamental to both implementing and sustaining your scorecards, since employee work teams will be using them to both track and improve performance. They will also be responsible for generating any data analysis from their work stream, which is done by imbedding the reporting process into the daily activities, rather than put together by exception.

✔ **Structure improvement initiatives to enable real-time corrective actions.** The key aspect here is *real-time*, where, when a work team sees an improvement opportunity, there is a simple, quick, and effective means to initiate, assess and formalize the improvement, and build it into the daily tracking method and local scorecard.

✔ **Train your supervisors in the art of coaching their employees to assess, understand, and improve their performance.** Supervisors in leading companies spend less time supervising and more time coaching and working with their work teams on performance and improvement. Following this example will help your scorecard's success also, because supervisors will have more time to look at the overall performance perspective of the operation or function. Additionally, supervisors will be able to tie-in the legs that much better, since they will be relying on the team members more for the detailed work, and collaborating and working together to achieve the team's performance goals and objectives.

✔ **Establish a deliberate employee-involvement program.** Getting employees involved in understanding, assessing, and improving the performance of their work team is critical to your scorecard's success, for many reasons, but primarily because employees are the most knowledgeable about what can be improved and how. An employee-improvement program can involve simply getting together daily to discuss events, issues, performance, who is missing, and any new developments within the workplace. Some teams create boards or other media (for example, this could be a white board, or an electronic one-page activity register) to track daily performance; hold daily meetings to share ideas, status, and current workload; and provide team and continuous-improvement training.

✔ **Get actively involved as a leader.** Provide resource support — both internally and externally when needed — to assure success and demonstrate your commitment to employee involvement and empowerment.

Be Flexible

To implement Balanced Scorecards throughout your organization, you must have a good, strong plan in place. But you must realize that flexibility adds to the ease of implementing changes and lends real strength to your plan.

For a company to quickly respond to changes, several things must be in place:

✔ You must have a system that can detect changes quickly and feed information to those who need it right away.

✔ Your employees must understand the importance of flexibility in both the creation and the delivery of your products and services — especially as demand and order behavior shifts.

✔ Your company's leadership team has to be closely involved. Provide continuous energy to the system, and work with employees to make changes to your tactics and activities — changes required by today's fast-changing business environment.

Apply Psychology

Change can be both exciting and terrifying to your employees — especially when the change will undeniably impact them in some way, even if they don't know how. So, take some time to understand what motivates your employees, and see if you can align their work needs and desires with those of the organization. If you tie company performance to personal and organizational achievements, you can overcome some of the basic barriers to change through involvement and recognition.

For your Balanced Scorecard applications, you can sync personal and organization goals by doing the following:

✔ Align measures of recognition, good leadership, employee involvement, fair treatment, and competitive wages with the appropriate scorecard legs, and make sure these are the focus of the organization's management practices.

✔ Continually assess how well or how poorly these measures are aligned, checking the alignment of these measures regularly, and correcting the alignment when they get off course or revert _k to motivating purely by financial means

✔ Establish the external competitor as the focus and target for any and all competitive activities within the organization, and discourage any type of internal competition wherever possible. In this way, you will be harnessing the competitive spirit of your workforce in the right direction.

Identify and Use Influential People

Get the people on your side who always seem to know who to talk to; where to get needed resources; how to get tasks accomplished; and who they can rely on to always get things done. These people can help you overcome resistance within your company — either as advocates themselves or as champions who solicit others to buy-in to the scorecard methods, even if it is for their own purposes. For instance, operations managers will want to support a Balanced Scorecard if it positively reflects their performance across the four legs.

Limit the Use of Force

Your natural tendency may be to force your employees to implement score-cards and then let them discover the attributes of scorecards afterwards. In some limited situations, this can work — for instance, in pilot changes where you want to try something to see what happens. By forcing a behavior, you run the risk of the people in the process disassociating themselves with that very process. If they aren't confident or don't believe the process will work, they'll disassociate themselves with the process even more.

We recommend that, even when you need to implement a controversial set of behaviors, you provide the members involved with a way to give input and assessments and to participate in the review and adjustments of the score-card changes. In this way — even as certain processes feel "forced" — the people involved can retain levels of authority in determining how best to fit their styles and performance into the new processes. (See the section "Empower Your Employees" and the following section for more topics related to this.)

Don't Shoot the Messenger; Make Everyone the Messenger

When you first start developing and implementing Balanced Scorecards, be prepared to find out how bad some processes really are in your organization! Balanced scorecards reveal performance at a more detailed level than you may have measured in the past; as a result, you may get some surprises in the form of problems that were covered up before. What you must remember is that this is actually a good thing. You need to make sure you don't assign blame for these discoveries and for anything that may seem a little questionable.

Ask your employees to get involved — to become messengers of change, in other words. As they realize that they can raise issues about anything — even things previously "owned" by management — your employees will bring up other issues that impact performance. Through this, you may discover that you have policies that need revising or eliminating, and employees may eliminate chronic issues you thought you could never get resolved. Just by not placing blame you can create more change.

Implement Stage-Gate Reviews

Stage-gate review systems give companies a regular review process that allows them to find out how they're doing when it comes to performance. With these reviews, you can periodically revisit your strategy, actions, and performance and adjust as appropriate.

As stage-gate reviews become more and more a part of the normal operations of your organization, Balanced Scorecards become commonplace and reflect the ever-increasing awareness of the business and its key performance indicators. The reviews also help your organization overcome a lot of the resistance people experience. Your employees realize that Balanced Scorecards aren't just the latest fad; they're a cornerstone of the way you run your business.

Reward, Recognize, and Celebrate Success

One of the most effective ways to motivate people and break down barriers to change is to show them how using scorecards and dashboards can benefit them. Of course, anything new is a risk, so when a team succeeds in improving performance and demonstrates the improvement via a scorecard, you need to recognize the team for its work and success and share the news with as many people and organizations as possible and appropriate.

When a team receives recognition for its success, the team members will talk about the experience and what they achieved in positive ways. This positivity will spark additional interest from people who may otherwise hesitate to try something new on the job. They may become excited to explore options, given the possibility for success and further recognition.

You can hold periodic celebrations to recognize members of the organization who have participated in, supported, or championed improvements based on scorecards in order to avoid appearing selective in who you reward and how. You don't want to foster an internally competitive atmosphere; instead, you want to focus scorecards and dashboards on the metrics that focus your energy and resources on defeating your external competitors.

Communicate, Communicate, Communicate (And Don't Forget to Talk)

You need to communicate to your organization continuously and constantly about what a Balanced Scorecard is, what it does internally for a company, how it creates a competitive edge, and how it improves performance in creating and delivering value for the customer.

By sharing your thoughts about scorecards, establishing two-way, interactive discussion opportunities, sharing the concepts, vision, and intent of Balanced Scorecards, you can overcome the fear, uncertainty, and misunderstanding common in organizational transformations.

Be aware, though: Haphazard, unstructured communication can do more damage than no communication at all.

Provide Structure for Coaching, Mentoring, and Learning from Mistakes

A well-known and equally well-practiced motto from the United States Marine Corps is "improvise, adapt, and overcome." In business, living by this motto is just as important due to the fast-changing, highly complex environments. In order to survive, global companies have adapted formal structures to enable rapid learning, understanding, and quick turnaround from mistakes. They also provide real-time coaching and mentoring from leaders as situations develop.

The structures you create must mirror your organizational structures to be effective. In other words, if your organization is set up with a corporate headquarters and several divisions, your support structure must involve players from both the corporate and division functions. It also has to include levels of management to ensure alignment and consistency with the goals and objectives of your organization, as they relate to the four legs of the Balanced Scorecard.

Index

BUSINESS, CAREERS & PERSONAL FINANCE

0-7645-9847-3

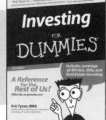

0-7645-2431-3

Also available:
- Business Plans Kit For Dummies
  0-7645-9794-9
- Economics For Dummies
  0-7645-5726-2
- Grant Writing For Dummies
  0-7645-8416-2
- Home Buying For Dummies
  0-7645-5331-3
- Managing For Dummies
  0-7645-1771-6
- Marketing For Dummies
  0-7645-5600-2

- Personal Finance For Dummies
  0-7645-2590-5*
- Resumes For Dummies
  0-7645-5471-9
- Selling For Dummies
  0-7645-5363-1
- Six Sigma For Dummies
  0-7645-6798-5
- Small Business Kit For Dummies
  0-7645-5984-2
- Starting an eBay Business For Dummies
  0-7645-6924-4
- Your Dream Career For Dummies
  0-7645-9795-7

HOME & BUSINESS COMPUTER BASICS

0-470-05432-8

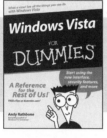

0-471-75421-8

Also available:
- Cleaning Windows Vista For Dummies
  0-471-78293-9
- Excel 2007 For Dummies
  0-470-03737-7
- Mac OS X Tiger For Dummies
  0-7645-7675-5
- MacBook For Dummies
  0-470-04859-X
- Macs For Dummies
  0-470-04849-2
- Office 2007 For Dummies
  0-470-00923-3

- Outlook 2007 For Dummies
  0-470-03830-6
- PCs For Dummies
  0-7645-8958-X
- Salesforce.com For Dummies
  0-470-04893-X
- Upgrading & Fixing Laptops For Dummies
  0-7645-8959-8
- Word 2007 For Dummies
  0-470-03658-3
- Quicken 2007 For Dummies
  0-470-04600-7

FOOD, HOME, GARDEN, HOBBIES, MUSIC & PETS

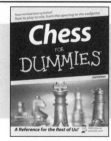

0-7645-8404-9

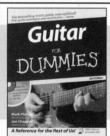

0-7645-9904-6

Also available:
- Candy Making For Dummies
  0-7645-9734-5
- Card Games For Dummies
  0-7645-9910-0
- Crocheting For Dummies
  0-7645-4151-X
- Dog Training For Dummies
  0-7645-8418-9
- Healthy Carb Cookbook For Dummies
  0-7645-8476-6
- Home Maintenance For Dummies
  0-7645-5215-5

- Horses For Dummies
  0-7645-9797-3
- Jewelry Making & Beading For Dummies
  0-7645-2571-9
- Orchids For Dummies
  0-7645-6759-4
- Puppies For Dummies
  0-7645-5255-4
- Rock Guitar For Dummies
  0-7645-5356-9
- Sewing For Dummies
  0-7645-6847-7
- Singing For Dummies
  0-7645-2475-5

INTERNET & DIGITAL MEDIA

0-470-04529-9

0-470-04894-8

Also available:
- Blogging For Dummies
  0-471-77084-1
- Digital Photography For Dummies
  0-7645-9802-3
- Digital Photography All-in-One Desk Reference For Dummies
  0-470-03743-1
- Digital SLR Cameras and Photography For Dummies
  0-7645-9803-1
- eBay Business All-in-One Desk Reference For Dummies
  0-7645-8438-3
- HDTV For Dummies
  0-470-09673-X

- Home Entertainment PCs For Dummies
  0-470-05523-5
- MySpace For Dummies
  0-470-09529-6
- Search Engine Optimization For Dummies
  0-471-97998-8
- Skype For Dummies
  0-470-04891-3
- The Internet For Dummies
  0-7645-8996-2
- Wiring Your Digital Home For Dummies
  0-471-91830-X

* Separate Canadian edition also available
† Separate U.K. edition also available

Available wherever books are sold. For more information or to order direct: U.S. customers visit www.dummies.com or call 1-877-762-2974.
U.K. customers visit www.wileyeurope.com or call 0800 243407. Canadian customers visit www.wiley.ca or call 1-800-567-4797.

SPORTS, FITNESS, PARENTING, RELIGION & SPIRITUALITY

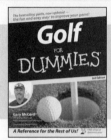

0-471-76871-5

0-7645-7841-3

Also available:
- Catholicism For Dummies
  0-7645-5391-7
- Exercise Balls For Dummies
  0-7645-5623-1
- Fitness For Dummies
  0-7645-7851-0
- Football For Dummies
  0-7645-3936-1
- Judaism For Dummies
  0-7645-5299-6
- Potty Training For Dummies
  0-7645-5417-4
- Buddhism For Dummies
  0-7645-5359-3

- Pregnancy For Dummies
  0-7645-4483-7 †
- Ten Minute Tone-Ups For Dummies
  0-7645-7207-5
- NASCAR For Dummies
  0-7645-7681-X
- Religion For Dummies
  0-7645-5264-3
- Soccer For Dummies
  0-7645-5229-5
- Women in the Bible For Dummies
  0-7645-8475-8

TRAVEL

0-7645-7749-2

0-7645-6945-7

Also available:
- Alaska For Dummies
  0-7645-7746-8
- Cruise Vacations For Dummies
  0-7645-6941-4
- England For Dummies
  0-7645-4276-1
- Europe For Dummies
  0-7645-7529-5
- Germany For Dummies
  0-7645-7823-5
- Hawaii For Dummies
  0-7645-7402-7

- Italy For Dummies
  0-7645-7386-1
- Las Vegas For Dummies
  0-7645-7382-9
- London For Dummies
  0-7645-4277-X
- Paris For Dummies
  0-7645-7630-5
- RV Vacations For Dummies
  0-7645-4442-X
- Walt Disney World & Orlando
  For Dummies
  0-7645-9660-8

GRAPHICS, DESIGN & WEB DEVELOPMENT

0-7645-8815-X

0-7645-9571-7

Also available:
- 3D Game Animation For Dummies
  0-7645-8789-7
- AutoCAD 2006 For Dummies
  0-7645-8925-3
- Building a Web Site For Dummies
  0-7645-7144-3
- Creating Web Pages For Dummies
  0-470-08030-2
- Creating Web Pages All-in-One Desk
  Reference For Dummies
  0-7645-4345-8
- Dreamweaver 8 For Dummies
  0-7645-9649-7

- InDesign CS2 For Dummies
  0-7645-9572-5
- Macromedia Flash 8 For Dummies
  0-7645-9691-8
- Photoshop CS2 and Digital
  Photography For Dummies
  0-7645-9580-6
- Photoshop Elements 4 For Dummies
  0-471-77483-9
- Syndicating Web Sites with RSS Feeds
  For Dummies
  0-7645-8848-6
- Yahoo! SiteBuilder For Dummies
  0-7645-9800-7

NETWORKING, SECURITY, PROGRAMMING & DATABASES

0-7645-7728-X

0-471-74940-0

Also available:
- Access 2007 For Dummies
  0-470-04612-0
- ASP.NET 2 For Dummies
  0-7645-7907-X
- C# 2005 For Dummies
  0-7645-9704-3
- Hacking For Dummies
  0-470-05235-X
- Hacking Wireless Networks
  For Dummies
  0-7645-9730-2
- Java For Dummies
  0-470-08716-1

- Microsoft SQL Server 2005 For Dummies
  0-7645-7755-7
- Networking All-in-One Desk Reference
  For Dummies
  0-7645-9939-9
- Preventing Identity Theft For Dummies
  0-7645-7336-5
- Telecom For Dummies
  0-471-77085-X
- Visual Studio 2005 All-in-One Desk
  Reference For Dummies
  0-7645-9775-2
- XML For Dummies
  0-7645-8845-1

HEALTH & SELF-HELP

0-7645-8450-2

0-7645-4149-8

Also available:

Bipolar Disorder For Dummies
0-7645-8451-0

Chemotherapy and Radiation
For Dummies
0-7645-7832-4

Controlling Cholesterol For Dummies
0-7645-5440-9

Diabetes For Dummies
0-7645-6820-5* †

Divorce For Dummies
0-7645-8417-0 †

Fibromyalgia For Dummies
0-7645-5441-7

Low-Calorie Dieting For Dummies
0-7645-9905-4

Meditation For Dummies
0-471-77774-9

Osteoporosis For Dummies
0-7645-7621-6

Overcoming Anxiety For Dummies
0-7645-5447-6

Reiki For Dummies
0-7645-9907-0

Stress Management For Dummies
0-7645-5144-2

EDUCATION, HISTORY, REFERENCE & TEST PREPARATION

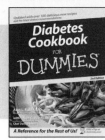
0-7645-8381-6

0-7645-9554-7

Also available:

The ACT For Dummies
0-7645-9652-7

Algebra For Dummies
0-7645-5325-9

Algebra Workbook For Dummies
0-7645-8467-7

Astronomy For Dummies
0-7645-8465-0

Calculus For Dummies
0-7645-2498-4

Chemistry For Dummies
0-7645-5430-1

Forensics For Dummies
0-7645-5580-4

Freemasons For Dummies
0-7645-9796-5

French For Dummies
0-7645-5193-0

Geometry For Dummies
0-7645-5324-0

Organic Chemistry I For Dummies
0-7645-6902-3

The SAT I For Dummies
0-7645-7193-1

Spanish For Dummies
0-7645-5194-9

Statistics For Dummies
0-7645-5423-9

Get smart @ dummies.com®

- **Find a full list of Dummies titles**
- **Look into loads of FREE on-site articles**
- **Sign up for FREE eTips e-mailed to you weekly**
- **See what other products carry the Dummies name**
- **Shop directly from the Dummies bookstore**
- **Enter to win new prizes every month!**

* Separate Canadian edition also available

† Separate U.K. edition also available

Available wherever books are sold. For more information or to order direct: U.S. customers visit www.dummies.com or call 1-877-762-2974.
U.K. customers visit www.wileyeurope.com or call 0800 243407. Canadian customers visit www.wiley.ca or call 1-800-567-4797.